MAKING THE NEWSMAKERS

Making the Newsmakers

INTERNATIONAL HANDBOOK ON JOURNALISM TRAINING

Philip Gaunt

Sponsored by Unesco

GREENWOOD PRESS
Westport, Connecticut • London

Library of Congress Cataloging-in-Publication Data

Gaunt, Philip.
    Making the newsmakers : international handbook on journalism
training / Philip Gaunt.
       p. cm.
    Sponsored by Unesco.
    Includes bibliographical references and index.
    ISBN 0-313-27984-5 (alk. paper)
       1. Journalism—Study and teaching—Handbooks, manuals, etc.
2. Journalists—Training of—Handbooks, manuals, etc.
3. Journalism—Political aspects—Handbooks, manuals, etc.
4. Political socialization—Developing countries—Handbooks,
manuals, etc. I. Title.
PN4785.G38 1992
070.4'07—dc20   92-10618

British Library Cataloguing in Publication Data is available.

Copyright © 1992 by Philip Gaunt

Library of Congress Catalog Card Number: 92-10618
ISBN: 0-313-27984-5

First published in 1992

Greenwood Press, 88 Post Road West, Westport, CT 06881
An imprint of Greenwood Publishing Group, Inc.

Printed in the United States of America

The paper used in this book complies with the
Permanent Paper Standard issued by the National
Information Standards Organization (Z39.48-1984).

10 9 8 7 6 5 4 3 2 1

Contents

Preface

This book has grown out of a previous book of mine, *Choosing the News*, a comparative study of factors influencing the way in which journalists select and process information in different countries. One of the most influential factors is training. Not all press systems are the same, and journalism training varies considerably from one system to another. As the reflection of journalism, training is shaped by the social, cultural, economic and political conditions in which it is conducted. It is affected by press laws, government controls, ownership, competition and, above all, the perceived function of journalism in any given society.

As a study of training needs, programs and facilities in 70 countries, *Making the Newsmakers* is the first worldwide survey of its kind since 1958. As an up-to-date directory of almost 600 training establishments in every region of the world, it is also a work of reference. Collecting, processing and analyzing the data needed for this study has been a tremendous task that would have been impossible without the generous cooperation and able assistance of a large number of people and institutions.

First and foremost, I want to thank UNESCO for sponsoring the research required to complete the study. In particular, I wish to acknowledge the friendly assistance and enlightened advice of Morten Giersing, Chief of UNESCO's Section of Free Flow of Information and Communication Research, and Alan Hancock, Director of the Division of Communication.

I also want to thank the administrators and scholars of a number of regional communication centers who have so generously worked to provide me with reports, studies, articles and papers about training structures in their particular part of the world. In particular, I want to express my gratitude to Crispin Maslog of the University of the Philippines, Sankaran Ramanathan of the Mara Institute of Technology in Malaysia, Edgar Jamarillo of the Center of Advanced Studies in Communication for Latin America, Batilloi Warritay and Kwame Boafo of the African Council on Communication Education and Alex Quarmayne, UNESCO Chief Communication Adviser for Africa, as well as the staff of the Asian Mass Communication and Information Center and the Press Foundation of Asia. I am also indebted to Stanislav Perkner, former director of the International Institute for the Training of Journalists in Prague, for sharing his encyclopedic knowledge of training in Eastern and Central Europe, and to Folu Ogundimu of Michigan State University for his insightful comments on African training structures.

Handling all the information supplied by these various sources, as well as creating the original database for both the survey and the directory, entailed much tedious but essential work. During the early stages of the project, Cathy Culot, a very capable graduate student from Belgium, carried the burden of this work with determination and cheerfulness. At a later stage, Phillip Bloomquist, then a graduate student but now the head of his own computer consulting firm, demonstrated a gift for database management that greatly facilitated the production of the final draft.

To all who have contributed to this book—and they are too numerous to mention by name—I extend my warmest thanks. Needless to say, any errors or omissions are my fault, and mine alone.

Finally, I want to ackowledge the encouragement and intellectual support of Vernon Keel and the entire faculty of the Elliott School of Communication at the Wichita State University. I feel fortunate to be a member of such a united team of outstanding teachers and scholars.

MAKING THE NEWSMAKERS

Chapter One

Introduction

Journalism training perpetuates or modifies professional journalistic practices and molds the perceptions journalists have of the role and function of the media. Because journalism training influences the selection and processing of news, it also has an indirect effect on the way in which we view the world around us. In times of crisis, as events in Eastern and Central Europe and elsewhere have shown, those who process the news play a key role in informing mass audiences and shaping public opinion. But it has also become obvious that not all newsmakers are alike. They do not all share the same objectives, procedures or role perceptions. This work seeks to explain some of these differences by analyzing journalism training needs and structures in the various regions of the world. It is to be noted that the use of the term "newsmakers" when referring to journalists is deliberate. It has become fashionable to use this term to describe sources or persons who are "in the news." But, as I have argued elsewhere,[1] journalists effectively "make the news" when they gather, select and process information.

Obviously, journalism training structures and the different models of journalism that support them are strongly influenced by the political, cultural and social contexts in which they exist. In the United States, for example, journalists are viewed as "watchdogs," keeping a close eye on the workings of government and democratic processes. In some West European countries, journalists function as reporters but also as interpret-

ers of information. In others, they are seen as literary figures, more akin
to artists than to hard-boiled newshounds. In the poorer nations, they are
often government employees serving as instruments of progress and
national unity in the unending struggle for development. In the communist
countries of Eastern Europe, journalists were given the task of dissemi-
nating ideological propaganda and fostering support for the regime. In the
wake of pro-democracy movements, things are now changing, but the
ways in which they change may prove to be unexpected.

The study presented in this book takes a detailed look at the concepts
and traditions that lead to different media systems and journalism training
structures, and it also examines a number of preoccupations and tensions
that are common to all systems. Indeed, whatever the geographic area or
sociopolitical context, journalism educators and media professionals have
had to come to terms with the same problems.

DIFFERENCES IN TRAINING SYSTEMS

The most common area of debate and dissension has always been
curriculum. Should training concentrate solely on professional and technical skills, or should it include liberal studies, law, ideological awareness,
ethics or other areas of general interest? Do communication studies, media
studies, public relations, public information, advertising or media management belong in journalism programs, or should they be taught elsewhere? Should curriculum be determined by educators, professional
associations, media owners, unions or government agencies or by a
combination thereof? Although these questions may be answered differ-
ently in different cultures, they remain a common source of preoccupation.

And then there is the vexed question of print versus broadcast journalism. The answer to this question will not always be the same. Demand for
broadcast personnel is likely to be greater in developing countries than in
the industrialized nations. Again, should broadcast production be taught
alongside broadcast news, or is it part of engineering? Today, the old
division of print versus broadcast media ought perhaps to be couched in
terms of "traditional" versus "new" media. How should journalism training respond to the demand for expertise in video, desktop publishing,
interactive media and sophisticated combinations of computers and communication satellites? Are these really questions of curriculum or questions of new orientations in human behavior?

There has also been a parallel debate over where journalism training
should be dispensed. In some countries, notably in Western Europe, it has
not been considered a fit subject for university study and has been

relegated to "trade schools" or polytechnics. On the other hand, media studies or communication studies are accepted as academic areas in the university tradition. In some regions, there are major differences too between public and private institutions of higher education. This debate has also been tempered by such local factors as immediate and projected needs, length of study programs, financial resources, existing media structures and availability of teachers and teaching materials.

This raises two other related problems common to most systems of journalism training. Who are the educators, and who are the students? In university settings, educators tend to have advanced academic degrees as well as professional experience, but there are wide variations from country to country. Teachers in professional schools and in less formal "on-the-job" training situations typically rely on practical experience and, as a result, focus more on technical than on analytical skills. Here again, though, wide variations exist.

Student profiles vary considerably, too, but constitute a common area of concern. Students taking basic journalism skills training courses are likely to want to become journalists or may already be journalists on release from their jobs. In university journalism schools, students are more academically inclined and may not even wish to enter a communication-related career. Graduate students, at the master's level, are usually interested in acquiring better communication and/or management skills. At the doctoral level, most students are more interested in becoming educators or researchers.

The intriguing question here is whether particular programs produce or attract a certain type of student. For example, in some Latin American countries, the public universities, which offer programs in communication studies, produce, or possibly attract, politically motivated students, many from lower socioeconomic levels, who view the media as defenders of the ruling class and perpetuators of the status quo and who are not particularly interested in working as journalists. On the other hand, the private universities, which offer skills-oriented programs, are frequented by students from older, wealthier families, many of whom have connections with established media owners. These students are more likely to want to enter the profession, often with the ambition of rising to upper management positions.

Many of these differences are variations on similar themes, but one concern runs like a common thread through all journalism training systems, and that is the prospect of change. As an important social institution, journalism is sensitive to cultural trends, political and social upheavals and economic development. It has already been affected and will continue to be affected by far-reaching technological innovations and changes in media ownership. Because of all these changes, journalism training in most countries is now faced with a series of major challenges.

RELATED STUDIES

These issues are complex and difficult to analyze, which may be why there is a dearth of research on the topic. Much of the research that has been done predates the changes that have occurred in recent years. It is hoped, however, that the comparative focus of this present study will shed some light not only on the problems involved but also on possible outcomes.

Most of the comparative studies done to date have been conducted under the aegis of UNESCO or the regional training and research centers set up as a result of UNESCO action. The most comprehensive is a 1975 study by May Katzen.[2] Although based on a worldwide survey, it is limited to mass communication teaching in universities and does not, therefore, cover the many different types of journalism training programs offered outside universities. A much older UNESCO publication, *The Training of Journalists*, dating back to 1958, contains mainly a collection of individual national studies by various authors. Although largely out of date at this point, it presents a point of departure for future comparative research.[3] Other studies published in UNESCO's "Reports and Papers on Mass Communication" are relevant but more limited in their scope.[4]

A few regional studies provide detailed information on selected countries within their regions. *La Formación de Los Periodistas en América Latina* (The Training of Journalists in Latin America), sponsored by CEESTEM (The Center for Third World Economic and Social Studies) and FELAP (Federación Latinoamericana de Periodistas), takes a critical look at journalism training in Mexico, Chile and Costa Rica.[5] *Ausbildung für Kommunikationsberufe in Europa* (Training for the Communication Professions in Europe), published in 1977, is a straightforward review of journalism training programs in 14 countries in both Western and Eastern Europe as well as Japan; but it does not, of course, take into account recent developments in the formerly Communist states.[6] *Reports on Journalism Education in Europe*, published by Tampere University and edited by Kaarle Nordenstreng, goes a long way toward filling in some of these gaps and is particularly good on the East European countries.[7] The Press Foundation of Asia's *Communication Education in Asia*, edited by Crispin Maslog, provides an excellent update of recent trends in India, Indonesia, Malaysia, Nepal, the Philippines and Thailand.[8] Stephenson and Mory's recent study, published by the Commission of the European Communities, has added a valuable new source of information on journalism training in Western Europe.[9]

A number of other book-length publications include at least some comparative research on journalism training in various countries,[10] while yet others provide information on training programs in individual countries.[11] But most recent research has been published in the form of scholarly articles, book chapters and papers. It is interesting to note that many of these studies focus on Latin America, Africa, Asia and the developing world in general, as well as Australia.[12] Meanwhile, American scholars continue to produce research on journalism training within the United States. This almost constitutes a separate body of literature and is far too vast to review here. However, the interested reader is directed to *Journalism Quarterly*, *Journalism Educator* and *Journal of Communication* as well as to trade publications such as *Presstime* and *Editor and Publisher*.

Finally, two unpublished doctoral dissertations throw some light on training problems in the developing world. One, by Abdallah Taher Eljerary, studies training programs in Arab countries and identifies a number of reasons why they have either failed or not lived up to their expectations—in particular, inadequate planning, apathy and lack of human and material resources.[13] The other, by Dennis Cooper, surveys journalism curricula in developing countries and concludes that, while many programs appear to be based on the U.S. model, which combines skills with liberal studies and theory, they also differ from that model in that they often contain a strong "developmental" orientation.[14]

AREAS OF CONCERN

Although this body of research may appear to be somewhat disparate, several preoccupations clearly emerge. In the United States, which has well over 300 schools of journalism and which has provided a journalism training model for much of the world, a great deal of research has focused on the relationship between educators and media professionals, especially those in the newspaper industry. As has already been mentioned, this relationship has been affected by a long-standing debate on curriculum. Recent research, however, has concentrated also on the changing needs of the profession and new enrollment patterns. The introduction of electronic news management systems, often as a result of competition and the concentration of media ownership, requires new skills in entry-level journalism graduates. At the same time, as the health of the newspaper industry languishes, more students are enrolling in broadcast, public relations and advertising sequences.

This pattern also partly holds true in Western Europe; but, because of the traditional division between communication and media studies in universities and skills training in professional training establishments, journalism graduates are more focused in their ambitions and more likely to enter the profession. In general, the type and numbers of students produced by these schools are more closely matched to actual needs. Research reflects some of the areas of tension peculiar to Western European media systems: the relationship between the media and the "establishment," the political orientation of newspapers, state controls on broadcasting, official media policies and the importance of labor unions, all of which affect the training of journalists.

Scholars in developing countries have other concerns, in particular the heritage of former colonial powers or the influence of the American model. Many training programs in Africa, Asia and parts of Latin America were instituted decades ago by well-meaning media professionals who saw the need for training but who also, inadvertently or not, passed on the values and priorities of Western journalism, which have since proven to be inappropriate and, in some cases, quite contrary to the needs of the Third World. In Latin America, communication researchers who subscribe to the "dependencia" theory view the U.S. journalism training model as another tool of Western cultural hegemony. Also of concern to Third World educators is the lack of teachers and suitable educational materials. Many scholars regret that some developing countries, without national training facilities, are obliged to send their most promising students to the United States or Europe, where they acquire Western ideas and values of little relevance to domestic needs and where they are tempted not to return home.

In Eastern Europe, research in journalism training has been relatively limited and has often focused on matters of ideological or "official" import. Since the emergence of democracy and new press freedoms, however, scholars have been attempting to define priority issues and orientations. The functions of journalism in Eastern European countries as they grope their way toward democratic rule, a free market economy and fundamental press freedoms may not be the same as in the West. These countries do not have the same media laws, the same patterns of ownership or the same management structures. More importantly perhaps, their media do not have the same advertising revenue. As a result, government press subsidies may be needed for some time to come. It may be tempting to assume that the removal of Communist rule has left a total vacuum, but that would be to ignore the vigorous press systems that existed long before Communism.

SCOPE OF THE STUDY

The preceding overview may give some idea of the complexity of journalism training in various parts of the world. This complexity makes it extremely difficult to do comparative research on the subject. An initial difficulty is that of correctly identifying training facilities around the world. Most directories, and there are few of them, are incomplete or sadly out of date. The regional directories printed in this book, the result of much work, are the most accurate and up-to-date available at the present time. A second difficulty met with in seeking to survey these institutions is that of creating a survey questionnaire that will have meaning in different languages and different cultural and political settings. A third difficulty is that of collecting accurate information in an area that is subject to rapid and far-reaching change. A final difficulty is that of interpreting data generated by different and sometimes conflicting concepts of journalism.

The information presented in the following chapters was gathered from many different sources, including an analysis of current research, a survey of some 600 journalism schools, materials contributed by a number of regional and international organizations and consultations with individual scholars, educators and media professionals.

Chapter 2 describes the factors governing training needs, such factors as journalistic functions, journalistic traditions, types of press systems, media structures and socioeconomic influences. These needs determine the training structures that are analyzed in Chapter 3, which also examines the history and development of journalism training, the different types of training structures in place in various parts of the world, and some of the international and former colonial influences behind them.

Chapters 4 through 10 give more detailed information on journalism training in each of seven major regions of the world, with particular emphasis on historical developments, current training structures and internal influences. A list of the most important training establishments in each of these regions is included in an appendix at the end of the book.

Chapter 11 introduces some comparative perspectives and discusses some of the challenges facing journalism training in the world today in view of the changes taking place not only in political and technological structures but also in ownership patterns and foreign news coverage. The study concludes that, despite differences in the social, cultural and political functions of the press and despite a continued and growing information

8 Making the Newsmakers

gap between industrialized and developing nations, journalism and journalism training are likely to follow the same trend toward homogenization.

NOTES

1. Philip Gaunt, *Choosing the News: The Profit Factor in News Selection* (Westport, CT: Greenwood Press, 1990).

2. May Katzen, *Mass Communication: Teaching and Studies at Universities* (Paris: UNESCO Press, 1975).

3. UNESCO, *The Training of Journalists: A World-wide Study on the Training of Personnel for the Mass Media* (Paris: UNESCO, 1958).

4. UNESCO, *Education for Journalism*, Reports and Papers on Mass Communication, no. 8 (Paris: UNESCO, 1954); UNESCO, *Professional Training for Mass Communication*, Reports and Papers on Mass Communication, no. 45 (Paris: UNESCO, 1965); UNESCO, *Training for Mass Communication*, Reports and Papers on Mass Communication, no. 73 (Paris: UNESCO, 1975).

5. José Baldivia Urdininea, Mario Planet, Javier Solís, and Tomás Guerra Rivas, *La Formación de los Periodistas en América Latina: México, Chile, Costa Rica* (Mexico City: Editorial Nueva Imagen, S. A., 1981).

6. Heinz-Dietrich Fischer and Otto B. Roegele, eds., *Ausbildung für Kommunikationsberufe in Europea: Praktiken und Perspektiven* (Düsseldorf: Droste Verlag, 1977).

7. Kaarle Nordenstreng, ed., *Reports on Journalism Education in Europe* (Tampere: University of Tampere Department of Journalism and Mass Communication, 1990).

8. Crispin C. Maslog, ed., *Communication Education in Asia* (Manila: Press Foundation of Asia, 1990).

9. Hugh Stephenson and Pierre Mory, *Journalism Training in Europe* (Brussels: Commission of the European Communities, 1990).

10. Georges Bohère, *Profession: Journalist* (Geneva: ILO, 1984); John C. Merrill, ed., *Global Journalism*, 2d ed. (White Plains, NY: Longman, 1991); Kaarle Nordenstreng and Hifzi Topuz, eds., *Journalist: Status, Rights and Responsibilities* (Prague: International Organization of Journalists, 1989); Michael Kunczik, *Concepts of Journalism North and South* (Bonn: Friedrich-Ebert-Stiftung, 1988); Ronny Adhikarya, *Knowledge Transfer and Usage in Communication Studies: The U.S.–ASEAN Case* (Singapore: Asian Mass Communication Research and Information Centre, 1983); Mohamamad Nur Alkali, Jerry Domatob, Yahaya Abubakar and Abubakar Jika, eds., *Mass Communication in Africa: A Book of Readings* (Enugu, Nigeria: Delta Publications, 1988).

11. Lee Becker, Jeffrey Fruit and Susan Caudill, with Sharon Dunwoody and Leonard Tipton, *The Training and Hiring of Journalists* (Norwood, NJ: Ablex, 1987); David H. Weaver and G. Cleveland Wilhoit, *The American Journalist: A Portrait of U.S. News People and Their Work*, 2d ed. (Bloomington: Indiana

University Press, 1991); Edwin Emery and Joseph McKerns, *AEJMC: 75 Years in the Making*, Journalism Monographs, no. 104 (Columbia, SC: AEJMC, 1987); Bernard Voyenne, *Les Journalistes Français: D'où viennent-ils? Qui sont-ils? Que font-ils?* (Paris: Les Editions CFPJ, 1985); Jeremy Tunstall, *Journalists at Work* (London: Constable, 1971); Frank Barton, *African Assignment* (Zurich: IPI, 1969); UNESCO, *Communication in Africa* (Paris: UNESCO, 1977); Vladimir Hudec, *Education and Training of Journalists at Higher Educational Establishments in the Czechoslovak Socialist Republic* (Prague: Faculty of Journalism, Charles University, 1984).

12. The following list is by no means exhaustive, but it represents some of the best research published in recent years. Colin Sparks and Slavko Splichal, "Journalistic Education and Professional Socialization," *Gazette* 43, no.1 (1989), pp. 31–52; Ramon Sala-Balust, "Journalists' Training: A FIEJ Survey," *FIEJ Bulletin* 144 (September 1985), pp. 9–12; Enn Raudsepp, "Reinventing Journalism Education," *Canadian Journal of Communication* 14, no.2 (May 1989), pp. 1–14; Joon-Mann Kang, "Reporters and Their Professional and Occupational Commitment in a Developing Country," *Gazette* 40, no.1 (1987), pp. 3–20; Don Woolford, "Third World Journalism Training," *Australian Journalism Review* 6, no.1 (January 1984), pp. 63–67; Jerry Komia Domatob, "Communication Training for Self-reliance in Black Africa: Challenges and Strategies," *Gazette* 40, no.3 (1987), pp. 167–82; Chen C. Chimutengwende, "The Role of Communications Training and Technology in African Development," in George Gerbner and Marsha Siefert, eds., *World Communications: A Handbook* (New York: Longman, 1984); Onuma O. Oreh, "Developmental Journalism and Press Freedom: An African Viewpoint," *Gazette* 24, no.1 (1978), pp. 36–40; A. Carlos Ruótolo, "Professional Orientation among Journalists in Three Latin American Countries," *Gazette* 40, no.2 (1987), pp. 131–142; John A. Lent, "Journalism Training in Cuba Emphasizes Politics, Ideology," *Journalism Educator* 39, no.3 (Autumn 1984), pp. 12–15; Ray Newton, "J-Education Mexican Style," *Journalism Educator* 27, no.3 (October 1972), pp. 16–17; Beverly Keever, "Journalism Education Grows by Leaps and Bounds in China," *Journalism Educator* 43, no.1 (Spring 1988), pp. 29–31; Elizabeth Schillinger, "Journalism at Moscow State: The Impact of Glasnost," *Journalism Educator* 43, no.2 (Summer 1988), pp. 52–56; Sankaran Ramanathan and Katherine T. Frith, "Mass Comm Young and Growing in Malaysia," *Journalism Educator* 42, no.4 (Winter 1988), pp. 10–12; Florangel Rosario-Braid, "Journalism Education: Responding to New Challenges," *Media Asia* 13, no.4 (1986), pp. 195–199; Lynn Failing, "The Changing Scene in Communication Education," *Media Asia* 13, no.4 (1986), pp. 183–188; John Warren and Adchara Khotanan, "Communication Education at Thai Universities," *Journalism Educator* 45, no.4 (Winter 1991), pp. 28–33; Terry Davidson, "Ed Emery: Teaching Journalism in China," *Community College Journalist* 13, no.4 (Fall 1985), pp. 2–7; Larry Taylor, "Journalism Education at the *Times of India*," *Community College Journalist* 15, no.2 (Spring 1987), p. 3; Robert Scheibel, "Five Dimensions Explain Differences in British-American Journalism Education,"

Community College Journalist 15, no.4 (Fall 1988), pp. 10–11; Doug Ramsey, "Educating Professional Journalists: Their Wants and Needs," *Newspaper Research Journal* 11, no.4 (Fall 1990), pp. 72–79.

13. Abdallah Taher Eljerary, "The Design of a Mass Media Training Program: The Formulation of a Paradigm for the Developing Nations with Particular Application to the Libyan Example" (Ph.D. diss., University of Wisconsin-Madison, 1981).

14. Dennis R. Cooper, "Basic Training for Third World Journalists" (Ph.D. diss., University of Tennessee-Knoxville, 1987).

Chapter Two

Training Needs

Training needs vary from country to country as a function of a wide range of factors, most of which will be discussed in this chapter. It needs to be said at the outset, however, that this chapter will deal only with general concepts and definitions common to most cultures and not specific to any individual country or region. A more detailed analysis of individual needs will be given in later chapters.

The first question that should be addressed is a definitional one. Are we discussing training needs for journalism, mass communication or communication as a whole? In general, terminology reflects successive developments in communication structures. At the beginning of the century, at a time when mass communication was virtually limited to the printed media, the first training establishments were called schools of journalism and were largely devoted to producing recruits for the newspaper industry, which needed reporters, editors, layout people and photographers. The film industry, which can certainly be regarded as a mass medium but not perhaps as a channel for the deliberate delivery of specific messages, had its own apprentice-type training systems concentrating almost exclusively on the technical aspects of cinematography.

Over the years, with the appearance of radio and television, new needs have emerged, and schools of journalism have adapted their programs to include broadcast production and broadcast news courses. Some of these courses are strictly technical, but the broadcast media have also developed their own communication languages and styles. More recently, public relations and advertising, offspring of both the print and electronic media, have made their appearance in certain schools of journalism, although not without controversy. Today, newer forms of communication, associated with computers, satellites and interactive linkages, are raising the question of expanding or adapting curricula even further.

It is interesting to note in parenthesis that over the last few decades the terminology employed by UNESCO, the largest sponsor of comparative research in this area, has also mirrored these shifts. In the 1950s, emphasis was placed on journalism training.[1] By the mid-1970s, mass communication had become the focus.[2] Today, many of its technical meetings are concerned with communication.[3] Of course, historically, UNESCO's approach to the whole area of communication has viewed information as a potential agent of economic development, cultural identity, social change and political domination. Along these lines, it has defined communication training as "the planned process of inducing those attitudes and transmitting those skills necessary for the effective mass movement of ideas, the sharing of information, and the transfer of experience."[4]

This approach is an interesting one in that it often implies some other aspects of communication, in particular the notion of communication and development.[5] Other issues that emerge from this approach include the whole idea of cultural imperialism, the role of interpersonal communication in the preservation and transmission of traditions, and the importance of mediated communication as a vehicle for cultural values, to name but a few. These ideas have universal application, but, perhaps regrettably, they are debated more often with reference to developing countries than to the industrialized nations. For the purposes of this study, however, these ideas will be treated as side issues except insofar as they affect the conceptual context in which training occurs.

In practical terms, this means that the focus of the study will be on journalism, which is at the core of mass communication and the mass media. As has already been pointed out, though, there is a growing tendency for schools of journalism to offer curricula that take in a wide variety of different communication disciplines. In many cases, journalism training goes beyond traditional journalistic skills and procedures.

In most countries, journalism training covers two main areas, practical skills and general education, to which may be added purely technical knowledge needed to operate the specialized equipment used in some branches of journalism. The thinking behind this is that, although it is difficult to communicate effectively without having mastered the basic skills of writing, editing and information gathering, it is equally important to have the general educational background that enables the journalist to understand, analyze and interpret the information gathered. In some circumstances, general education may also include ideological teachings necessary to understand the political context in which a particular type of journalism is practiced. The relative proportion of theory, skills, technical expertise and liberal studies varies from system to system.

CONCEPTS OF JOURNALISM

One of the most important factors in determining this mix of subject matter is the perceived function of journalism in any given society, which is a reflection of the type of media system in place. Media systems themselves are the result of press laws, economic and political variables, cultural and social influences and such basic considerations as demographic distribution, literacy or personal income levels.

Many attempts have been made to classify press systems. The oldest typology, developed by Siebert, Peterson and Schramm in 1956, defined four theories of the press, the Authoritarian, the Libertarian, the Social Responsibility and the Soviet Communist "concepts of what the press should be and do."[6] This influential typology, written at the height of the Cold War, is now considered to be out of date, particularly since the emergence of press freedoms in Eastern Europe, but it is easy to see how different countries could be neatly classified under this system. Even today, it is possible, for example, to place China, Cuba and Vietnam under the Soviet Communist heading; a few Latin American and several African countries under Authoritarian; and most Western European nations under Libertarian. The Social Responsibility concept, which reflects the thinking of the Hutchins Commission,[7] has traditionally included the United States (with some serious reservations); but some elements of it could also be applied to a number of emerging press systems in the developing world, which often place emphasis on information as a means of education and social progress. However, it will be obvious that such a typology fails to take into account some of the developments that have taken place since the 1950s.

William Hachten set out to remedy this situation with a work called *The World News Prism*, which first appeared in 1981.[8] In this study, Hachten kept the Authoritarian and Communist models but combined the Libertarian and Social Responsibility concepts under a Western model. More importantly, he added two other concepts, the Revolutionary and the Developmental. Under the Revolutionary heading, Hachten includes such examples as *Pravda*, at its origin the quintessential revolutionary newspaper, the underground press in Nazi-occupied France during World War II, and *samizdat* publications in the Soviet Union. One could add any number of examples from anticolonialist movements, particularly in Africa.

The Developmental model, which in some cases has grown out of revolutionary situations, views the communication process as a tool for nation building and economic development. Obviously, the subordination of all means of communication to development goals often implies some form of autocratic control by a central government, which is why this model has been criticized by the West. The Developmental model, which can also be classified as an offshoot of the Authoritarian concept, has been closely linked to the notion of a "New World Information Order" and Third World criticisms of the West and its transnational media. This issue was hotly debated in UNESCO conferences in the 1970s and continues to be a subject of much controversy. Although a large number of Third World countries fall naturally under the Developmental heading, the Developmental concept itself remains, as Hachten remarks, "an amorphous and curious mixture of ideas, rhetoric, influences and grievances. As yet, the concept is not clearly defined."[9]

Other media scholars have offered other models,[10] but, on the whole, the five concepts outlined above cover most of the press systems in place today. However, a sixth concept, offered by Robert Picard in *The Press and the Decline of Democracy*,[11] is now of particular relevance to the new press systems emerging in Eastern Europe. Picard argues that Hachten's Western model, which includes the Libertarian and Social Responsibility concepts, should also include a "democratic socialist" concept. This Democratic Socialist theory recognizes the need for pluralism but also allows state intervention, if necessary, to protect the interests of the people, a notion that is entirely abhorrent to the advocates of Western libertarianism. Versions of this model already exist in Scandinavia, and it is also a concept that underlies public ownership of the broadcast media in many parts of the world.

Picard's concept, which has been little more than a subcategory of the Western model, now takes on a whole new significance as the press systems of Eastern Europe grope their way toward some kind of freedom. Indeed, most Eastern European countries have reinstated freedom of the press; but, until a free market economy can be built, there will be little or none of the advertising revenue necessary to support the kind of free press systems that exist in the West. Inevitably, therefore, if the press is to survive in Eastern Europe, it will be forced to accept some form of state subsidy. In light of the total government controls that existed under communist rule, it is likely that any new form of state subsidy will be regulated by law, so as to protect the new-found freedoms of the people. If this is the case, then the kind of system that will emerge will look more like Picard's Democratic Socialist model than the traditional libertarian Western model.

Another method of classification, developed by Donald Brod,[12] is worthy of attention because it is very simple and easily applied to most press systems. Brod believes that all systems can be divided between the One-Step and the Two-Step approach. The One-Step approach refers to the Western tradition of simply reporting the news. The Two-Step approach involves (1) determining the desired effect of communication and (2) sending a message to achieve it. Deceptively simple. In the best libertarian tradition, Western journalists believe that the greatest good will result if the public has unlimited access to information. On the other hand, argues Brod, journalists in the rest of the world, whether they are operating in systems labeled Authoritarian, Communist, Developmental, or even Revolutionary, see information as a means to an end that cannot be left to faith.

Brod points out that the "desired effect" in the Two-Step approach is not necessarily evil. That approach may of course be intent on keeping a tyrannical government in power, but it may also seek no further than to help farmers to produce greater yields or encourage citizens to participate in the arts. Brod's conclusion is relevant to our analysis of the perceived function of journalism. "Where journalists have the Two-Step attitude," he writes, "very little outside control is needed. And where journalists have the One-Step attitude, relatively little outside control is possible."[13]

It should be stressed that the foregoing discussion of press systems and press freedoms is applicable mainly to the print media. With the notable exception of the United States, broadcast systems in almost every country in the world are subjected, or have been subjected at some time in the past, to some type of state control, in the form of government censorship, ownership or subsidy. Even in the United States, radio and television stations, while free to broadcast virtually any kind of program content, are subject to licensing and regulation by the Federal Communications Commission.

Historically, in most other countries in the world, broadcast systems were first created and subsequently controlled by governments or governmental bodies. Although many governments have indeed used broadcasting systems to further their own aims, the reasoning behind initial government intervention was less repressive than philosophical and, in some cases, was merely practical. In smaller countries, government support was made necessary by the huge cost of building expensive transmitters, relays and studio facilities. But, in more general terms, broadcasting was viewed as a public service and as too powerful a tool to be placed in the hands of possibly unscrupulous private interests. Only government control, it was thought, could protect the interests of the public.[14]

For this reason, resistance to commercial broadcasting has remained strong. Only in recent years have certain governments in Western Europe allowed independent broadcasting systems to develop, and it is doubtful whether this would have happened without the phenomena of pirate radio, transborder broadcasting and direct broadcast satellites. In other parts of the world, where communication continues to be viewed as an instrument of education and development, strong government controls remain firmly in place. It is interesting to note that in Eastern Europe governments have hastened to install press freedoms for the print media but have been reluctant to extend these freedoms to broadcasting.

POLITICAL AND ECONOMIC INFLUENCES

As will be evident, the various types of press systems described above are sensitive to political upheavals and economic change. It is easy to understand how a new political regime can introduce either sweeping reforms or stricter controls or how existing systems can be totally transformed by new laws. Such extreme political changes are more likely to occur in unstable societies, particularly in certain areas of the Third World where coups are relatively common. In more settled countries, change will be more gradual and is likely to be associated more with economic than with political developments.

In free market economies, competition for advertising revenue has led to concentration of ownership, which for a variety of reasons has resulted in increased homogenization of news content, a greater reliance on electronic news sources and the "de-skilling" of journalists, all of which will have a profound effect on journalistic practices and consequently on journalism training.[15]

Another feature that characterizes group ownership is that its financial net is spreading wider and wider. In the face of competition, press groups were initially content to buy up radio and television stations, weeklies, magazines and other competing media. But now, their financial interests have extended to cable systems, newsprint manufacturing, printing and timberlands, as well as to entertainment, oil, banking, manufacturing and other activities unrelated to the media. It could be argued that such diversification provides greater financial strength; and it is true that, on more than one occasion, losing newspapers have been subsidized by profits from nonmedia holdings. On the other hand, because of this diversification, decisions governing the future of individual news organizations may be influenced by factors that are foreign or even downright hostile to the media. The dangers of "interlocking directorates" and a "private ministry of information" have been well documented.[16]

Another economic consideration that affects all press systems is the amount of disposable income the public can afford to spend on media products. In many countries, rising production costs and dwindling advertising revenues have contributed to the demise of many daily newspapers, thus compromising pluralism and forcing choices between entertainment and news. In poorer societies and in the absence of substantial advertising revenue, the newspaper may be an elite medium reserved for those who can afford it, in which case the broadcast media, and especially radio, become important vectors of free public information and education, that is, when they do not require viewing or listening licenses. Finally, newspaper and periodical distribution networks, cable television and pay-as-you-view programming are all destined to become significant terms in the overall equation of consumer economics.

Within these different contexts, then, journalists emerge as key figures responsible for conveying information about the society in which they work to those who live in it. But journalists are also affected by the traditions of their profession, shaped by progress and revolution, laws, cultural factors and socialization. In this sense, they belong both to the historical fabric of the past and the modern realities of the system in which they function.

And so, depending on the past history, the traditions, the current political structure and the economics of the press system in which they operate, journalists may be perceived as having distinct roles: reporters, interpreters, disseminators, artists, thinkers, informers, government employees, political workers, nation builders, defenders of the truth, public watchdogs or the guardians of morality. It is this definition, or combination of definitions, that will determine the type of communicator to be produced by a country's training facilities, placing lesser or greater emphasis on practical skills, analytical abilities, general or specialized knowledge, loyalty to government, political correctness or, in a few cases, professional certification.

NEEDS ASSESSMENT

Such considerations, which to this writer's knowledge have never been seriously included in needs assessment for communication training, are of course qualitative in nature and fall within what could be termed societal needs. In general terms, these needs will be either factual or developmental. In the first case, information is viewed as part of the democratic process and, as such, contributes to the greater happiness of the public by achieving true representation and by promoting truth, equality and access to the elected government. It is doubtful whether this kind of information system can exist, given the commercial nature of the media in most "democratic" nations, but certainly some societies aspire to it. The needs of such societies will be for communicators who can function as reporters, government watchdogs and disseminators; and these communicators will require a specific set of skills that can be produced by a specific program of training.

Developmental needs, on the other hand, are primarily concerned with improving society. UNESCO's report *Training for Mass Communication* identifies three main categories of development-oriented material.[17] The first is *cultural*, involving the development and preservation of a society's arts, music, history and traditions as a basis for cultural identity when faced with a flood of "alien" material from other societies. The second is *informational* in nature. The media almost always supply information; with planning, it is possible to select from the range of facts available those which have a useful meaning for the audience. Western critics frequently argue that this process injects value judgments into content, but it could also be argued that all media, even in "free" systems, cannot report all the facts and have to make some kind of selection. The third category is *instructional*. Examples of this are broadcasting for schools or other forms of educational programming.

The needs of societies seeking these types of communication will be for communicators who are able to entertain while they educate, who are able to keep in mind the permanent interests of their audience and who have a firm grasp of the whole development process. These communicators will require a somewhat different set of skills than those needed by communicators in industrial democracies.

Whatever the nature of the communication process, training must be able to satisfy six need levels.[18] The first is *orientation*, which enables new communicators to understand the system in which they will work. The second level involves *basic skills*, which include mainly language-handling abilities but also certain types of manual dexterity. The third level focuses on *technical skills*, which take in programming, writing and production skills and which will probably require the use of equipment. It is to be noted, though, that this kind of knowledge extends only to the use of equipment and not to its repair or maintenance, which remains the domain of technicians. The fourth level concerns the *upgrading of skills*, either for those whose skills may have deteriorated over time or for those who are being called upon to work with new equipment or procedures. The fifth level seeks to build a *liberal background* so that communicators can develop an ability to process a variety of information and understand social, cultural and economic issues affecting their audience. The final level extends to *specialized applications* in the various fields of mass communication.

The quantitative side of needs assessment is affected by a variety of social and professional factors. The numbers and types of communicators needed by the media industry of a society will depend on the structure of that industry. For example, is the media system dominated by the print media, or is broadcasting an important avenue of communication? In most industrialized nations, there is a fairly balanced mix of media, controlled to a certain extent by the degree of advertising allowed in the broadcast media. In other countries, there may be technical difficulties associated with the availability of newsprint or printing presses, or social problems such as illiteracy, which are bound to alter prevailing media structures. In some countries, geographic considerations may make it difficult to distribute newspapers or transmit broadcast messages effectively. In a few societies, media consumption patterns may be shaped by strong cultural or religious traditions.

In summary, then, the training needs of different societies will be affected by any number of factors associated with their political and social systems, their economies and their media systems, as well as the traditions and perceived roles of the communicators that work in them. It is obvious that such training needs will vary considerably and that very different training structures will be needed to meet them successfully.

NOTES

1. UNESCO, *The Training of Journalists: A World-wide Study on the Training of Personnel for the Mass Media* (Paris: UNESCO, 1958); UNESCO, *Education for Journalism*, Reports and Papers on Mass Communication, no.8 (Paris: UNESCO, 1954).

2. UNESCO, *Training for Mass Communication*, Reports and Papers on Mass Communication, no.73 (Paris: UNESCO, 1975); May Katzen, *Mass Communication: Teaching and Studies at Universities* (Paris: UNESCO Press, 1975).

3. For example, "International Meeting of Experts on Regional Approaches to Communication Training," UNESCO House, Paris, June 12–14, 1991.

4. UNESCO, *Training for Mass Communication*, p. 9.

5. See, among others, Everett Rogers, *Communication and Development: Critical Perspectives* (Beverly Hills, CA: Sage, 1976); Robert L. Stevenson, *Communication, Development and the Third World* (White Plains, NY: Longman, 1988); Robert C. Hornik, *Development Communication: Information, Agriculture and Nutrition in the Third World* (White Plains, NY: Longman, 1988); Hamid Mowlana and Laurie J. Wilson, *Communication Technology and Development*, Reports and Papers on Mass Communication, no. 101 (Paris: UNESCO, 1988); Ithiel de Sola Pool, *Technologies of Freedom* (Cambridge, MA: Belknap Press/Harvard University Press, 1983).

6. Frederick Siebert, Theodore Peterson and Wilbur Schramm, *Four Theories of the Press* (Urbana: University of Illinois Press, 1956).

7. Commission on Freedom of the Press, *A Free and Responsible Press* (Chicago: University of Chicago Press, 1947).

8. William A. Hachten, *The World News Prism: Changing Media, Clashing Ideologies* (Ames: Iowa State University Press, 1981), 2d ed., 1987.

9. Ibid., 2d ed., p. 30.

10. Among others, Ralph Lowenstein in John C. Merrill and Ralph L. Lowenstein, *Media, Messages and Men*, 2d ed. (New York: Longman, 1979), p. 164; John C. Merrill, *The Imperative of Freedom* (New York: Hastings House, 1974), p. 42; J. Herbert Altschull, *Agents of Power* (New York: Longman, 1984), pp. 279–299; Raymond Williams, *Communications*, 3d ed. (Harmondsworth, Middlesex, U.K.: Penguin Books, 1976), pp. 130–131.

11. Robert G. Picard, *The Press and the Decline of Democracy* (Westport, CT: Greenwood Press, 1985).

12. Donald F. Brod, "Classifying the World's Media: The One-Step and Two-Step Approaches," *International Communication Bulletin* 22, nos. 3–4 (Fall 1987), pp. 8–11.

13. Ibid., p. 11.

14. For further information on broadcasting systems, see Donald Brown, *International Radio Broadcasting* (New York: Praeger, 1982) and Sydney W. Head, *World Broadcasting Systems: A Comparative Analysis* (Belmont, CA: Wadsworth, 1985). For European broadcasting policies, see Denis McQuail and Karen Siune, eds., *New Media Politics: Comparative Perspectives in Western Europe* (Beverly Hills, CA: Sage, 1986).

15. Philip Gaunt, *Choosing the News: The Profit Factor in News Selection* (Westport, CT: Greenwood Press, 1990). See, in particular, chap. 4.

16. Ben Bagdikian, *The Media Monopoly*, 2d ed. (Boston: Beacon Press, 1987).

17. UNESCO, *Training for Mass Communication*, p. 14.

18. Ibid., pp. 13–14.

Chapter Three

Training Structures

It would be logical to assume that training structures are the natural outcome of training needs, which, as was suggested in the last chapter, can be either social or professional. In many countries, this is indeed the case; in other countries, training structures may also be subject to the availability of human or technical resources or, infrequently, to government or professional regulation. For this reason, while the wealthier nations often produce more communicators than are needed, some less fortunate countries, which tend to view communication as an essential tool for social and economic development, remain desperately short of trained personnel.

Education administrators, even in the most affluent societies, always complain about the resources that are allocated to them. Of course, it could be argued that there is never enough money spent on education. But there is a question of degree. Educators in the industrialized nations may claim with justification that their salaries and facilities are inadequate, but in many parts of the Third World even the most fundamental needs remain unsatisfied. The most frequent complaints recorded in researching this study had to do with the dearth of such basic teaching materials as textbooks. It can be imagined how difficult it must be in these circumstances to teach some of the more advanced communication skills requiring word processors, computers, cameras, projectors, recorders and other expensive equipment.

Many developing countries also have a chronic shortage of qualified teachers, and the training of trainers has become a familiar part of the development process. This raises problems because, without qualified local educators, future trainers have to be trained either in a foreign country or by visiting "experts." In both situations, trainees are almost inevitably exposed to alien cultures, professional values and press philosophies, which may clash with their own national priorities. In some cases, they may be taught to work with equipment and technologies that are just not available in their own country.

Another, less obvious problem outside the West is the shortage of suitable students. In the developing world, students often lack the basic educational skills required to take advanced courses in writing, reporting, editing and other more technical areas of communication. The situation is improving, thanks to the efforts of regional and international training institutions, but the shortage of qualified students not only in communication but also in other areas of education remains a real challenge in many developing countries. In other countries, as was traditionally true in Eastern Europe, there is sometimes a shortage of students who are willing to study for careers in communication. Journalists in most formerly Communist countries enjoyed little prestige because they were viewed as tools of the system; as a result, for several years prior to independence, enrollments in journalism schools showed a steady decline. Since the emergence of more democratic forms of government, interest in journalism has soared; but it will be some time before existing training structures can be modified to meet the demands of a freer and more commercial press system.

TYPES OF TRAINING STRUCTURES

Training structures vary considerably from country to country, but it is possible to identify three main categories that are a reflection of the size and strength of the economies in which they occur.

Major Industrial Democracies

Major industrialized democracies usually have a large number of training institutions to meet the needs of complex press systems. However, although they have emerged from the same traditions of pluralism and press freedom, their training structures are not necessarily identical. Any variations that occur tend to be the result of differences in the relationships that have developed among various key actors: educators, media owners, government agencies and unions or other professional associations. Of these, the most important is that between training establishments and media professionals, which in many cases has determined not only the nature of the training given but also the place in which it is dispensed, that is, the university, the specialized trade school, the workplace or some combination thereof. These differences will be addressed in detail in later chapters.

The number of countries enjoying democratic freedoms and economies large enough to support complex training structures remains relatively small, but historically they have had a considerable influence on the way in which training structures have developed in other countries.

Smaller Industrialized Countries

Many smaller countries with lower populations and more limited press systems are able to satisfy their training needs with one or two national schools. Examples of these are the Scandinavian nations, which, although they value press freedom, do not always have enough advertising revenue to support a pluralistic press or independent training structures without some form of government subsidy. Other examples are to be found in Eastern Europe, where, until recently, training establishments were limited to a small number of government-controlled schools. The new training structures that are beginning to emerge are likely to be limited by other, economic considerations and will almost certainly have to be subsidized by the government, however ideologically distasteful this may be to the supporters of new press freedoms.

Developing Nations

The developing nations, which are by far the most numerous and which also have the greatest and most urgent needs, may be further divided into subcategories that, once again, reflect economic and social development. The categories are:

1. larger and economically stronger countries that have their own well-developed national training institutions
2. countries that have no training establishments of their own but are able to send their students to training centers in their own geographic region
3. countries that have no training establishments of their own but are obliged, for various reasons, to send their students to training centers outside their geographic region, usually in the West

Each of these subcategories presents problems that will be discussed later under the section on external influences, but suffice it to say here that numerous international and regional training initiatives have already made progress in solving these problems.

The three main categories identified above cover most of the different types of training structures in place today, but a few countries, like China, still stand apart. Until recently, it would have been possible to include a fourth category covering the Communist countries, but this bloc has now disintegrated, with many Eastern and Central European nations moving toward capitalistic or at least social-democratic political systems and the press freedoms that go with them.

Despite *glasnost* and independence, however, the systems in place in many parts of the former Soviet bloc are still not entirely free of certain forms of press control, and it may take some time to change completely the existing training structures. China, which experimented briefly with limited freedoms in the 1980s, has now reverted to strict press controls. A few other authoritarian regimes in Latin America and Africa remain apart, too, but on the whole most systems fall into the three categories or will tend to move toward them in the future.

Many variations exist within these various structures; but, as has already been suggested, most of these revolve around two principal factors, the perceived role and function of journalism and the type of relationship that exists between educators and the communication industry. Taken together, these two factors help to shape what is taught, how it is taught and where it is taught, as well as who teaches it and who studies it.

REGULATION

Another factor that should be taken into account is regulation by either government or professional bodies. In all Western countries and in many countries in other parts of the world, no professional qualifications are required to practice journalism, which means that journalists are not obliged to have any formal training. In actual fact, a large and growing percentage of journalists in these countries do choose to undergo some form of specialized training, particularly in the more technical areas of communication. At the same time, an increasing number of journalists entering the profession are university graduates. It should be emphasized that, in these countries, such qualifications, while desirable, are not required either by law or by employers. In some cases, union membership may be considered an informal prerequisite to working in the profession, but this is as close as these countries come to regulation.

On the other hand, quite a few countries do have a mechanism for licensing journalists. In these situations, journalists are allowed to work only if they hold an official license, which is usually granted directly by the government or, in some cases, indirectly through unions or other professional bodies. Although such practices are abhorred in the West, they are common in countries that espouse the concept of developmental journalism and in which journalists are government employees.

Another interesting form of regulation is provided by the *colegios* in about a dozen countries in Latin America. Practicing journalists are required by law to belong to one of these organizations, and in order to belong they must have a journalism degree from a recognized national university. This system has been criticized by press freedom advocates such as the Inter American Press Association, which argues that it provides governments with a potential means of controlling the press. However, Latin American journalists have traditionally supported *colegio* laws because they provide a degree of protection by restricting entry into the profession and by keeping salaries at acceptable levels.

EXTERNAL INFLUENCES

So far this analysis has centered on internal factors affecting training structures, but external influences may also come into play. On the whole, the older industrialized nations are the least likely to be affected because they already have well-established training structures, some of which have been in place since the beginning of the century. But the developing countries are particularly vulnerable to outside influences, which may take several forms.

In the preceding discussion of training structures in developing countries, three subcategories were identified. Each is subject to outside influences, either directly or indirectly. Obviously, those countries that have no training establishments of their own and are obliged to send students to training centers in the West are the most vulnerable because students often encounter cultural and ideological conflicts. In one typical situation, students from Latin America are trained in print journalism in the United States and are taught the virtues of a free press, investigative reporting, adversarial interviewing, sunshine laws and the accountability of public officials. These are all worthy concepts; but when the students return home and attempt to apply them in a society that condones press controls and authoritarian rule, they are likely to find themselves in trouble.

In another typical situation, African students are sent to London to learn television reporting techniques. Although the London training centers try to be sensitive to the needs of journalists from developing countries, many educators claim that it is impossible to teach such basic techniques as framing, angles and editing without also imparting values that may be alien to foreign cultures. Indeed, very few journalistic procedures, whether they are technical or editorial in nature, are entirely free of values since they imply choices that make sense only in a certain cultural context.

Those nations that have no training establisments of their own but are able to send their students to regional training centers are more fortunate because costs tend to be lower. But it would be wrong to assume that all countries within a single geographic region share the same cultural values or the same political ideologies. There is often more conflict within regions than between regions, which is particularly true of some of the religious and ethnic differences that divide countries. Most regional training centers attempt to accommodate these differences, but for reasons of sheer practicality some form of shared paradigm has to be adopted.

Finally, those countries with their own national or local schools are better equipped to meet their own communication training needs, but even these are not always totally free of external influences. Many national training centers were originally set up by former colonial powers or are still staffed by educators who were trained in Western centers. In their efforts to free themselves of colonial influences, school administrators, reinforced by government officials, have sometimes felt obliged to develop curricula and approaches that are as far removed as possible from Western models, and this has not always been constructive. It should be added, however, that regional training bodies have made much progress in developing training structures that are more realistically geared toward local and intraregional needs.

Another form of external influence is economic in nature and, in some cases, still related to former colonial ties. In order to fill gaps in infrastructure, some Western nations have donated communication hardware and other training equipment to a number of developing countries. Though such initiatives may have been disinterested and may have truly benefited the recipients, they have also created technological dependencies favorable to the development of profitable markets. For example, telephone networks, printing facilities and entire broadcasting systems in a number of African countries have been supplied by former colonial powers. There are some very good technological reasons for this, but the result is a lingering influence long after former colonial ties have been officially broken.

MULTISTAGE SYSTEMS

Historically, formal journalism training emerged around the turn of the century, first in the United States and then in France and other Western European countries. In its early stages, training was largely limited to basic newsroom and printroom skills and duplicated the kind of informal on-the-job training that had existed in newspapers for generations. As training needs grew with the development of the mass media, curricula were expanded to take in new skills and nontechnical areas such as ethics, law, media management and communication and society, particularly when training was given in universities, as was the case in the United States. Generally speaking, formal training initiatives in the West were financed by a variety of sources that included media owners, government agencies, unions and other professional bodies. At the same time, a number of private schools were created, but their diplomas and programs were often not accredited.

Training institutions also appeared at an early date in many Latin American countries, some of them as the result of efforts by religious organizations, but in other parts of the world they were slow to develop. Before independence, in many African and Asian countries, on-the-job training was the norm; but, whether owners and editors were European or local, training tended to be based on Western news practices and European languages. There were some exceptions, particularly as independence approached and locally owned newspapers became outlets for anticolonial grievances and nationalistic aspirations; but on the whole the press remained firmly in the hands of the colonial powers right up until independence. When independence came and the colonial powers went home, most of these countries were left with an acute shortage of trained journalists.

Some newly independent countries, such as India, Ghana and Nigeria, quickly moved to establish their own schools; but in most cases they had to rely on Europeans to initiate training programs, with the result that European journalistic practices continued to be perpetuated. Many countries that did not have their own schools were obliged to send trainee journalists to London or Paris, where they acquired styles and approaches that were quite out of touch with the people. In the 1960s, as training needs continued to grow, a number of organizations jumped into the breach. Among them were the International Press Institute, the International Organization of Journalists, the International Federation of Journalists, the Thomson Foundation, the American Press Institute and UNESCO. These organizations designed intensive short courses that succeeded in producing hundreds of journalists equipped with at least some basic skills, but very few of these organizations were "value free." Almost all of them were intent on transmitting not only technical skills but also strong ideological convictions.

When regional training centers were set up later, they were still staffed either by Westerners or by people who had been trained by Westerners, so that for several decades the influence of Western values was felt first directly and then indirectly through multistage training systems. Naturally, these values often clashed with the nation-building needs of the developing world, but it was not until relatively recently that notions of developmental journalism grew strong enough to threaten traditional Western journalistic practices. There is now some debate, even in the Third World, as to the value of developmental journalism, and efforts to create agencies producing development news have not met with notable success. The conflicts that remain and continue to shape training in many developing countries are more between the ideal of press freedom and the reality of government ownership of the media.

Chapter Four

The United States and Canada

As in so many other areas, communication training structures in the United States and Canada are now quite similar but spring from very different traditions. The United States is the home of university-based journalism training programs that have become a model for countries all over the world. On the other hand, Canada, which has maintained very strong ties with Britain and France, has, until relatively recently, favored European training methods based on the apprenticeship system. Needless to say, journalism and journalism training in Canada and the United States share the same beliefs in a free and pluralistic press.

THE UNITED STATES

The United States can be said to have the oldest and strongest system of journalism education of any country in the world, with roots going back to the end of the nineteenth century.[1] As early as 1873, Kansas State College offered a course in printing; and in 1876 and 1877 Cornell University ran a series of lectures on journalism. In 1908, the University of Missouri opened the first independent school of journalism, soon to be followed by the creation of limited programs at the universities of Pennsylvania and Illinois.[2]

After these modest beginnings, journalism education in the United States quickly gained strong support from the newspaper industry. Joseph

Pulitzer of the *New York Daily World* gave over $2 million to Columbia University to found the Pulitzer School of Journalism, which opened in 1912. In 1918, William Murphy, the publisher of the *Minneapolis Tribune*, set up an endowment fund for journalism education at the University of Minnesota. Three years later, the owners of the *Chicago Tribune* established the Medill School of Journalism at Northwestern University. Many other schools and departments of journalism were created or developed with the help of state press associations and individuals.[3]

As is not the case in Western Europe or Canada, the strong relationship that has developed between the media, the newspaper industry in particular, and the universities has virtually eliminated any influence by unions or government agencies. In any case, direct government intervention in the workings of the media is prohibited by the First Amendment. On the other hand, even though media managers take great pains to separate the newsroom from the business office, there is little doubt that commercial interests have at least an indirect effect on the total communication process, and that includes training.[4]

The media industry also continues to exercise a strong influence on communication training through the Accrediting Council on Education in Journalism and Mass Communications (ACEJMC), which is formed of about two-thirds media professionals and one-third educators. Accreditation is granted to those institutions meeting the Council's standards, which emphasize innovative educational and training techniques and which insist that students take a minimum of 90 semester hours in courses outside their major area of journalism or mass communication, including at least 65 hours in the basic liberal arts and sciences, with 30 hours in journalism or mass communication.[5]

This 90–65 standard, which was adopted by the ACEJMC in 1985, still has a lot of support in both the universities and the profession. However, the fact that only about 25 to 30 percent of a student's classes may be taken in a department of journalism or mass communication has tended to isolate training institutions from the true intellectual life of the university. Some administrators also argue that certain types of nonskills communication courses, although taught in departments of journalism or mass communication, should be considered as social science subjects and could therefore be removed from the 30 hours in the area major, thus freeing more hours for purely skills courses. Today, there is a growing split between schools of journalism, with their emphasis on training for the media, and schools of communication, which offer a more integrated approach toward the different areas of the communication process.

Naturally these accreditation standards apply only to those schools that are accredited or that seek accreditation. According to the latest annual survey of journalism and mass communication programs performed by Professor Lee B. Becker of Ohio State University, there are 91 accredited programs in the country. There are also 92 schools that are members of the Association of Schools of Journalism and Mass Communication (ASJMC) but are not accredited by the ACEJMC. Finally, there are 212 schools without accreditation or ASJMC membership.[6]

The same survey showed that for the autumn of 1989 the number of students enrolled in the programs offered by these 398 schools was estimated at around 155,000. Of these, about 145,000 were enrolled in undergraduate programs, 8,500 in master's programs and 900 in doctoral programs. These figures showed an overall increase in enrollment of 5.6 percent, an increase of 4 percent in master's programs and 11.7 percent in doctoral programs. The number of degrees granted for the same period was approximately 30,500 undergraduate degrees, 2,500 master's degrees and 100 doctoral degrees. This was a 2.5 percent drop for the undergraduates but a substantial increase of around 12.5 percent for graduate degrees.

With regard to the type of degrees granted, 21.1 percent of all undergraduate degrees were in advertising, 14.3 percent in public relations, 13 percent in news-editorial, 9.9 percent in radio-television, 9 percent in broadcast news and 4.1 percent in journalism. Although these figures certainly represent a common trend over the last few years, it should be pointed out that the percentages shown do vary. At the accredited schools, which of course are the most influenced by the profession, the top specialties were advertising, news-editorial, public relations, broadcast journalism and radio-television. At the nonaccredited but ASJMC membership schools, the top five were radio-television, public relations, news-editorial, advertising and broadcast news. Finally, at the nonaccredited programs that were not members of ASJMC, the top ranking specialties were journalism, radio-television, public relations, advertising and news-editorial.

The figures mentioned certainly indicate that communication training is still extremely healthy in the United States, even with the slight dip in the number of undergraduate degrees awarded. Indeed, seen from a European perspective, the numbers seem enormous; but it must be remembered that not all communication graduates enter the communication industry. Some 1988 figures show that of all those students earning bachelor's degrees in communication, fewer than 50 percent find media-related jobs and, if new hires in public relations and advertising are discounted, fewer than 30 percent enter what could be defined as truly journalistic jobs in newspapers, broadcasting or periodicals.[7] Even so, if we are to take the 1989 figures that would still mean that some 12,000 to 14,000 are entering jobs in some area of communication. A growing proportion of these jobs are to be found in public information, public affairs, consumer relations, marketing and other areas of public relations.

Although healthy, communication training is still plagued by a number of problems, the most pervasive of which springs from the fact that journalism and mass communication are usually taught in universities, which have increasingly stringent requirements for the hiring, tenure and promotion of academics. Up until the 1950s, many educators were former professionals; although they had good firsthand knowledge of the profession, they usually lacked higher degrees or any appreciation of the theoretical issues in communication.

While, by this time, journalism courses were being offered in some 400 colleges and universities, newspapermen and journalism educators alike were concerned about the lack of properly trained teaching personnel, which is why early accrediting procedures were initiated by such bodies as the American Council on Education for Journalism, created in 1945.[8]

Since then, doctoral programs in journalism and mass communication, which first began in the 1930s, have spread to a number of universities, many of them in the Midwest; and today, even if the Ph.D. is not yet held by a majority of educators, it is certainly fast becoming the standard educational requirement, especially for promotion to full professor. All faculty are usually expected to have several years of professional experience; but, generally speaking, faculty who do not have the doctorate have double the mass media experience of those with doctorates. Given these various requirements, it is perhaps surprising that only 55 percent of all mass communication faculty have undergraduate degrees in journalism, radio-television or communication, but this figure rises to 71 percent for higher degrees. [9]

This problem is further complicated by the fact that many media professionals believe that journalism education should largely be conducted by experienced journalists, particularly those with a reportorial background. In a recent survey done by the American Society of Newspaper Editors (ASNE), 64 percent of the 381 editors responding to the survey stated that their top priority for the improvement of journalism schools would be to see more media professionals on the faculty. This response is consistent with a long-held belief among editors that journalism is itself a scholarly activity and that those who have practiced it with distinction should be recognized by universities as having academic experience equivalent to those who have earned Ph.D.s.[10]

Whatever the arguments on both sides, it is clear that the journalism schools have won the battle. Today, the vast majority of new newspaper hires are journalism graduates, and journalists with journalism or communication degrees are a majority in the newsroom. If anything, journalism schools have been the victim of their own success. With a sixfold increase in enrollments between 1966 and 1986, journalism schools have been hard put to keep up, not only because of inadequate faculties, facilities and budgets but also because of the need to match the computerization that has come to daily newspapers and other areas of the communications industry.[11]

With regard to curriculum, few schools offer exactly the same programs, although those that are accredited by the ACEJMC all tend to follow a similar pattern. Many schools, accredited or not, follow the old 75:25 ratio of nonjournalistic and journalistic courses; and most of them provide instruction in news-editorial, broadcast journalism, public relations and advertising, with an emphasis on writing, editing and information gathering. Some of them also offer courses in photojournalism and magazine journalism. At the same time, most programs provide an introduction to mass communication as well as courses in communication history, media law and/or ethics.[12]

However, while educators believe that a solid grounding in the liberal arts, the ability to write well and some familiarity with technical equipment are essential, increasingly beginning journalists will also need good backgrounds in the sciences and computers. It is felt that the industry will need more journalists trained in law, economics and business.[13] For this reason, many departments are now encouraging their students to take related courses in business subjects as well as psychology and sociology. Students specializing in public relations or advertising are often required to take one or more courses in marketing.

Courses in broadcasting vary considerably according to whether emphasis is on news, production, presentation or management. At its beginnings, radio required good oral skills, which is why early broadcast courses tended to be found in departments of speech communication. But as news became an increasingly important part of broadcasting, schools of journalism began to offer courses specializing in broadcast news. Production techniques have also become much more complex and sophisticated with the result that, in many universities, broadcast production is taught in departments of telecommunications while broadcast news is taught in journalism departments.[14]

Because communication training has been adopted by the universities, it has moved away from the apprenticeship-type system that was in use until the last quarter of the nineteenth century and is still common in some Western European countries. However, because of pressure from the communication industry, most students are expected to acquire practical experience either from student newspapers and broadcast stations or from internships in local media and advertising and public relations firms. Some of the student newspapers and broadcast laboratories are quite sophisticated and provide valuable experience in a variety of editorial, technical and management roles. They also allow students to put together clip files or demonstration broadcast tapes that can be useful when seeking employment. Students who fill the top editorial or management slots in these student organizations usually have no trouble finding jobs.

Internships or work-study placements in professional media vehicles are sometimes problematical because they depend on the school's relationship with the local media industry. Many schools are located in small college towns or other areas that do not have a large media network; although the local media are usually happy to cooperate, they are able to offer only a limited number of opportunities. In many cases, students are obliged to seek summer internships in their home towns. Even in major media markets, schools have to work hard to establish good relationships with the media, and supervising internships can be a time-consuming task for faculty. All in all, though, internships are valued by educators, students and communication professionals alike; and, today, more than 80 percent of graduates finding jobs in newspapers have worked as interns.[15]

The size and complexity of training structures in the United States are the reflection of a large and flourishing communications industry. Even though there has been a steady decline in evening newspapers, morning newspapers and Sunday newspapers have continued to grow both in number and in circulation. At the beginning of 1990, the total number of daily newspapers stood at 1,626. Their circulation has remained steady at around 62 million.[16] According to the American Society of Newspaper Editors, newsroom staffs at daily newspapers are growing at a rate of 2.3 percent each year and in 1987 stood at a total of 55,300 professional reporters and editors. [17] At the end of 1990, there were also 10,794 radio stations in operation as well as 1,469 television stations, which together accounted for total advertising revenues of almost $30 billion. More than 92 million homes have at least one television set, and there are an estimated 541 million radio receivers.[18]

The demand for trained college graduates remains high, partly because of the strength of the communications industry and partly because of turnover caused by job dissatisfaction.[19] The following figures will give some idea of the relative strength of demand in the various communications fields. In 1989, 19 percent of new journalism school graduates found jobs in newspapers and news services, 16.1 percent in radio and television, 13.5 percent in advertising, 12.2 percent in public relations and a total of 39.2 percent in other communications areas.[20]

CANADA

Journalism training in Canada developed much later than in the United States and today strikes an uneasy balance between the apprenticeship system favored in Britain and the prestigious university model provided by Columbia's Graduate School of Journalism. In this sense, like many Canadian institutions, its roots are divided between Europe and its powerful neighbor to the south.

Although the University of Western Ontario offered a few basic journalism courses in the 1920s, formal journalism education did not begin until after World War II. Carleton University in Ottawa, which was founded in 1942 as a nondenominational liberal arts, science, commerce and engineering college, started the first journalism program in Canada in September of 1945 and granted its first degrees in journalism a year later. The University of Western Ontario in London followed suit in 1945–46 and awarded its first degrees in 1948. Ryerson Polytechnical Institute in Toronto also began to offer courses shortly thereafter and, thanks to extensive equipment for the teaching of typography, printing, engraving, radio and television, soon achieved large enrollments.[21]

In 1970, a Senate report on the mass media noted that most training programs were located in central Canada and recommended that courses should be available in all parts of the country.[22] As a result, programs were introduced in the University of King's College in Halifax, Concordia University in Montreal, Université du Québec in Montreal, Laval University in Quebec City, the University of Regina in Saskatchewan and the University of Moncton in New Brunswick.[23] Today, there are seven university-level programs in English Canada and three French-language university-level programs in Quebec.[24] A small number of community colleges, such as Vancouver City College, Humber in Toronto and Fanshawe in London, have also earned a reputation for sound teaching at the junior level. All together, the Canadian journalism schools turn out more than 300 students every year.[25]

From the start, the two founding fathers of journalism education in Canada, Wilfrid Eggleston at Carleton and George McCracken at the

University of Western Ontario, both consciously adopted the curriculum of Columbia's Graduate School of Journalism, which involved the study of reporting practices and issues of politics and society as well as journalism history, ethics and law. Both men sought to establish programs that would combine journalistic skills training with broader study in the humanities and social sciences.[26]

The split between journalism educators and the industry appears to be more pronounced in Canada than in the United States. One reason is that when today's senior journalists entered the profession twenty or thirty years ago, journalism education was less common. Having come up through the apprenticeship system, many believe that the university is too far removed from the realities of everyday journalism and that educators are out to "control the agenda." Another reason is that, in a country that has had to fight hard for its press freedoms, some elements of the industry view educational diplomas as being only one step removed from the licensing of journalists.[27]

While the industry as a whole remains critical of journalism programs, individual media organizations have done little to provide alternative forms of organized training. Some of them have supported professional development programs. For example, the Southam Fellowship for Journalists enables up to five experienced journalists to spend a year at the University of Toronto. The Michenor Awards Foundation provides study-leave fellowships and the Atkinson Fellowship in Public Policy funds a journalist for a one-year research project. At the same time, a few professional associations, such as the Daily Newspapers Publishers Association and the Fédération Professionnelle des Journalistes du Québec, sponsor a number of workshops and seminars. About a dozen other associations, including the Centre for Investigative Journalism, give awards for outstanding journalism.[28]

Such initiatives, while obviously beneficial to individual journalists, are essentially media-oriented and do little to support formal journalism education. The kind of industry funding that is made available to journalism programs in the United States is practically nonexistent in Canada even though the media are starting to realize that, in the absence of organized in-house training schemes, they are becoming increasingly dependent on journalism schools for new recruits. At the same time, the concentration of ownership, the trend toward monopolies and other developments in the media have been the subject of much public scrutiny.[29] Unfortunately, the industry has come to associate such criticism with the universities, which has further widened the split between them.

Right from the start, the decision to adopt the Columbia model placed formal journalism education firmly in the university tradition and signaled an allegiance not to the industry but rather to the public interest. The thinking was that journalism could thus leave the trade schools and take its place alongside medicine and law in the hallowed halls of academe. The fact that Columbia became exclusively a graduate school in 1935 further reinforced this shift toward professionalism.

Along the same lines, almost all university level programs in Canada now have graduate courses leading to a "first professional degree." The University of Western Ontario has eliminated its undergraduate program altogether, while Carleton is considering the possibility of a Ph.D. program in journalism.[30] Since the late 1960s, both Carleton and Western Ontario have been recruiting faculty with Ph.D.s, which has consolidated the academic underpinnings of professional training.[31]

It would be untoward to leave the subject of journalism training in Canada without at least some reference to the situation in the province of Quebec, where, by the very nature of the profession, the question of language poses particular problems. A few years ago, educators, faced with scarce resources and inadequate results, sought to consolidate the three French-language university level programs into a single central institute of journalism training, somewhat along the lines of the Centre de Formation des Journalistes in Paris.[32] The existing programs were all 30-credit minor options within other departments and as such were typically underfunded and understaffed. At the Université de Montréal, classes were relegated to the evening extension program and were taught by part-time instructors. In contrast with programs in English Canada, which enjoyed considerable administrative autonomy, the French journalism programs at both Laval University and Université du Québec à Montréal were located within the communications studies departments and were thus accorded little priority.[33]

This situation was unsatisfactory on its own, but it was made even worse by the fact that graduates of English-language programs seemed better qualified to find jobs, perhaps because their training was more suited to industry needs. The attempt to consolidate the French programs failed when the Bourassa Government refused to underwrite a feasibility study, and today the situation remains much as it was in the early 1980s.

In conclusion, while journalism education remains relatively healthy, it is still beset with problems, in particular the "dialogue of the deaf" between the academy and industry. One contributing factor is the absence of any accreditation mechanism. In the United States, the existence of the ACEJMC has done a great deal to heal the rift between educators and the media by involving industry professionals in the accreditation process. In Canada, the industry has few formal channels through which to express its needs and priorities, and has to rely on open criticism, a situation that obviously leaves a great deal to be desired. Meanwhile, the system remains uncomfortably poised between the traditions of the Ivy League and the school of hard knocks.

NOTES

1. Frank Luther Mott, *American Journalism, A History: 1690–1960*, 3d ed. (New York: Macmillan, 1982), pp. 604–605.

2. Burton W. Marvin, "United States of America: Journalism," in UNESCO, *The Training of Journalists: A World-wide Study on the Training of Personnel for the Mass Media* (Paris: UNESCO, 1958), p. 111.

3. Edwin Emery and Michael Emery, *The Press and America: An Interpretive History of the Mass Media*, 6th ed. (Englewood Cliffs, NJ: Prentice-Hall, 1988), pp. 581–582.

4. Philip Gaunt, *Choosing the News: The Profit Factor in News Selection* (Westport, CT: Greenwood Press, 1990). See chap. 7.

5. Ron Thornburg, "The Liberal Arts and Sciences," in Robert H. Giles, ed., *Journalism Education: Facing Up to the Challenge of Change* (Washington, DC: American Society of Newspaper Editors Committee on Education for Journalism, 1990), p. 12.

6. Lee B. Becker, "Enrollments Increase in 1989, but Graduation Rates Drop," *Journalism Educator* 45, no.3 (Autumn 1990), p. 5.

7. The Dow Jones Newspaper Fund, *1988 Journalism Career and Scholarship Guide* (Princeton, NJ: Dow Jones Newspaper Fund, 1988), pp. 12–13.

8. Marvin, "United States," pp. 111–112.

9. David H. Weaver and G. Cleveland Wilhoit, "A Profile of JMC Educators: Traits, Attitudes and Values," *Journalism Educator* 43, no.2 (Summer 1988), pp. 15–41.

10. Jerry Ceppos, "Media Professionals as Teachers," in Giles, *Journalism Education*, p. 17.

11. Maxwell McCombs, "Testing the Myths: A Statistical Review 1967–1986," *Gannett Center Journal* 2, no.2 (Spring 1988), pp. 101–108.

12. Lee Becker, Jeffrey Fruit and Susan Caudill, with Sharon Dunwoody and Leonard Tipton, *The Training and Hiring of Journalists* (Norwood, NJ: Ablex, 1987), p. 12.

13. *Communications 1990*, a report of the Future Committee (Columbia: School of Journalism, University of Columbia, MO, 1980).

14. Warren K. Agee, Phillip H. Ault and Edwin Emery, *Introduction to Mass Communication*, 7th ed. (New York: Harper and Row, 1982), p. 315.

15. *1991 Journalism Career and Scholarship Guide* (Princeton, NJ: The Dow Jones Newspaper Fund, Inc., 1990), p. 18.

16. *1990 International Yearbook* (New York: Editor and Publisher, 1990).

17. *1991 Journalism Career and Scholarship Guide*, p. 16.

18. *The Broadcasting Yearbook 1991* (Washington, DC: Broadcasting Publications, Inc., 1991), p. A-3.

19. David H. Weaver and G. Cleveland Wilhoit, *The American Journalist: A Portrait of U.S. News People and Their Work,* 2d ed. (Bloomington: Indiana University Press, 1991), pp. 88–103.

20. *1991 Journalism Career and Scholarship Guide*, p. 19.

21. Wilfrid Eggleston, "Canada," in UNESCO, *The Training of Journalists*, p. 98.

22. Government of Canada, *Special Senate Committee on Mass Media*, Davey Commission Report (Ottawa: Queen's Printer, 1970).

23. Paul Adams and Catherine McKercher, "North America," in John C. Merrill, ed., *Global Journalism*, 2d ed. (White Plains, NY: Longman, 1991), p. 354.

24. Enn Raudsepp, "Reinventing Journalism Education," *Canadian Journal of Communication* 14, no.2 (May 1988), p. 3.

25. G. Stuart Adam, "The World Next Door: A Commonwealth Perspective," *Gannett Center Journal* 2, no.2 (Spring 1988), p. 113.

26. Ibid., p. 110.

27. Raudsepp, "Reinventing Journalism Education," p. 5.

28. Adams and McKercher, "North America," p. 355.

29. Government of Canada, *Royal Commission on Newspapers*, Kent Commission Report (Hull: Minister of Supply and Services, 1981).

30. Raudsepp, "Reinventing Journalism Education," p. 11.

31. Adam, "The World Next Door," p. 114.

32. See the section on France in the following chapter.

33. This section draws on Raudsepp, "Reinventing Journalism Education."

Chapter Five

Western Europe

Journalism training throughout North America and Western Europe is based essentially on the same general principles of press freedom, truth and professional integrity. However, these seemingly unambiguous principles are subject to many shades of interpretation that have grown out of different legal systems, cultural traditions, social needs and economic circumstances. In general terms, all the countries in this group are "Western democracies." They espouse democratic principles and, to a greater or lesser extent, believe that a free press is part of the democratic process. Their media are mostly financed by some form of advertising, but, in several countries, political affiliations and subsidies from political parties or governments are considered normal. Communication training varies considerably within this group, with each national system located somewhere along a continuum between on-the-job skills training on one end and communications-oriented university-based media studies on the other.

THE MAJOR POWERS

The United Kingdom

Formal journalism training did not emerge in the United Kingdom until well after World War II, although some earlier attempts to introduce university-level training were made during the interwar period. At this time, between 1919 and 1939, London University offered a two-year

Journalism Diploma course, which produced a total of 400 graduates, several of whom rose to prominent positions at the *Times*, the *Observer* and the BBC.[1] Formal journalism education, which did not begin until 1952, was a joint initiative of the government, through the National Council for the Training of Journalists (NCTJ) and the National Union of Journalists (NUJ). Today, almost all training is given outside the universities, either in colleges of technology or in units run by individual newspapers.

Training focuses mainly on professional skills with very little emphasis on theory, except for law. In the past, the NUJ has succeeded in keeping a very tight control over the training and "qualification" of journalists, to the point of achieving a virtual closed shop. In recent years, however, tensions have arisen between the NUJ and newspaper owners who wish to reserve the right to hire "unqualified" recruits, that is to say, highly educated and specialized writers who have not gone through the hands of the NCTJ. This development is consistent with a rise in the status of journalists, created, in part, by the influx of increasing numbers of university graduates into the profession. A degree, although not necessarily in a communications-related field, is gradually becoming a desirable qualification and, in some cases, university graduates are able to bypass the old apprenticeship system in which new recruits started in a small local newspaper and, if lucky, were able to work their way up to a national daily in Fleet Street. However, the trainee system still remains very strong.

The media industry, which employs about 30,000 full-time journalists, recruits some 700 trainees each year, most of whom are employed by small local weeklies. As trainees, they must take courses accredited by the NCTJ. They can either attend part-time courses or take a one-year, full-time course at one of seven non-university colleges in England and Wales. These seven colleges are Darlington College of Technology in Durham; Harlow College in Essex; Highbury College of Technology in Portsmouth; Lancashire Polytechnic in Preston; Stradbroke College in Sheffield; South Glamorgan Institute of Higher Education in Cardiff, Wales; and the College of Business Studies in Belfast. Other institutions, such as the Polytechnic of Central London, offer degrees in media studies. Postgraduate courses are offered at University College, Cardiff, City University in London and South Glamorgan Institute of Higher Learning in Cardiff. Accredited in-company training schemes are also run by seven newspaper groups: Croydon Advertiser Group, Herald Group, Express and Star in Wolverhampton, Kent and Sussex Courier, Eastern Counties Newspapers, Thomson Regional Newspapers and Westminster Press, although the last two have recently announced their intention of leaving the national training scheme and developing their own qualifications.[2]

Also, since September 1989, direct entrants to newspaper journalism, both graduates and nongraduates, have been able to qualify through a distance learning system set up by the NCTJ. As soon as they start work, trainees undertake a foundation course based on a distance learning pack that is sent to their editor or employer. The pack consists of 15 units of printed learning material with self-assessment tests, a video tape, eight audio tapes and a newspaper stylebook. After completing the foundation course, which usually takes about six months, the trainees attend a 12-week block release course at an accredited college.[3]

Another innovation is the new National Certificate, which superseded the old Proficiency Certificate in the autumn of 1990. In order to take the National Certificate examination, candidates must have first completed two years of full-time on-the-job training and passed seven preliminary examinations organized by the NCTJ. The National Certificate will become the main, universally recognized professional qualification for newspaper journalism.

It should be noted that the NCTJ, which was set up mainly as a result of the 1949 Report of the Royal Commission on the Press, is concerned exclusively with newspaper journalists. Training for journalists working in periodicals and "trade" publications is organized by the Periodicals Training Council (PTC). In the past, broadcast journalists tended either to move into the electronic media from newspapers or take the excellent training courses organized by the BBC or the Independent Television Authority. Since 1977, the London College of Printing has also offered broadcast training courses. The Joint Committee for the Training of Radio Journalists (JCTRJ) coordinates the training of journalists for local radio. The Polytechnic of Central London, which began a journalism course in 1949, has since expanded its activities to take in broadcasting.

On the whole, despite a growing interest in communication and media studies at the university level, training is still very much industry driven. In order to become fully qualified, journalists must complete six preliminary NCTJ examinations, a shorthand test and a final proficiency test. The continued existence of a shorthand test in a world of electronic aids is some indication of the profoundly practical orientation of the NCTJ courses. Each year, the proficiency test is taken by about 650 reporters and 35 photographers. On an average, 70 percent of the reporters and 85 percent of the photographers pass the test. According to the NCTJ, the aims of the newspaper journalism syllabus are to enable trainees:

- To recognize, obtain and select important, relevant and newsworthy facts from either written or verbal sources, using appropriate skills or techniques
- To write clear, vigorous and balanced reports in a form that will attract and interest the reader
- To gain a general knowledge of a newspaper's departments (for instance, production, advertising, circulation and finance, as well as editorial) and an understanding of the industry's structure and economics[4]

In order to acquire these skills, trainees take courses in news gathering and processing, writing, reporting, law, public administration and the role of the newspaper in society. In all these courses, the main emphasis is on practical skills. For example, in the law courses, trainees are taught not only about libel and defamation but also how to understand and interpret legal proceedings, an essential skill for those assigned to courthouse beats. Similarly, in reporting courses, they are taught how to ask questions, make use of shorthand and properly address members of the clergy and aristocracy as well as civic leaders. Law courses are particularly detailed because British journalists are not protected by anything like the First Amendment and are, as a consequence, far more vulnerable to legal action.

Unlike the United States, but like other West European countries, the United Kingdom is small enough to know quite precisely how many journalism students should be trained in order to meet industry needs. The small number of training insti،،،tions also makes it possible to determine how many each should train to fill these needs. As a result, the selection process for students can afford to be very rigorous. For example, the Polytechnic of Central London has about 2,000 applicants for 50 places. Birmingham Polytechnic has around 1,500 for approximately the same number of places. At Highbury College near Portsmouth, 250 applicants take an entrance exam. Of these about half pass and are interviewed. The final intake is only 30. Entrance into in-company training schemes is even more competitive, although there are no academic limits. Of the 400 who apply, four to ten are accepted. The results of this system of careful selection are hard-working students, very low dropout rates and almost guaranteed employment in the field.[5]

Journalism is still a long way from being recognized as a university discipline, even though a number of universities and polytechnics do offer degree courses in mass communications and media studies. At the same time, the proportion of university graduates entering the field is steadily rising. Seventy-five percent of all new hires in magazine and radio journalism have a degree or an equivalent qualification. In provincial newspapers, once the impregnable bastion of the apprenticeship system, the proportion of new entrants with degrees has risen from 5 to 10 percent 15 years ago to 53 percent today.[6] These are telling figures that will inevitably affect the way in which journalists are trained in the United Kingdom.

In conclusion, it can be said that, even though the situation is evolving, British training structures are essentially industry driven, heavily controlled by the National Union of Journalists and still firmly attached to the apprenticeship model. In contrast to the American system, which turns out thousands of graduates who have no intention of entering a media-related profession, the British system produces only enough trained professionals to satisfy industry demand.[7]

France

The French system occupies a place somewhere between the British and American models. The media industry still prefers an apprenticeship-type approach and is prepared to grant accreditation only to those institutions giving emphasis to practical skills, but, at the same time, journalism programs have existed in universities for many years. Communications and media studies also exist as part of university programs. New programs are springing up both inside and outside the universities to meet the growing demand for trained personnel, particularly in the field of broadcasting.

The choice of schools offering serious journalism programs is, however, limited. Although some forty or fifty establishments describe themselves as "schools of communication," most of them are small private institutions offering programs leading to diplomas well below the university-degree level.[8] Only seven of them are "recognized by the Collective Convention on Journalists," an accrediting body set up jointly by the government, the journalists' union and the industry.

The study of the mass media, particularly in the universities, has been influenced by a number of peculiarly French academic pursuits: structuralism, semiology and film. The Institut Français de Presse has successfully undertaken empirical studies of the French and foreign press from a political science perspective, but most other university research in the field has been preoccupied with the psychological and physiological impact of messages or the symbolic structure of the mass media as creators of contemporary culture. French journalism skills training, as most editors and many journalists are happy to report, has kept well away from such lofty preoccupations. On the other hand, despite increasing professionalism, French journalism is still very much attached to its literary traditions, and this is evident in the programs offered by journalism training institutions.

The first journalism school in France, L'Ecole Supérieure de Journalisme, dates back to 1899 but was attached to the Ecole de Hautes Etudes en Sciences Sociales a year later. By all accounts, this school concentrated more on intellectual studies than skills training and was better fitted to produce publicists than real journalists.[9] The Ecole Supérieure de Journalisme de Lille (ESJ), created in 1924 as part of that city's Catholic University, sought to emphasize the moral foundations of journalism. The ESJ is still considered to be one of the best schools in France, but never accepts more than about forty or fifty students each year. The most prestigious school, without any doubt, is the Centre de Formation des Journalistes in Paris (CFJ), which was founded in 1946 by representatives of the unions, the industry and the university. This school, which accepts only about fifty or sixty selected students each year, has produced some of the best-known names in French journalism. Both the ESJ and the CFJ concentrate mainly on practical aspects of journalism, and both insist on a two-month internship between the second and third years. Applicants must have a two-year college degree to qualify for the competitive entrance examination.

Three other accredited schools located within universities offer programs that focus more on an academic knowledge of journalism. They are the Institut des Hautes Etudes de l'Information et de la Communication (known as CELSA), which is part of Paris University IV; the Centre Universitaire d'Enseignment du Journalisme (CUEJ), which is part of Strasbourg University III; and the Centre Transméditerranéen de la Communication (CTMC) at the University of Aix-Marseille. These schools, which require a two-year college degree and an entrance examination, run courses that last from one to three years and also provide a trainee program.[10]

University Institutes of Technology (IUTs) exist in many French universities, and several of them offer courses in "information careers." Most, however, are narrowly focused on training documentalists and public relations officers.[11] Only two of them are accredited and provide training for the mass media. They are the IUT at Bordeaux III, which was founded by the veteran journalist, teacher and writer Robert Escarpit, and the IUT at Tours. These two schools offer programs similar to those provided by CELSA, CUEJ and CTMC, but only require a high-school diploma to qualify for the entrance examination. A growing number of provincial universities now offer communications programs, the best known of which are located in Rennes, Besançon and Nantes. Finally, the Centre de

Perfectionnement des Journalistes (CPJ), located in the same building as the CFJ in Paris, provides for the further training of professional journalists. This accredited program was begun in 1969 by the CFJ in collaboration with the ESJ in Lille.

The CFJ, which offers a two-year program, has a curriculum that is typical of accredited schools. The first year is devoted to basic editorial and layout skills. Working alongside professional journalists, students do copy-desk assignments, interviews and reporting. During the second term, these skills are applied to school newspapers. There is also a seven-week course on broadcast and news agency journalism. Over the summer vacation, students are required to do a two-month internship with a local newspaper. In keeping with the national convention on journalists, second-year students are considered as first-year professional probationers. During their second year, students specialize in broadcast news, editing or agency work. At the same time, they take part in seminars on economics, politics, international relations and sports. To graduate, a good working knowledge of English is also required.

A similar curriculum is offered at the ESJ in Lille, although rather more emphasis is placed on general knowledge, particularly during the first year when students have to take courses covering political, economic and cultural aspects of the contemporary world; current affairs; the contemporary press in France and abroad; the history of information; and information law, as well as foreign languages and basic journalism skills such as news gathering and writing. During their second year, following the obligatory two-month internship with a provincial newspaper, students concentrate more on practical aspects of journalism but continue to develop their knowledge of current affairs, press laws and economics.

Entry into these two schools is extremely competitive and involves a stiff entrance examination. In 1987, the ESC took only 40 students from among 518 applicants, and the CFJ accepted 64 from among 766. Once in, the standards are high, but students are virtually guaranteed employment when they qualify, which is more than can be said for other minor schools. While a diploma from one of the top schools usually opens the door to the best jobs, a good level of general education is sometimes more highly prized than formal training in a journalism school. The results of a survey published in *Le Monde de l'Education* show that, of 684 journalists hired between 1980 and 1984, 74 percent had received university training of some kind but only 40 percent were graduates of accredited journalism schools.[12] Of those having received university training, 25 percent had completed literary or social science studies, 17 percent political science,

21 percent law, 13 percent languages, 11 percent history and 4 percent science.

These figures are eloquent because they not only show the kind of recruits editors like to hire but also give a clue as to the kind of intellectual preparation seen as desirable by would-be journalists, as well as to the general perception that the public at large has of journalism. Indeed, tradition has established the French journalist either as a literary figure or as a powerful interpreter of events.[13] The image of the journalist as an interpreter or commentator springs from the fact that, historically, information sources have been closely controlled. Because of these restrictions, and some of them are still in force today, journalists have been unable to gather information for themselves and have thus been obliged to fall back on commentary. The literary image is still so strong, even today, that teachers at the CFJ in Paris sometimes have difficulty persuading new students that it is necessary to learn basic writing and reporting skills, because they see themselves as editorialists and paragraph writers. Some of them are even reluctant to learn how to type![14]

Generally speaking, teachers are recruited more for their professional qualifications than for academic credentials, particularly in the non-university-based accredited programs. Partly because of a strong tradition of literary journalism, journalists and teachers seem to be able to move very freely between journalism and the university. One striking example is Robert Escarpit, who not only founded the Bordeaux journalism program but who also wrote a front-page column for *Le Monde* for thirty years, as well as producing more than fifty books and leading an active political life.[15] As a consequence of this situation, French journalism schools have no difficulty in attracting working journalists to teach practices. Furthermore, as they are unhampered by the exigencies of academic research and service they can concentrate wholly on the task at hand.

The French journalists' union is nowhere near as monolithic or powerful as the NUJ in Britain, but it still has some influence on training through the accreditation process. The profession is regulated in a loose kind of way by the Press Card Commission, which issues the official press pass to qualifying journalists. There are no educational requirements. All a journalist has to do to qualify is to be employed as a professional journalist by a media organization. Of the approximately 21,000 journalists working in France, only about 65 percent are fully fledged permanent professionals. The rest are probationers or part-time employees or belong to such peripheral categories as cameraman, "reporter-illustrator" and "stenographer-writer."

The journalists' union is critical of the many new communication programs that are springing up because they do not meet the strict accreditation standards, but demand for trained professionals continues to grow. Newspapers no longer have the time to do traditional on-the-job training; and, while entry-level graduates of journalism schools are far from being experienced professionals, they are immediately operational and, in the eyes of editors, that is their strength.[16] Statistics published by the Press Card Commission indicate that the proportion of new recruits having undergone formal training is steadily rising, which suggests that schools of journalism are indeed playing an increasingly important role in the profession.[17]

Germany

Before reunification, there were distinct training systems in the two Germanys. In the German Democratic Republic, the system was similar but not identical to those in other parts of the Eastern bloc and consisted of two state-controlled institutes of journalism, one in Leipzig and the other in East Berlin, both of which were closed upon reunification. Efforts are now being made to reopen them along Western lines, but much remains to be done to reshape curricula. In the Federal Republic of Germany, the system was and still is similar to those of other Western European nations in that it is theoretically free of state control, emphasizes press freedoms and also takes part in the debate over whether training properly belongs in the newsroom, in professional schools or in universities.

The general perception of journalism—and it is one that has prevailed for a very long time—is that it is an occupation that requires talent and that no amount of training can provide a substitute for talent. On the other hand, it would be almost impossible even for the most talented to carve out a successful career without a thorough knowledge of the various technical skills involved.[18] Whatever the approach, it is true to say that journalism training has a long history in Germany. In fact, lectures on journalism were given at the University of Leipzig in as early as 1762.[19] At the beginning of the nineteenth century, however, the German university redefined its role as one of conveying intellectual knowledge rather than preparing students for practical professions. As a result, the study of the press disappeared from the universities and did not really reappear until the second decade of the twentieth century.[20]

During the Nazi regime, attempts were made to regulate journalism training and control access to the profession. Centralized standards were imposed on in-company training schemes, university training was pro-

moted and the government even set up its own school (Reichspresseschule)
to make sure that journalists were correctly trained in their "public
function." After World War II, the Allies determined that there were not
enough qualified journalists and created two schools of journalism to fill
the gap. These two schools, one in Aachen, in the north, and the other in
Munich, in the south, were based on the American model.[21]

Training now makes a distinction between *Zeitungwissenschaft* (newspaper science), taught in professional journalism schools, and *Publizistik*
(journalism and mass communication), taught in universities. In recent
years, the media have developed very rapidly, creating a sharply increased
demand for trained professionals. Furthermore, demand is no longer
limited to the classic media of press, radio and television. There is now a
need for people with expertise in public relations, public information,
media consulting and other areas of the communication industry. Today,
there are four main methods of communication training.

The most common form of training is still the "traineeship"
(Volontariat) completed in an editorial department of a media vehicle.
Standard guidelines set up by media owners and the unions give strong
emphasis to practical skills, but they also provide for theory courses.
On-the-job training in the press usually takes two years, but this may be
shortened for trainees having completed vocational courses or some form
of university education. The broadcasting networks, which began similar
courses a few years ago, offer only a few training positions, and university
qualifications may be required. These courses usually last eighteen
months. All traineeships both in the press and the electronic media are
paid, which enables trainees to devote themselves full time to their studies.
In any given year, there are somewhere between 1500 and 2,000 trainees
in the *Volontariat* system. Of these about 85 percent will be in daily
newspapers, about 7 or 8 percent each in periodicals and broadcast
organizations and the rest—usually only a handful—in news agencies.

Lee Becker and his colleagues have described in some detail the training
process in the print media.[22] The first three months of the two-year
program are probationary. During this period, the trainee is free to leave
or can be asked to leave by the company. After this probationary period,
which is spent in editorial departments both at the head office and at
regional offices, trainees undertake a year of full-time formal courses
devoted to the media and the social sciences, presenting a mix of both
theory and practice. Finally, students spend time in the different departments of the organization so as to gain familiarity with the coverage of
politics, sports, culture and other specialized areas.

Entry into the *Volontariat* is difficult and uses an elaborate screening process involving the personnel director, the chief editor and other specialized editors. Applicants are only considered if they have the *Abitur* or high school diploma, have already completed their military service and are able to type and take shorthand. Usually about half of the applicants are invited to an initial interview with the personnel director. Those that seem promising are then invited to come back for two days of testing and further interviews with specialized editors. Finally, about 10 percent of the original pool will be offered a trainee position. At the end of the training period, during which constant evaluations are made, contracts will be offered to those who have shown they have "the right stuff." This whole process is highly subjective and is based as much on personal qualities as professional skills. One reason that the selection process is so severe is that, because of strong labor laws, it is almost impossible to fire journalists once they have been given a contract.

The system of training in the broadcast media is rather less formal. Although some networks have adopted an 18-month *Volontariat*, many smaller stations use shorter programs to introduce trainees to their organizations. Here again, there is no lack of applicants. Those selected have usually had some exposure to the media and must have a good speaking voice. After the initial training period, promising recruits are offered freelance jobs to continue their professional development. Only about one in ten freelancers are eventually offered permanent contracts. This system allows broadcast organizations to circumvent the strict labor laws that make it difficult to fire journalists on permanent contract. Even permanent contracts have a one-year probationary period during which it is possible to terminate employment.

Although most journalists come out of the *Volontariat* system, a few very select students are fortunate enough to train at one of three prestigious private journalism schools. The German School of Journalism (Deutsche Journalistenschule) in Munich, founded in 1958, trains 45 students a year in a program that lasts 15 months. Thirty of them also take courses at the University of Munich. Two other schools are run by large publishing groups mainly to train their own recruits. The Springer-Verlag School of Journalism, which has branches in Berlin and Hamburg, trains 40 or 50 students over a period of 24 months. The Hamburg School of Journalism, funded by the Gruner & Jahr group and the weekly *Die Zeit*, also produces about 20 new journalists every year after completing an 18-month program. Generally speaking, the training capacity of these three schools is very limited, but their graduates always find jobs in the most prestigious news organizations in the country, which is why there is tremendous competition to get in. The lucky trainees are selected from literally thousands of applicants by a process of formal tests and interviews. Most of them are university graduates, and their average age is relatively high.

The course of study in these three schools involves intensive on-the-job training in newsroom settings, with a strong emphasis on news, editing and layout. Very little theory is taught, and what there is tends to be given a practical orientation. In fact, every effort is made to reproduce actual working conditions as realistically as possible, and a lot of work is done on the students' own newspaper. All the teaching is done by professional journalists.

Seven universities offer programs in media studies and communications, usually in combination with other subjects. They are the universities of Berlin, Bochum, Göttingen, Mainz, Munich, Münster and Erlangen/Nuremburg. The programs offered in these universities cannot be considered as full vocational preparation for careers in the communication industry because they do not have the technical equipment or facilities for practical training; as a result, they have been strongly criticized by media professionals. In the face of this criticism, some universities have made attempts to mix theory and practice in "integrated study courses." Such programs, offered at the universities of Bamberg, Dortmund, Eichstätt, Hamburg and Munich, seek to combine specialized academic concentrations in such fields as economics or political science with a working knowledge of journalistic methods, acquired both in student newsrooms and studios and in compulsory practical training periods in newspapers, broadcast organizations or public relations agencies.

A fourth avenue of training is provided by advanced courses and continuing education programs in a variety of institutions. For example, university graduates can take advanced research courses in communication sciences at the universities of Mainz and Hohenheim or at the College of Music and Theater in Hanover. The electronic media, which in fact recruit a lot of their personnel from newspapers and periodicals, have two central facilities for training and further training. The School of Engineering in Nuremburg provides instruction for up to 1,000 radio and television employees every year. The Central Agency for Further Training Programs, in Frankfurt, also runs some 80 to 90 seminars annually for radio and television journalists.

As the German communication industry expands, both as a result of technological developments and the new markets produced by reunification, demand for training continues to rise. Altogether, some 10,000 students graduate from communication training programs every year. Over the last ten years, 15 new study courses have been established, 12 of them in universities. In Germany, as in other expanding Western economies, it would seem that the increasing demand for communication workers cannot be met by traditional professional training schools and will have to be supplemented by hybrid programs situated in universities.[23]

Most other Western European countries have smaller populations, less extensive media systems and less elaborate training structures. There is usually a split between skills training, provided through apprenticeship-type schemes or specialized professional schools, and media or communication studies offered in universities. In a few countries with long-standing literary traditions, there is little training for journalists other than a grounding in the humanities. For these and other reasons, there is little information available on communication training in some of these countries.

THE NORDIC COUNTRIES

While information may be lacking in many countries of Western Europe, communication scholars in the Nordic countries are beginning to treat journalism training as a topic worthy of research. In particular, the Department of Journalism and Mass Communication at the University of Tampere in Finland has set out to centralize information in a series of reports edited by its director, Professor Kaarle Nordenstreng. The following sections draw heavily on this source. The author is also indebted to Professor Kim Minke of the Danish School of Journalism at Aarhus for information on journalism training in Denmark.

Denmark

The Danish system of communication training is distinguished by three main features. First, training has long been the monopoly of a single school, the Danmarks Journalisthøjskole (DJH) in Aarhus, although this situation is now changing. Second, the system offers a highly developed continuing education program for working journalists. Third, training is the result of negotiation between the national education authorities, a very strong journalists' union and powerful employers' associations.

After World War II, journalists were hired by newspapers for a three-year probationary period during which they had the option of taking a three-month training course at the Aarhus University School of Journalism, which was founded in 1946 as an independent institution in cooperation with the university and all Danish press organizations.[24] In 1962, the course was removed from the university and became the core offering of the newly created DJH. From 1964 on, the program became a compulsory part of the three-year probationary period. It is to be noted that, at this time, the employers insisted that the school should remain separate from the university to preserve the professional and vocational orientation of the curriculum. In 1970, the DJH became part of the system of higher education, with 95 percent of its budget provided by the state. Since 1971, it has awarded a diploma equivalent to a bachelor's degree after a four-year course of study.

The program consists of three semesters of basic instruction at Aarhus, followed by three semesters of practical work in a media organization and a final year of specialized study at Aarhus. During their 18-month internships, students are paid 80 percent of a normal starting salary. About 1,700 applicants take the entrance examination every year, but only 210 are accepted. Although there are no age limits, the average age of new students is about 25. More than half of them have had at least two years of university education. The school produces about 195 graduates every year.

Today, the DJH is the only professional journalism school in the country to be recognized by the national education authorities, the employers' associations and the journalists' union. It is estimated that 80 percent of all new journalists in any given year are DJH graduates, although this figure fluctuates somewhat as a result of industry needs. The virtual monopoly enjoyed by the DJH has been of some concern to the Ministry of Education, which is of the opinion that some kind of competition would be beneficial. However, the employers' organizations and the journalists' union are convinced that in a small country such as Denmark it is better to devote scarce available resources to a single school, over which, incidentally, they maintain a considerable degree of control. Indeed, if the school's governing board is chaired by a person appointed by the Ministry of Education, its other 17 members are mainly representatives of the journalists' union, the employers' associations, the broadcasting companies, the periodical and trade press and the school itself.

Traditionally, as a professional college, the school has sought to produce well-rounded generalists able to function in any of the media; because of that, while the main focus of the curriculum remains the print media, students are also given a grounding in radio and television. In fact, a new wing containing two television studios and extensive ENG facilities was added on in 1985. However, some employers believe that the curriculum devotes too much attention to radio and television for those entering the print media and not enough for those entering the broadcast media. One of the most vocal critics has been Danmarks Radio (DR), which would like to see more emphasis given to broadcast areas, particularly during the final year of the course, when students return to school after 18 months of on-the-job training. Because of this and growing competition from the newly deregulated broadcast media, there is likely to be increased pressure for specialized radio and television courses either at the DJH or at other facilities. Such courses are already being offered at the Aalestrup Education Center in North Jutland and the Viborg Video School.

Other changes are likely to occur, too, because of developments in Danish higher education. In 1990, the Ministry of Education introduced a new three-year bachelor's degree for the five universities located in Aarhus, Odense, Aalborg, Copenhagen and Roskilde, replacing the old first degree, which took five years to complete. This is expected to be popular with those students who do not wish to pursue advanced degrees, in particular those considering a career in journalism. However, there is now some debate as to whether journalism students with the new three-year bachelor's degree should be made to take the full four-year course at the DJH, which is the solution favored by many employers who insist that older and better-educated journalists are now needed, or whether the students may choose a shorter and cheaper option, which is the outcome favored by the Ministry of Education.

In another major development, the departments of Information Science or Mass Communications at the five Danish universities have recently begun to experiment with programs that combine journalism skills courses with more academically oriented mass communications courses aimed at those students who are interested in pursuing a career either in the media or in other, media-related areas such as public relations. Over the last four or five years, these programs have proved to be very popular and are yet another indication that the monopoly of the DJH will soon disappear despite opposition from the journalists' union and the media associations.

One area that seems likely to remain unchanged is further training for established journalists. In 1979, as part of the national salary negotiations between the journalists' union and the Newspaper Publishers Association, it was agreed that journalists should be entitled to one week's paid training leave every year, to be financed by employer contributions. The resulting program, known as Journalistisk Efteruddannelse, or JE, now offers 80 weeks of one- and two-week courses attended by some 1,100 journalists ever year. These courses, which are free for all members of the journalists' union, cover such areas as investigative reporting, layout and interviewing techniques. Journalists, who can accumulate training leave for up to six years, are thus provided with excellent opportunities to improve their professional skills.

The DJH provides a five-month course for university graduates wishing to learn enough about journalism, the media, and basic journalistic skills to enter general information positions. This program is offered twice a year for about 25 students. The school also runs a series of refresher courses for mid-career professionals.

In conclusion, the Danish system of training is based on a dynamic relationship between the education authorities, the journalists' union and the employers' associations. The union and the employers would like to maintain the kind of professional training traditionally provided by the DJH, but recent changes in media structures and needs are bound to move at least certain areas of journalism training into the universities, where they will be less subject to control by the industry.

Finland

The Institute of Social Sciences in Helsinki first introduced courses in journalism in as early as 1925, but, for decades, the great majority of journalists received no formal training in journalism before entering the profession.[25] The Institute appointed a permanent lecturer in journalism in 1943 and a professor in 1947, after which date students could combine journalism with other subjects for a graduate degree in social science. After the institute moved in 1960 and subsequently became the University of Tampere, the journalism department developed a vocational program leading to an undergraduate degree and an academic program in the Faculty of Social Sciences leading to an M.S. degree. In 1986, the University of Jyväskylä initiated a master's program in journalism and mass communication. The Department of Communication at the University of Helsinki also offers a degree program in communication theory with an emphasis on organizational communication.

The principal journalism degree at Tampere is the master's in communication studies, which "provides all students with basic knowledge and skills in both print and electronic media, with an option for specialization in each."[26] This degree, which grew out of earlier programs offering separate concentrations in both print and electronic media, involves a comprehensive course of studies lasting five years. It covers five main areas:

1. basic studies in journalism and mass communication
2. topics in mass communication
3. journalism theory and practice

4. research methods and theory
5. research work

   Although, as can be seen, there is a strong emphasis on theory, communication studies and research, the practical work undertaken is supposed to give students "the basic professional skills and qualifications of a journalist." Students are also required to take two minor subjects from among those offered by the five colleges of the university. The undergraduate degree is more strongly oriented toward vocational skills and in fact constitutes a common practical core for the master's degree.

   One peculiarity of the Finnish system is the existence of a flourishing Swedish-language press serving the country's 300,000-strong Swedish minority. The Swedish School of Social Sciences at the University of Helsinki has its own Swedish School of Journalism that offers an undergraduate degree program lasting three and one-half years, including a 14-week period of practical work in the media. The program is a small one, with only about 20 students each year, and consists of both theoretical and practical classes. Basic and general subjects are taken as part of regular political science or social science programs. Journalism subjects include news reporting and editing as well as press history, communication theory and journalism research and seminars. Students are also expected to take classes in political science, sociology and local administration.

   Although the Finns are among the most avid newspaper readers in the world, with sales of 532 copies per 1,000 persons, there are, in fact, only about 65 to 70 daily newspapers and 300 weeklies. At the same time, radio and television are state controlled and remain undiversified. In these circumstances, the demand for trained journalists, although rising steadily, is still relatively small and appears to be adequately served by existing training structures.

Sweden

   In 1945, the University of Göteberg began to offer occasional journalism study courses in conjunction with a number of local newspapers. A year later, the University of Stockholm introduced similar courses with the cooperation of the three leading press organizations, the Press Club, the Union of Swedish Journalists and the Newspaper Publishers' Association of Sweden. In the early 1950s, the two universities added a series of six- to eight-week courses for beginners, as well as specialized courses for experienced journalists.[27]

In October of 1955, a Committee for the Education of Journalists was set up to investigate existing training programs. Two years later, the committee recommended that journalism training should include three main components: general education, basic skills training following a brief period of professional experience, and advanced training after a longer period of work as a journalist. Out of these recommendations have evolved the two communication training programs now available at the universities of Stockholm and Göteberg.

The undergraduate programs offered by both these institutions last three years and are intended to prepare students for entry level positions in the media. Competition for available places is keen, but the only qualification is a high-school certificate. The graduate program, reserved for students having completed a university degree, lasts only one year and is designed to produce specialized journalists for newspapers and magazines. There is also a doctoral program for those who wish to pursue an academic career.[28]

The typical undergraduate program is divided into six semesters. The first two semesters form an introductory segment consisting of media rhetoric, media studies and media law as well as basic writing, editing, newspaper production and a survey of both radio and television journalism. The first semester also includes a one-week internship on a news desk. The third semester is almost entirely devoted to a longer internship but also includes a segment on journalism and society. During the internship, the student is supervised by a faculty member and a tutor at the place of work.

The theme of journalism and society is reinforced during the fourth semester with readings and research. The fifth semester covers journalistic sources, different forms of expression, including graphics and electronic publishing, as well as a specialization in either broadcasting, the daily press or the periodical press. The sixth and final semester, which serves as an advanced course, consists of two parallel tracks, one focusing on strengthening practical skills in specialized areas and the other offering a research option for those wishing to go on to a doctoral program.

Like other Scandinavian countries, Sweden also has a well-developed system of continuing education programs, often known as "institutes," funded by the unions and other industry associations. In this sense, the communication industry still remains attached to on-the-job professional training with the universities bridging the gap between practical skills and more theoretical communication studies.

Norway

Of all the Nordic countries, Norway has the largest professional school of this type, the Norwegian Institute of Journalism (NIJ), which has 20 full-time faculty members, ultramodern print and broadcast equipment as well as its own accommodation and restaurant facilities. The NIJ accepts working journalists from all the Scandinavian countries and even operates programs in the United States, the United Kingdom and Germany.[29]

After World War II, the Norwegian press organizations sponsored periodic short courses for young journalists, but they soon decided that there was a need for a longer, more structured program. In 1951, the Norwegian Association of Editors and Journalists and the National Federation of Norwegian Newspaper Publishers founded the Oslo School of Journalism, which offered a ten-month training course. The school was run by a professional journalist and was very professionally oriented, but the universities of Oslo and Bergen both had representatives on its governing board. The textbook developed by the school was also used by the Norwegian Correspondence School, the largest and most highly respected training school in the country.[30]

Today, the Norwegian School of Journalism (Norsk Journalisthøgskole) in Oslo offers a two-year training program dedicated to the promotion of high quality journalism. The courses offered by the school seek to meet the special needs of the Norwegian media system, which is characterized by a relatively small population, very strong newspaper readership, a large number of small newspapers, apart from the large circulation dailies in Oslo and Bergen, a high level of cabling and an autonomous, decentralized television network.

During the first year, training focuses on news reporting for both print and broadcast media. Particular emphasis is placed on news-gathering techniques and the evaluation of information from verbal and written sources. Students also take courses on ethics and press law. During the second year, students are taught not only how to develop their professional skills but also how to build their self-confidence as journalists. The format throughout the two years is based on workshops. The school also offers courses in specialized reporting areas such as sport, science and the developing world.[31]

The Regional College of Volda has also had a two-year journalism program since 1971. This school, which is particularly well-equipped for technical skills training, takes about 50 students each year, most of whom have had two or more years of university or professional experience. A similar program at Bodø, in northern Norway, with an intake of no more than 15 students each year, specializes in news and feature writing. There is also another two-year course in Stavanger supported by the powerful *Stavanger Aftenblad*, which trains about 20 students. Finally, the universities of Oslo and Bergen both offer programs in mass communication, but these are strictly academic in nature.

SOUTHERN EUROPE

Italy

As in many other Western European countries, communication training in Italy followed an apprenticeship model until after World War II. Then, in the absence of any national framework, several training facilities were established by universities, professional associations, religious bodies, newspaper chains and local journalists' groups. While there has been the usual split between university-based media and communication studies and practical skills training in professional schools, the most prestigious establishment is the Institute of Journalism Training in Milan, which was founded in 1977 by the journalists' association of Lombardy. It was felt at the time that traditional on-the-job training was no longer sufficient to provide the technical, cultural and ethical preparation required by developments in the journalistic profession.[32]

This school, which in many ways resembles the Centre de Formation des Journalistes in Paris, offers a two-year program combining both academic and practical courses taught by professional journalists from the Milan newspapers and professors from the city's three universities. In theory, students can apply for entrance with only a high-school diploma, but preference is usually given to students with a university degree. Competition to enter the institute is keen, with as many as 800 applicants vying for the 45 places awarded every two years. One peculiarity of the school is that it does not grant a diploma. However, the training given is accepted by the national journalists' association in lieu of the 18-month probationary period trainees have to complete before taking the examination that qualifies them as professional journalists. The Milan Institute for Journalism Training is the only establishment in the country to benefit from this arrangement.

The major emphasis of the institute's program is practical, with basic writing and editing courses in the first year and specialized sequences during the second year. The institute runs three student publications and a student radio news program. Students also have to complete at least three months of internships in various news organizations, and the institute has special arrangements with local radio and television stations. The training given at the institute is highly regarded by the industry; as a result, even without a diploma, "graduates" usually have no trouble finding jobs.

In the universities, academic journalism programs began earlier. The University of Urbino introduced the first such program in 1949 with the blessing of the Italian Press Federation, but it was perhaps a little before its time and thus failed to develop as expected. Another program, begun in Bergamo in 1960, was that of the (Catholic) Advanced School of Journalism and Audiovisual Media, which in 1986 became part of the Catholic University of Milan under the name of School of Specialization in Social Communications and today offers only a graduate program. The only other institution offering a complete journalism program is the University of Salerno, but several other universities, including those of Trent, Messina, Molisa, Verona and the Bocconi Economics University in Milan, provide isolated courses or mini-sequences in various areas of communication.

Since 1987, the department of sociology at La Sapienza University in Rome and the department of political science at the University of Naples have begun courses that could possibly develop into fully fledged programs of journalism and mass communication. Also in 1987, the Italian Ministry of Education asked the universities of Turin and Naples to study the creation of "schools of specialization" in journalism. These schools are expected to provide graduate level studies similar to professional-track master's programs to be found in American universities.

Although several universities offer academic programs in media studies, only two provide thoroughly professional training. The first is the previously mentioned School of Specialization in Social Communications at the Catholic University of Milan, which offers a three-year program with specialized studies in journalism, advertising/public relations and entertainment (radio-television, film and theater). Courses are taught either by permanent faculty or by media professionals hired on contract. Only 50 students are accepted each year from among a 100 qualified applicants holding undergraduate degrees in economics, law, informatics (information sciences), the humanities, sociology, statistics, political science and, perhaps surprisingly, architecture.

The emphasis of the program is decidedly professional. The school has its own student newspaper and television studio and, during the third year, students spend a great deal of time in local newsrooms and broadcast stations. The training given is so professionally oriented that the journalists' association of Lombardy is trying to obtain the same probationary-period waiver as that enjoyed by the Milan Institute of Journalism Training.

The other professional graduate program is provided by the School of Specialization in Journalism and Mass Communication at LUISS (Libera Universita Internazionale degli Studi Sociali) in Rome. The school was created within the Faculty of Political Science in 1983 by the Italian Federation of Newspaper Editors and the university, which is a nonreligious institution recognized by the state. The two-year program offers two specializations, one in print or broadcast journalism and the other in newspaper management and corporate publishing. Courses are taught by both communication professionals and academics. The school takes in only 40 or 50 graduate students each year, selected on the basis of academic records, an examination, professional experience, previous specialized study abroad and a knowledge of foreign languages. Successful applicants must be at least 27 years old.

A large number of other training programs are offered throughout the country by a variety of private groups and individuals. They range from brief training sessions or weekend courses to full-scale four-year programs organized by cultural centers, municipalities, design institutes, private business schools and groups of local journalists. Some of them are not known for the quality of their programs, but many others, particularly those associated with the provincial universities, adequately fill a well-defined and growing need for trained personnel in local media outlets and specialized sub-areas of the communication industry.

Finally, several communication groups have experimented with their own training courses. For example, *La Stampa*, the Monti Group, the Federation of Newspaper Editors, the National Federation of the Italian Press and Italian television have all created grants for in-house training schemes, which have proved to be very popular. In 1981, there were more than 7,000 applicants for the 65 grants offered by the two national federations.

One group, the Rizzoli-Corriere de la Sera Group, created its own school in 1987 along the lines of the Institute for Journalism Training in Milan. To begin with, only the high-school diploma was required. However, it soon became apparent that, while a year was long enough to teach the technical basics of journalism, it was not long enough to allow students to assimilate the kind of general culture necessary to be a successful journalist. Now, candidates are expected to have some kind of university training before they apply. In 1987, 2,242 candidates applied. Only the top 14 were given study grants.

Successful applicants undergo a year of rigorous training, after which they are given a six-week trial period. If they perform satisfactorily they are then put on the standard 18-month probationary period leading up to the final examination and qualification as a professional journalist. Many of the successful candidates are subsequently hired by the Rizzoli Group.

Although it has risen steadily since the war, the total number of journalists in Italy remains relatively low at just over 9,000, including about 1,000 probationers. Demand for trained journalists stands at around 400 every year. These figures reflect a fairly strict definition of the profession. Only those employed in a news or information organization have the right to call themselves journalists. On the other hand, the category known as "pubblicisti" (advertising/public relations) counts well over 20,000 and is rising rapidly. More women are entering the communication industry, particularly advertising and public relations, but are still very much a minority. At the same time a growing number of communication professionals have completed university degrees. These trends are bound to have an effect on the way in which communication training develops in Italy.

Spain

There was no formal communication training in Spain until 1941, when a national school of journalism was set up by the government and placed under the control of Franco's Falangist Party. The first courses taught had to be approved by the National Press Delegation, which organized a series of six-month training programs reserved for students with a university education or regular army officers. Over the next 30 years, the school developed a three-year program of study attended by students from all over the country. Other smaller schools emerged, but the national school was without doubt the largest and most important journalism training center in Spain. Although run by a supposedly independent governing board, it remained under government supervision right up until the early 1970s.[33]

In 1970, educational reforms paved the way for the creation of several new "faculties of information sciences," which ultimately led to the disappearance of all the old journalism schools associated with the Franco regime. In 1971, new faculties appeared at Universidad Complutense in Madrid, Universidad Autónoma in Barcelona and the University of Navarre. Others followed at Bilbao in 1977, Valencia in 1986 and Salamanca, Seville and Laguna in 1988. Another, private facility is the

Catholic San Pablo Center for University Studies in Madrid, which operates in conjunction with Complutense.[34]

These programs, which are mainly theoretical and which have attracted large numbers of students, lead to degrees in journalism, advertising or audiovisual techniques. Courses are taught either by permanent faculty, frequently transferred from departments of economics, political science, law, sociology or the humanities, or by adjunct instructors from the communication industry. The universities have been accused of being too theoretical, but they maintain that, with the country's new-found democracy, it is more than ever necessary to develop critical and analytical approaches to communication as well as intellectual breadth.

In response to professional pressures, many university programs have attempted to increase the amount of practical training dispensed. Most departments do not have the necessary technical equipment to provide much more than basic skills training but are able to arrange media visits and internships, particularly during the summer preceding the final year of study. Several major newspapers, the national broadcasting organization and the EFE news agency all take interns, and most offer supporting grants for outstanding students. On the whole, this compromise appears to be satisfactory to both sides, but supervision remains a problem.

One development that merits attention has been the creation of master's programs by private news organizations in conjunction with various universities. In 1987, the Prisa group, which owns *El Pais*, started a one-year professional master's program with the help of the Free University of Madrid. In the same year, *ABC* opened its Escuela de Praticas to train 25 carefully selected graduate students in its own newsrooms. A year later, the *El Correo* group began a similar program in conjunction with the Basque University of Bilbao. Both the national broadcasting organization and the Press Association have introduced master's programs with the assistance of Complutense in Madrid. Other projects are being planned by other companies, including the *Diario 16* group.

These one-year programs are very intensive and are mainly devoted to practical training. Students are hand-picked and are expected to perform. Obviously, the press organizations involved are primarily interested in having potential recruits trained the way they want them trained, but, even though the numbers of students selected are limited, not all of them are given jobs at the end of the training period. However, a large percentage of them find employment in the media, which is a tribute to the quality of the training received.

The same cannot be said for the more than 2,000 communication graduates produced yearly by the universities. Only about 25 percent of them find employment in journalism. With job opportunities limited to around 600 each year, training programs are faced with a serious demand problem that is likely to become even more acute as graduates from some of the more recently established schools enter the work force.

Portugal

As in Spain, the media were controlled by a repressive authoritarian regime until the mid-1970s. Before 1974, when the old order was replaced by a more democratic form of government, journalism in Portugal enjoyed little prestige. Journalists were badly paid and, because of government controls, were reduced to routine hack work. What training there was consisted of on-the-job socialization. But even before 1974, attempts to streamline and modernize the media were beginning to draw attention to a need for more professional training.

After 1974, with a free press and the creation of many new newspapers and periodicals, it became even more urgent to organize formal training structures, despite opposition from an older generation of journalists, who swore by on-the-job training, as well as from certain media owners somewhat reluctant to accept a form of training and recruitment freed of all ideological, social and political constraints. What has finally emerged is a system similar to those of other Western European countries, combining universities and professional schools.[35]

The New University of Lisbon is one of only two state universities to grant a degree in social communication. The department of social communication, created in 1979 as part of the Faculty of Social Science, offers a four-year program that includes two years of general studies followed by two years of specialization in print journalism, audiovisual techniques or theory and research. The general philosophy of the program is built on the premise that, in a democratic society, journalists must be independent of political and economic constraints. They need a knowledge of technical and professional skills, but they should also be able to analyze and interpret the mass of information available today. True to this philosophy, the program places great emphasis on critical thinking, particularly during the first three years. Practical training is provided by at least six months of internships in the media. The department accepts about 75 students at a time. The only requirement to apply is a high-school diploma.

The Higher Institute of Social and Political Science, also in Lisbon, offers a similar four-year degree program in social communication. This program, now heavily theoretical, grew out of an earlier three-year diploma program that was closed down during the 1974 revolution. It accepts no more than 35 students a year.

At the graduate level, the New University of Lisbon has the only master's program in social communication in the country, but the Portuguese Catholic University, located in Lisbon, offers graduate courses in information sciences that are not recognized by the Ministry of Education. The New University master's program, open to 30 students at a time, is largely theoretical. That of the Catholic University, which takes in about 40 students a year, includes a six-month internship. The courses are so rigorous that only about 25 percent of the students actually finish the program.

A number of professional schools provide courses leading to a baccalaureate after three years or a four-year diploma of specialized studies that is equivalent to a university degree. The Higher Journalism School of Porto was created in 1986 by the Center for Journalism Training, which seeks not only to promote professional training but also to improve the public image of the profession. Its program, approved by the Ministry of Education, attempts to strike a balance between theory and skills training. It accepts a maximum of 40 students a year, some of whom are already working journalists.

In 1979, the Higher School of Journalism in Lisbon became the Higher School of Social Communication. Its program is currently limited to advertising and marketing and public relations, but its journalism sequence might be reestablished in the near future. Meanwhile, the Center for Journalism Training in Porto, which already runs a four-year program, has introduced a new 12-month "basic" training course open to students and office workers holding a high-school diploma. Courses cover journalistic methods, computer skills and communication theory as well as law and ethics. A similar basic course is offered in Lisbon by CENJOR (Center for the Professional Training of Journalists) for students aged 18 to 24 who have not passed their high-school diploma. CENJOR also runs refresher courses for working journalists seeking to update their technical skills. Both CENJOR and the Center for Journalism Training in Porto have extensive continuing education programs in the print and broadcast media.

Greece

Communication training structures in Greece are far less developed than those of other Western European countries. The press, like many other Greek institutions, is dominated by Athens, which, with its 4.5 million inhabitants, accounts for almost half of the country's population as well as for most of its dailies, periodicals and broadcasting services. In the same way, journalism is dominated by the Union of Journalists of the Athens Daily Newspapers, which has long controlled the way in which most journalists are allowed to enter the profession.[36]

Traditionally, aspiring journalists are recruited on the basis of their personal contacts and taken on without pay for as long as seven or eight months, during which they have to demonstrate their talent and determination to become a professional. After that, successful candidates may move to a paid position. Generally speaking, journalists are badly paid; and many hold down more than one job, which, in a highly politicized press system, may lead to conflicts of interest.

Although the old system continues to be acceptable to most people in the profession, its associations with the patronage and corruption of the military regime overthrown in 1974 have prompted the current democratic government to reform journalism education. In 1990, the Greek Ministry of Education authorized the creation of two new undergraduate journalism programs at the University of Athens and the new Pantios University of Social and Political Sciences. Each of these programs would train between 100 and 140 students a year, a figure that bears little relationship to the actual annual demand for journalists, which, according to the Athens Union, is no more than 100. Furthermore, both the Union and the Athens Daily Newspaper Publishers Association have doubts about the nonvocational orientation of the new university courses and are studying the possibility of creating their own two-year professional course for a maximum of 30 university graduates. These two bodies already run seminars and refresher courses for working journalists in subjects such as law and economics.

SMALLER COUNTRIES

The Netherlands

Religious denominational divisions, long a feature of Dutch society, are present not only in the country's media system but also in the training of communicators. Shortly after World War II, formal journalism education was introduced at both the Institute of Press Studies at the University of Amsterdam and the Catholic University of Nijmegan. Both programs were strongly supported by the newspaper industry and provided a mix of professional training and communication studies.[37] The academic sides of these programs have survived as the Department of Mass Communication at the University of Amsterdam and the Institute for Mass Communication at the Catholic University in Nijmegan. These two institutions have also been joined by the Institute for the Science of the Press in Amsterdam, which functions essentially as a mass communication research center.[38]

Meanwhile, other professional schools have been created for each of the denominational tendencies. The first was the Journalism School of Utrecht, which was founded in 1966 as a public or nondenominational school. The second was the Catholic School of Journalism at Tilburg, created in 1980. The third was the reformed (protestant) school at Kampen, founded in 1981 and, finally, in 1982, the evangelical church set up its own school at Amersfoort. Of these, the most doctrinaire is ESJ Amersfoort, which is entirely supported by private funds, whereas the other three are subsidized by the national Ministry of Education. These four schools, which are in fact higher technical institutes, all offer four-year programs and, together, turn out about 300 graduates every year.[39]

Skills courses are taught by media professionals in simulated newsrooms, working broadcast studios and model layout rooms. Students thus gain realistic media experience before undertaking two mandatory three-month internships in a medium of their choice. Other courses are taught by specialists in communication and language as well as economics, law, history, politics and social geography. Although these four schools have slightly different study cycles, educational approaches and, of course, ideological positions, on the whole their programs are very similar. Recently, however, the Ministry of Education, in an effort to avoid duplication, has asked them to consider developing differentiated programs. As a result, Utrecht, Tilburg and Kampen have begun to investigate joint programs with the universities or higher technical institutes both inside and outside the country. Kampen is seeking to develop a higher institute for mass communication. Tilburg is strengthening its public relations emphasis. And Amersfoort is developing a program in business communication and telematics.

In 1990, the universities of Groningen and Rotterdam announced their intention to introduce journalism programs. This initiative has been met with considerable opposition not only from the Dutch Journalists' Association (NVJ), but also from the Ministry of Education, which argues that journalism is best taught in the professional schools. Furthermore, as the four professional schools are already in the process of expanding and adding new programs, it would be logical for them to develop academic courses, rather than the universities.

Finally, there is also a wide array of private and industry-sponsored institutions providing professional training, including correspondence courses, the Santbergen broadcast institute and the highly respected Radio Netherlands Training Center in Hilversum.

Austria

Austria was one of the first countries to offer "newspaper science" (*Zeitungwissenschaft*) courses at the turn of the century, but these were essentially academic.[40] Today, professional training remains firmly anchored in the traditional apprenticeship system. There are no specialized professional training institutes. Instead, trainees spend a three-year probationary period in the newsroom during which they learn the skills of the trade. In compliance with a collective labor agreement governing the employment of journalists, trainees are also expected to attend short courses offered by a number of professional development institutions.[41]

The most important of these is the Journalism Training Board (Kuratorium für Journalistenausbildung), which was founded by the newspaper publishers, the journalists' union and the ORF (the Austrian Broadcasting Corporation) and which provides four-week elementary courses as well as seminars for qualified working journalists. The Board also gives grants to students who wish to work at a newspaper during their vacation. Other professional development institutions include the Catholic Media Academy (Katolische Medienakademie), which specializes in religious journalism, and the Austrian Society for Journalism and Media Research (Österreichischer Gesellschaft für Publizistik und Medienforschung), which is associated with the trade unions. Some of the political parties also run educational establishments offering some form of journalism training. Finally, the ORF runs its own training programs for broadcast journalists.

Only 20 percent of Austria's 6,000 journalists hold a university degree, but as many as 40 percent have started at a university and then relinquished their studies, a phenomenon that is not uncommon in Western Europe. For those entering the profession with a university degree, the usual three-year probationary period is reduced to two years. Many degree holders have studied at the universities of Vienna or Salzburg, both of which have a department of mass communication. Vienna has some 5,000 communication students and Salzburg 1,000. About a third major in journalism and mass communication. Enrollments have increased sixfold since the beginning of the 1970s.

Communication programs cover not only journalism but also advertising, public relations and other related fields such as documentation and communication research. The journalism and mass communication program consists of one-third media theory, one-third practical training and one-third media science. Journalism majors also have to do an internship in a media organization. The four-year program leads to a degree that is equivalent to a master's. Since Austrian universities are state institutions, they enjoy considerable autonomy and the media have little direct influence over their programs.

Belgium

As in other northern European nations, higher education generally in Belgium is affected by religous considerations, and education in communication is no exception. Indeed, training programs are to be found in both Catholic and state-run institutions as well as in private nonreligious establishments. The situation is further complicated by the bilingual nature of Belgian society and the obligation to provide programs in both French and Flemish.

The oldest institution, the Belgian Journalists' Institute (Institut pour Journalistes de Belgique), was opened in Brussels in 1922 under the aegis of the General Association of the Belgian Press. Its programs were initially in French, and a Flemish department was added in 1934. At the time the institute was created, the Belgian press was essentially a partisan press. Journalists were little more than intellectuals eager to write about their beliefs. The founders of the institute were convinced that the time had come to train a new kind of journalist, capable of meeting the demands of a more sophisticated press and a more educated public. Early curricula provided university-level theory courses and a few practical classes, but the general assumption was that professional skills could only really be acquired by on-the-job training. Today, the two-year program places more emphasis on skills training, but it continues to value a broad liberal arts approach.[42]

The first universities to offer communication programs were the Free University of Brussels, in 1945, and the Catholic University of Louvain, in 1946. In 1962, the state university of Ghent entered the field, followed by the state university of Liège in the early 1970s. Today, all six Belgian universities (Ghent, Liège, Brussels-French, Brussels-Flemish, Louvain and Louvain-la-Neuve) offer four-year degree courses in communication. The universities remain strongly attached to their intellectual traditions and communication programs are essentially theoretical and critical in their approach. As a result of pressure from students, however, all the universities now provide some degree of practical training, either through internships or special classes taught by temporary adjunct professionals.

Alongside the universities and the Journalists' Institute in Brussels, four other "advanced schools" (écoles supérieures) were created in 1965 to provide four-year programs in radio, television, film, theater and other technical aspects of the entertainment industry. Three of them are located in Brussels and the fourth in Louvain-La-Neuve. The general orientation of these progams is creative and artistic, but many of the students they produce find work in journalism, particularly in the areas of layout, photojournalism and film editing. In these schools, courses are taught by specialists whose "professional notoriety" is recognized by the Ministry of Education. A number of other schools, four Flemish and three French, offer three-year courses in public relations, advertising, public information and social communication.

Switzerland

Another multicultural and multilingual nation, Switzerland has a diverse media system supported by large advertising revenues. The country has a relatively dense population; and there are flourishing newspapers in Zürich, Geneva, Lausanne, Lugano and Basle. Alongside 80 small bi-weeklies and triweeklies are several large-circulation weeklies as well as a state-run radio and television network serving the German-speaking, French-speaking and Italian-speaking communities. The system also includes private radio stations, pay television and cable. The size and diversity of the system create a sustained demand for trained journalists.

As a matter of record, the first journalism courses were given at the University of Zürich in 1903 and the University of Berne in 1904, but they were isolated and sporadic. Until the late 1950s, when the first real programs were created at the universities of Freiburg and Neuchâtel, on-the-job training was universal; it survives to this day in the form of lengthy probationary periods. Today, these are the only universities offering complete programs, but "seminars" and individual courses in journalism are to be found in the universities of Zürich, Berne, Geneva, Basle and Lausanne.[43]

The Institute of Journalism and Social Communication at the Catholic University of Freiburg runs courses, mainly of a theoretical and analytical nature, in both French and German. The four-semester program, following preliminary university studies in the humanities or law, includes a three-month internship but places little emphasis on professional skills training, which is amply provided for during the two-year probationary period every trainee must take before becoming a registered journalist. The Institute has approximately 250 students, about 60 percent of whom are

German-speaking. Classes are taught by two full-time professors and several adjunct professsionals.

The University of Neuchâtel's journalism program, created in 1959 and located in the Faculty of Letters, seeks to provide a general education as well as a theoretical and practical knowledge of the mass media. Again, because of the two-year professional probationary period, it makes no pretense of offering practical training. An internship is recommended but not required. The program, which lasts six semesters, is open to students and journalists wishing to improve their theoretical knowledge of the profession. Courses are taken by about a hundred students.

Although on-the-job training remains popular, various professional organizations have seen the need for more formal training. The journalists' unions have long felt that probationers are often used as cheap labor, while editors no longer have the time or inclination to provide training for beginners. For these reasons, the unions and publishers' associations have created three training schools, one in French, one in German and one in Italian, providing mainly practical but some theoretical courses taken during the probationary period.

The French school, the CRFJ (Centre Romand de Formation des Journalistes), in Lausanne, was founded in 1965 and offers eight weeks of courses spread over two years. It trains about 70 students each year. In 1986, it introduced an end-of-course certificate. Almost all beginning French-speaking journalists are trained at the CRFJ.

The German school, known as the Media Training Center or MAZ (Medienausbildungzentrum), is located in Lucerne and was founded in 1983. This center, which trains about 50 students, has a much more complete program, consisting of 33 weeks of courses spread over two years. Probationary journalists are allowed to take only 18 weeks. At the request of the publishers, the MAZ now offers a certificate similar to that provided by the CRFJ.

The Italian school, the Corso de Giornalismo, located in the Ticino and founded in 1987, is much smaller, given the size of the Italian-speaking community. It provides six weeks of courses spread out over two or three months and trains from 12 to 20 students each year. The center is heavily subsidized by the Ticino canton. Some form of collaboration with training centers in Italy has been rejected because journalists need to be familiar with Swiss institutions, law and journalistic practices.

The three language services of the Swiss broadcasting system all have their own training schemes that are part of the usual two-year probationary period. Most of the instruction given is technical and job specific. However, the French-speaking service sends probationers to the CRFJ for more general courses on journalism, and the German-speaking service has a similar arrangement with the MAZ. The Swiss broadcasting system has also developed a series of continuing education courses to enable journalists to update their professional skills or to prepare for a career move. This initiative has been followed by other professional associations, and the CRFJ has been particularly active in providing educational support.

Finally, two private programs have been introduced by press groups. In 1974, the multimedia Ringier group began an 18-month training scheme involving six months of formal courses and twelve months of placements in the various publications belonging to the group. The program is open to anyone, but most of the 20 students trained at any given time are probationers with Ringier. Courses are taught by a combination of media professionals and university teachers.

The Saint Gall Journalism School, which was taken over by the Zollikofer group at the beginning of 1989, runs a four-semester program for preprobationers over the age of 18. Apart from attending courses, students have to spend 60 days in a newsroom or write at least 30 lengthy news stories.

Ireland

Despite a population of only three and a half million, Ireland has a flourishing media industry. Indeed, the Irish have one of the highest newspaper reading rates in Europe, bolstered partly by the ready availability of British publications. For a long time, the training of journalists was modeled after the British apprenticeship system and, as in Britain, the National Union of Journalists has had a strong influence on the profession. The first full-time journalism course, established at the Rathmines College of Commerce in 1969, was adapted from training schemes run by the National Council for the Training of Journalists in the United Kingdom. The one-year course, which emphasized reporting and sub-editing, was extended to two years in 1974 and leads to a Certificate of Journalism. The College, now part of the Dublin Institute of Technology, takes 25 to 30 students each year.[44]

Since 1982, the School of Communications at Dublin City University has had a one-year graduate program leading to a Graduate Diploma in Journalism. The course, open to students with a good undergraduate degree, combines academic and practical subjects and includes an eight-week internship. The Graduate Center for Journalism at University College in Galway offers a similar one-year graduate course with options in both journalism and public relations.[45]

With all three of these institutions providing only 60 to 70 places each year, there is still an unsatisfied demand for communication training. As a result, several private colleges of journalism, mainly in the Dublin area, are now offering short courses or one-year programs, but such institutions are not popular with the National Union of Journalists, which maintains a virtual if unofficial closed shop.

Luxemburg

Luxemburg, even smaller than Ireland, with a population of only about 375,000, has a robust press system that is characterized by linguistic diversity and strong political affiliations. The country has enjoyed freedom of the press since 1848, but advertising revenues are just too limited to allow smaller media vehicles to survive without some form of government subsidy. Furthermore, because of the country's size and geographic location, French, German and Belgian media are easily accessible.

There are no formal journalism training facilities in Luxemburg, which is understandable given the size of the press corps. The total number of journalists, including probationers and retirees, foreign journalists working in Luxemburg and Luxemburg journalists working outside the country, is somewhere between 150 and 160. Some journalists go abroad for training; and the Luxemburg media employ graduates from schools in Germany, France, Belgium, Austria and Switzerland. However, the vast majority of journalists working in Luxemburg today are the products of on-the-job training. Perhaps the main reason for this is that the Luxemburg language is used not only in everyday life but in formal press conferences and other media events. Training in foreign countries and in "foreign" languages may not be considered useful. Many journalists, particularly those covering local news, have little more than a high school diploma, but there is a marked tendency to hire university graduates for specialized reporting areas.[46]

THE EUROPEAN JOURNALISM TRAINING ASSOCIATION

The disparity of communication training systems in Europe has been a source of concern to many educators as the European Community moves towards even greater integration. In November 1990, 22 journalism schools from 11 West European countries met in Brussels to create the European Journalism Training Association (EJTA), whose future role will be to "encourage the emergence of a European consciousness" in its training centers.[47] One of the main aims of the association will be to standardize training curricula and methods, but it is already obvious that member institutions strongly favor a professional rather than an academic approach to training. When the EJTA finds its feet, it will almost certainly foster ties with training institutions in Eastern and Central Europe. As it develops, it is certain to play a major role in communication training in Europe.[48]

NOTES

1. Frederic N. Hunter, "Grub Street and Academia: The Relationship between Journalism and Education, 1880–1940" (Ph.D. diss., City University, London, 1984).

2. National Council for the Training of Journalists, *How Journalists Are Trained* (London: NCTJ, 1989), p. 8.

3. Ibid., p. 2.

4. *Newspaper Journalism Syllabus: Aims* (London: National Council for the Training of Journalists, May 1984).

5. Bob Scheibel, "Five Dimensions Explain Differences in British-American Journalism Education," *Community College Journalism* 15, no.4 (Fall 1988), pp. 10–11.

6. John Tulloch, "The United Kingdom," in Kaarle Nordenstreng, ed., *Reports on Journalism Education in Europe* (Tampere: University of Tampere Department of Journalism and Mass Communication, 1990), p. 52.

7. Philip Gaunt, "Overcoming Obstacles to Regional and International Cooperation for Communication Training" (Paper presented to the UNESCO International Meeting of Regional Training Institutes for Communication Development, Paris, June 12–14, 1991).

8. Isabelle Hernett, "Les Ecoles de Communication," *EPP*, June 16, 1986, pp. 60–64.

9. Bernard Voyenne, *Les Journalistes Français: D'où viennent-ils? Qui sont-ils? Que font-ils?* (Paris: Les Editions CFPJ, 1985), pp. 227–228.

10. Jacques Bourdonnais, "France," in Nordenstreng, *Reports on Journalism Education*, pp. 39–42.

11. May Katzen, *Mass Communication: Teaching and Studies at Universities* (Paris: UNESCO Press, 1975), p. 100.

12. "Les patrons préfèrent embaucher des universitaires," *Le Journaliste* 194 (February-March, 1985), p. 3.

13. Philip Gaunt, *Choosing the News: The Profit Factor in News Selection* (Westport, CT: Greenwood Press, 1990). See chap. 2, "Journalistic Traditions," pp. 19–33.

14. These views were expressed in interviews with the author at the CFJ in Paris.

15. Interview with Robert Escarpit at Indiana University West European Studies Center in 1989.

16. Bénédicte Haquin, "Les entreprises de presse: des employeurs insatisfaits," *Presse-Actualité* (June-July 1985), p. 24.

17. Jean Savary, "Les écoles de journalisme: permis de conduire ou leçon de conduite?" *Presse-Actualité* (June-July 1985), p. 19.

18. Georg Hellack, *Newspapers, Radio and Television in the Federal Republic of Germany* (Bonn: Inter Nationes, 1987), pp. 20–21.

19. Walery Pisarek, "Central and East European Countries: Overview," in Nordenstreng, *Reports on Journalism Education*, p. 60.

20. Jürgen Wilke, "The Federal Republic of Germany," in Nordenstreng, *Reports on Journalism Education*, pp. 29–33.

21. John Sandford, *The Mass Media of the German-Speaking Countries* (London: Oswald Wolff, 1976), p. 21.

22. Lee Becker, Jeffrey Fruit and Susan Caudill, with Sharon Dunwoody and Leonard Tipton, *The Training and Hiring of Journalists* (Norwood, NJ: Ablex, 1987), pp. 165–167.

23. Gaunt, "Overcoming Obstacles."

24. Troels Fink, "Denmark," in UNESCO, *The Training of Journalists: A Worldwide Study on the Training of Personnel for the Mass Media* (Paris: UNESCO, 1958), p. 181.

25. Osmo Mäkeläinen, "Finland," in UNESCO, *The Training of Journalists*, p. 183.

26. Most of this information comes from Kaarle Nordenstreng's own section on the Nordic countries in Nordenstreng, *Reports on Journalism Education*.

27. Sven Sandstedt, "Sweden," in UNESCO, *The Training of Journalists*, pp. 195–196.

28. Nordenstreng, "Sweden," in Nordenstreng, *Reports on Journalism Education*, pp. 13–16.

29. Manny Paraschos, "Europe," in John C. Merrill, ed., *Global Journalism*, 2d ed. (White Plains, NY: Longman, 1991), p. 115.

30. Carl Just, "Norway," in UNESCO, *The Training of Journalists*, pp. 185–187.

31. Nordenstreng, "Norway," in Nordenstreng, *Reports on Journalism Education*, p. 21.

32. Much of this section is drawn from Hugh Stephenson and Pierre Mory, *Journalism Training in Europe* (Brussels: Commission of the European Communities, 1990), pp. 241–253.

33. Stephenson and Mory, *Journalism Training*, pp. 86–92.

34. Juan Beneyto, "Spain," in UNESCO, *The Training of Journalists*, pp. 191–193.

35. Stephenson and Mory, *Journalism Training*, pp. 119–132.

36. Ibid., pp. 337–344.

37. Jacques Bourquin, "Europe," in UNESCO, *The Training of Journalists*, pp. 173–174.

38. International Organization of Journalists, *Journalistic Training Centres* (Prague: IOJ, 1986), p. 200.

39. Gabriella Meerbach, "The Netherlands," in Nordenstreng, *Reports on Journalism Education*, pp. 35–37.

40. Bourquin, "Europe, p. 155.

41. Heinz Hans Fabris, "Austria," in Nordenstreng, *Reports on Journalism Training*, pp. 25–27.

42. Bourquin, "Europe," pp. 161–162.

43. Ibid., pp. 267–268.

44. Ibid., pp. 316–326.

45. Francis Xavier Carty, "Ireland," in Nordenstreng, *Reports on Journalism Training*, pp. 43–46.

46. Stephenson and Mory, *Journalism Training*, pp. 225– 227.

47. Ibid., pp. 207–214.

48. James A. Crook, "Europeans Form Training Association with Help from European Community," *Journalism Educator* 45, no.4 (Winter 1991), pp. 92–96.

Chapter Six

Eastern and Central Europe

At this writing, it is still too early to predict with any certainty what kind of press systems and what kind of communication training structures will emerge in the former Soviet bloc. In an incredibly short period of time, between the end of the 1989 and the end of 1991, the countries of this region experienced the triumph of pro-democracy movements, the breakup of the Soviet Union and the creation of a new "commonwealth" of independent republics. In the wake of these momentous events, political instability, ethnic strife, civil unrest and bleak economic prospects point to the likelihood of continuing change and at least the possibility of further serious upheavals.

In these circumstances, it is obvious that press systems and communication training will change. What is less obvious is how far they will change and in what directions they will develop. In order to appreciate what they may become, it is necessary to understand what they were.

THE OLD SYSTEM

Throughout the Cold War and right up until the dissolution of the Soviet Union, popular imagination tended to view Eastern and Central Europe as a uniform, homogeneous whole, dominated by a central authority that dictated everything from economic policy to political behavior. In this context, press systems were believed to be identical, all slavishly following the Marxist-Leninist model imposed by Moscow. In the same way, it was firmly believed both in the East and in the West that the education of socialist journalists followed the same pattern in all the countries of the Soviet bloc. The very use of the term "bloc" suggested a faceless uniformity that belied the enormous cultural and linguistic diversity of the peoples of Eastern and Central Europe. Needless to say, while media systems were strictly controlled and were expected to conform closely to Communist Party dictates, they also differed from country to country.

It is certainly true that journalism training throughout the region was permeated by Marxist-Leninist ideology, but clear differences were apparent in such areas as length of training, the kind of institutions involved and entrance qualifications. For example, in a major study of eight Eastern and Central European countries (Bulgaria, Czechoslovakia, German Democratic Republic, Hungary, Poland, Romania, Soviet Union and Yugoslavia), Walery Pisarek found that, at the end of the 1980s:

- Seven countries (all but Hungary) had university undergraduate degree programs in journalism lasting from three to five years.

- Five countries (Bulgaria, Czechoslovakia, Poland, USSR and Yugoslavia) had two-year graduate programs in their universities.

- Three countries (Hungary, GDR and Yugoslavia) had professional training schools organized by national associations of journalists.

- All eight countries had some form of supplementary education and professional training for journalists.[1]

Pisarek is quick to point out that, despite these differences, training programs shared a number of common features, the most obvious of which was the overtly political nature of the training given. In socialist systems, journalists were always classified as political workers and as such were expected to be thoroughly familiar with Marxist-Leninist ideology. All journalism programs in the Soviet system, especially those taught in the universities, were built along the same lines. Curricula were standardized and were refined at yearly meetings attended by deans from all the socialist countries. Moscow provided assistance to schools to standardize curricula as much as possible, and there were attempts to impose Soviet textbooks in all programs. However, standardization was mainly limited to ideology and theory, and individual programs were allowed to develop specific specializations. For example, public relations was not offered at Moscow State or Leningrad State but was available at other institutions such as Charles University in Prague. On the whole, though, most programs followed the same pattern.[2] A typical curriculum would consist of three parts:

I. Ideology
   a. Marxist-Leninist political economy
   b. Marxist-Leninist philosophy
   c. Marxist-Leninist scientific socialism

II. Theory
   a. History of communication
   b. Concepts of communication
   c. Personal versus mass communication
   d. Foreign languages, with compulsory Russian

III. Specialization
   a. Operation of technical equipment
   b. Art of speech
   c. Theory of genres
   d. Writing
   e. Editing
   f. News agency journalism

In the 1960s, educators were often professionals; but in the 1970s and 1980s efforts were made to hire faculty with qualifications in economics or the social sciences and with good teaching skills. However, political qualifications were even more important, with the result that many teachers were well able to teach theory based on Marxist-Leninist principles but were less qualified to teach practical skills. This deficiency was partly compensated for by compulsory month-long summer internships. Typically, the first summer would be spent in a local newspaper, the second at a news agency and the third at a radio or television station, but there was considerable flexibility of choice. After the third year, students could work for money during the summer months.

To enter a program, students had to be politically active. It helped too if their parents were also politically active. On the other hand, children of dissidents were not allowed to enter any program of higher education, especially not journalism. Academic results were important, too, but only if political credentials were satisfactory. Most students attended regular daytime classes, but evening classes were also taught. In some countries, almost one-fourth of the day students were foreign, many of them from developing countries. In Bulgaria, in the late 1980s, this proportion rose as high as 50 percent of all day students. Another common feature of the socialist system, centralized planning, sought to match the production of journalism graduates with industry demand. In theory, this virtually guaranteed employment for all those who successfully completed training.

INTERIM INITIATIVES

Such, in general outline, was the system before independence. A more detailed description of the various programs offered in each country would be somewhat academic, given the fact that most of them now have been heavily modified or closed down altogether. At this point, it is still too early to predict what kinds of training structures will eventually develop. What is certain, though, is that the rebuilding of training programs, as both the reflection of newly emerging democratic press systems and a reaction to the past, will take years to accomplish. But, even at this early stage, it is possible to identify some of the needs and priorities that will guide the direction of future training programs.

Inevitably, following independence, most journalism programs, which were seen as bastions of communist ideology, were suspended or removed, in a greatly diminished form, to social science faculties. Despite attempts by some new governments to limit reprisals, many journalism educators, particularly those who taught Marxist-Leninist "theory," found themselves out of a job. All graduates of the old training system came under suspicion. In the euphoria of new press freedoms, the demand for "untainted" journalists soared. Very quickly, many of the new newspapers that appeared found that they could get along perfectly well with writers holding degrees in economics, political science or the humanities. Who needed journalism training?[3]

Those departments that were allowed to survive hastily set about revamping their curricula to reflect the new values. For the most part, this action was limited to removing ideology classes. Many programs lost their students. For example, faced with plummeting enrollments, Moscow State's Department of Journalism, one of the largest in the entire system, suddenly discovered a vocation for communication research. Almost overnight, journalism training was confronted with a troublesome paradox. Throughout the 1980s, enrollments had been steadily dropping as the prestige of journalism sank lower and lower, particularly in the hard-line countries. When independence came, many people were tempted to flirt with this now glamorous profession but were reluctant to seek training at institutions that still bore the stigma of socialist ideology and privilege. The resulting hiatus poses a serious threat to the harmonious development of quality press systems.

In the immediate future, as press systems learn to cope with the harsh realities of a free-market economy, and until universities succeed in developing appropriate curricula, which could take a long time, specialized training programs for practicing journalists would appear to hold out the best hope for improving the quality of journalism. A group of Eastern European journalists meeting in Prague in July, 1990, identified those areas in which training needs are the most urgent. They are, in order of priority, investigative reporting, newsgathering techniques, news writing, news editing, graphic design and interviewing.[4] They further indicated that, in a democratic regime, they would need to acquire expertise in covering business and economic affairs, government, international affairs, science, medicine and environmental issues. At the same time, with press systems that are moving from government subsidized funding to competitive commercial funding, there is going to be an urgent need for training in various areas of media management, including advertising sales, circulation development, accounting and general business practices.

There has been no shortage of foreign media companies, government agencies, professional associations and universities willing to provide training in all of these areas. In 1990, at least 80 U.S. groups launched aid projects ranging from joint-venture publications and exchanges to technical seminars and gift subscriptions to U.S. publications.[5] While many of these initiatives are genuinely altruistic, there is little doubt that some of them are motivated either by ulterior profit motives or by a desire to replace socialist ideologies with Western ideologies. In this respect, it would be well to remember that however much Eastern Europeans may need Western know-how, they remain suspicious of Western values. And not all Western journalism or journalistic practices are worthy of imitation. Furthermore, the unseemly speed with which Western press moguls have bought into Eastern European media systems has alerted leaders to the potential dangers of foreign ownership.

Among those bodies that have offered immediate training assistance are UNESCO, the International Press Institute, the Thomson Foundation, Reuters and the International Federation of Newspaper Publishers. The United States has been particularly active and has launched numerous programs funded by the Agency for International Development (A.I.D.), the U.S. Information Agency (USIA) and other government agencies as well as by private foundations. The Association for Education in Journalism and Mass Communication (AEJMC) is also working with USIA's International Media Training Center to bring Eastern European journalists to U.S. campuses for a year of professional development. The Center for Foreign Journalists in Reston, Virginia, the World Press Freedom Committee, the National Forum Foundation and Freedom House were active in promoting press freedoms and supporting independent press initiatives long before the pro-democracy movements began, and it could be argued that their efforts may have helped to force the Soviet leadership into introducing *glasnost* and *perestroika*.

The International Media Fund, created in 1990 with the support of the U.S. government, advises private organizations on how best to help the Eastern European media. Although it functions primarily as a clearing house for grants, it has also become involved in training initiatives, including the American Journalism Center in Budapest. Run by the College of Journalism at the University of Maryland, the Center provides short courses, seminars and workshops for journalists in Hungary, building a base upon which longer courses will be offered for university students interested in journalism and mass communication careers. It is hoped that ultimately it will become a school of journalism within the Hungarian university system.[6]

The Center has held seminars not only for journalists but also for government officials, media executives and future journalism educators. They have been organized with the cooperation of the Hungarian Association of Journalists, the Hungarian Press Union, the International Monetary Fund, Elte University in Budapest and the Hungarian College of Crafts and Design. Seminar topics have included Government-Press Relations, How Democratic Governments Work with a Free Press, Journalism Ethics and Women in Journalism, as well as Newspaper Design and Layout, Desktop Publishing and Managing Publications for Profit. This initiative is particularly interesting in that it has involved appropriate professional organizations, thus making sure that local needs are addressed.

FUTURE PROSPECTS

One of the concerns associated with foreign training initiatives is that local needs are not always properly understood. Offers of help have sometimes been based on the erroneous assumption that East European countries want to adopt all the features of Western press systems. This is not always the case. Not all Eastern European journalists believe that absolute freedom is desirable. Many believe that some form of mixed government-private ownership is preferable, particularly for the electronic media. There is also a very strong feeling that the rights to gather, process and disseminate information should all receive legal definition and protection, which runs counter to American libertarian traditions.[7] Indeed, some Eastern European countries feel less affinity for the United States than for Western Europe, which has its own firmly entrenched traditions, including the subsidizing of newspapers by political parties. Such traditions are bound to affect training.

In these circumstances, then, it seems likely that communication training in Eastern and Central Europe will move through three stages. The first stage, which we are now witnessing, is an emergency stage during which most programs have been suspended or radically changed, and every effort is being made to provide stopgap courses in journalistic practices that are very different from those that prevailed under Soviet rule. The main problem during this stage is that no one knows what kind of press systems and what kind of journalism will emerge. The seminars and workshops offered by the West are unabashedly based on Western practices. The programs that are being developed by the Eastern European countries, either on their own or in conjunction with foreign organizations, are based on what are believed to be the principles of "free" journalism but may fail to understand completely what is involved. For example, definitions of investigative journalism, which is perceived as a priority area for training, may differ widely not only between the East and the West but also among the Eastern European countries. Despite the well-meaning earnestness of all those involved, until new press systems emerge and until the resulting journalistic practices and training needs can be defined with accuracy, training will continue to be an ad hoc activity characterized by little more than its non-Sovietness.

The second stage, which is already beginning to appear, will involve regional initiatives based on a more realistic understanding of what the communication training needs of Eastern Europe will be. One such initiative is the Central and Eastern European Center for Communication in Warsaw, Poland. The creation of the center was proposed by the Polish Journalists Association (SPD) following an informal meeting of some 90 Eastern and Central European journalists at UNESCO headquarters in Paris in February 1990. The meeting stressed the inadequacy of training available for journalists in the region, particularly in the context of new media structures.[8] The center, which opened in March of 1991, was set up with the assistance of UNESCO and financial support from the International Federation of Journalists (IFJ), the World Press Freedom Committee, the United Nations Development Program and the governments of the United States and the Netherlands. As it develops, the center will organize training programs in journalism, media management and foreign languages and will also serve as a link between professional organizations in Eastern and Western Europe.

Another regional initiative is the proposed Central European University, which would offer graduate courses to Czechs, Slovaks, Poles, Hungarians and possibly Austrians and Germans.[9] Instruction would be in English. It is thought that the university would also be an ideal forum to train practicing journalists in urgently needed specialties, such as economic journalism. With the addition of an endowed chair, the university could eventually develop a complete graduate program in journalism. A possible site for the university would be Bratislava in Czechoslovakia.

The third stage would see the creation of new programs both in the universities and in professional training centers, based on the "real" rather than the perceived realities of pluralistic press systems. Journalists' associations and unions, which have been traditionally strong in Eastern Europe, will no doubt have a hand in shaping the programs as will private media owners. How far governments will intervene will depend on political and economic developments. The main problems associated with the third stage will revolve around the production of textbooks, the training of qualified educators and accreditation.

The outlook for communication training in Eastern and Central Europe is full of promise. It is to be hoped that the press freedoms that have already emerged will continue to be preserved, thus contributing to the growth and stability of the whole region. The way in which training is developed and supported will be crucial to the preservation of these freedoms.

NOTES

1. Walery Pisarek, "Overview," in Kaarle Nordenstreng, ed., *Reports on Journalism Education in Europe* (Tampere: University of Tampere Department of Journalism and Mass Communication, 1990), pp. 59–80.

2. Interview with Stanislav Perkner, former Dean of the School of Journalism at Prague University, April 9, 1991.

3. Interview with Melor Sturua, November 8, 1991.

4. Everette E. Dennis, "Eastern Europe and the Media: Some Views of Insiders," in Everette E. Dennis and John Vanden Heuvel, *Emerging Voices: East European Media in Transition* (New York: Gannett Foundation Media Center, 1990), pp. 95–98.

5. Cynthia F. Wilson, "There Are Various Ways to Help," *Presstime*, March 1991, p. 26.

6. Information supplied by Ray E. Hiebert, Director of the American Journalism Center, Budapest, and Professor of Journalism at the University of Maryland.

7. Dennis, "Eastern Europe and the Media," p. 96.

8. UNESCO, *Perspectives for Regional and International Cooperation*, Conference Document CII-91/CONF CC-609 (Paris: UNESCO, April 30, 1991), p. 24.

9. Dennis, "Eastern Europe and the Media," p. 42.

Chapter Seven

Asia and the Pacific

It is not a simple matter to analyze communication training in a region as vast and diverse as Asia and the Pacific. The countries within it reflect enormous differences in size, population, wealth, literacy, political regimes, press systems and journalistic concepts. It contains some of the most populous countries, including India and China, which by 2025 will account for one-third of the world's total population, and also some of the smallest island nations. Japan, Australia and New Zealand enjoy high living standards, followed closely by Taiwan, Hong Kong and Singapore, while Afghanistan, Bangladesh, Cambodia and Nepal are among the poorest nations on earth. Political regimes range from the totalitarian to the most democratic, with press systems that vary from the freest to the most repressed. Japan has one of the largest circulation dailies in the world, while several of the smaller nations have no newspapers at all.[1]

Because of this diversity, it is difficult to find points of comparison among communication training structures in the region. They do, however, share some common features as well as a number of problems. Although it is easy to overgeneralize, it can be stated that most countries, with very few exceptions, are moving from limited craft-oriented training schemes toward broader university-based programs. There are some good reasons for this. In the region as a whole, the need for trained communicators has risen dramatically, partly because media systems have expanded so rapidly, but also because many governments have come to view communication as a vital development tool. Existing training structures have expanded too, but they have not been able to keep pace with demand. In seeking to create new training programs, governments have turned, logically enough, to the state-funded universities.

A parallel trend, again with some exceptions, has been the move from the British model to the U.S. model. Former British colonies or territories, and there are many in this region, have continued to favor on-the-job training; but, as new university courses have been created, they have tended to adopt the kind of programs used in American universities, with their emphasis on liberal arts subjects alongside skills training. One reason is that the American model has shown itself to work well in university settings. Another is that consultants called in to develop new programs are often American. Finally, many leading educators in the region have received their training in the United States.[2]

The creation of new university programs presents a number of problems, however. Often the level of funding is such that only very few faculty positions can be provided, which limits enrollments. Many universities do not have the technical facilities necessary to teach newsroom or studio skills. At the same time, there is a chronic shortage of qualified university teachers. In many countries, this lack of facilities and trained educators, combined with high demand for communication courses, has prompted the creation of private schools, which are not always good and frequently expensive.

Another common thread is a lack of indigenous teaching materials, especially textbooks. Some countries are beginning to develop their own textbooks, but it is a task that is considerably complicated by the number and variety of local languages. The problem is particularly acute with regard to training for community newspapers, which are invariably published in local languages. In India and the Philippines, teaching is given in English, which simplifies matters somewhat but tends to favor the larger, elitist, urban media. The problem remains intact for smaller, local-language publications, where communication training needs are the most urgent.

Other common features include high enrollments, lack of support from the media industry and inadequate funding. Another noteworthy feature is the role that UNESCO has played in communication training throughout the region at local, national and regional levels. Finally, in summary, it could be said that the more a country of this region is developed, stable, literate and free, the less formal its communication training will be. Conversely, the more urgent its developmental needs, the more structured and formal its communication training is likely to be.

After such a series of overgeneralizations, formulated, let it be said, in an attempt to make sense of the diversity of this vast region, it would be appropriate to take a more detailed look at some of the main countries within it. This analysis will adopt a subregional approach, examining in turn South Asia, Southeast Asia, East Asia and, finally, the Pacific.

SOUTH ASIA

Formal communication training in South Asia is somewhat less developed than in other parts of the region for a variety of reasons that will be discussed below. As in many other areas of activity, it is largely dominated by India, the first major country to be examined.

India

According to some sources,[3] the origins of communication training in India go back to 1941 with the creation of a department of journalism at the Punjab University in Lahore (now in Pakistan). This program was transferred to Delhi in 1947 and then to Chandigarh in 1962. Madras University also opened a department of journalism in 1947. A number of other communication training courses were begun in the 1950s at the universities of Mysore, Nagpur, Osmania and Calcutta. Partly as a result of the 1954 Press Commission, which recommended that persons with formal qualifications should be given preference when seeking jobs, many more training establishments were created in the 1960s and 1970. Today, there are over 40 universities offering courses in various areas of specialization including print journalism, photo journalism, broadcast journalism, advertising, public relations, media management and communication research.[4]

Most university departments offer courses that tend to be more academically oriented than skills based. This bias is largely due to a chronic shortage of educators with suitable professional experience, but it is further compounded by a lack of technical equipment and teaching materials. Many departments are still heavily print oriented because they do not have any broadcast or audiovisual equipment. Even when they do, they often lack the trained personnel to use it effectively. Most departments actively seek internships in newspapers, magazines and news agencies, but, unfortunately, news organizations are often reluctant to accept interns. In fact, most newspaper editors criticize course curricula in universities on the grounds that they are obsolete. Attempts by universities to bring senior-level professionals into course design, teaching and practical work are frequently unsuccessful because of poor cooperation from the media industry. The situation is particularly difficult outside of major metropolitan areas.

The current state of communication training in Indian university departments appears to be the result of bad planning and inadequate coordination.[5] Many universities have rushed into the field without proper preparation and have discovered too late how difficult it is to find qualified faculty and how expensive it is to acquire the right kind of equipment. The University Grants Commission (UGC) has laid down that training programs should have a minimum of one professor, two readers and four lecturers, but these requirements are rarely met. Some departments at otherwise respectable institutions are run by one or two part-time faculty. At the present time, about 50 percent of communication faculty positions in Indian universities are not filled. The UGC is, of course, painfully aware of this situation and has done its best to organize refresher courses and workshops in cooperation with the Indian Institute of Mass Communication and the Press Institute of India.

Despite these problems, many departments run successful programs, and there is a growing demand for university communication courses. For example, at Osmania University in Hyderabad, there were 1,145 applications for 40 seats in 1988–89. Although the demand is there, partly because fees are low, most universities can offer only a very limited number of places, for example, Himachal eight, Calicut ten, Poona 30, Marathwada 35 and Herhampur 33. Karnataka has turned out only 25 graduates since 1983. On the other end of the scale, Mysore confers as many as 80 bachelor's degrees and 30 graduate degrees every year. All in all, universities train about 1,500 graduates annually, an average of 30 students for each department.[6]

There are a number of well-established graduate programs at the universities of Madras, Mysore, Marathwada and Herhampur as well as newer programs at a dozen other institutions. Some critics believe it is unwise to launch new graduate courses before undergraduate programs have been properly streamlined and coordinated,[7] but the acute shortage of qualified educators is likely to sustain demand for all but the most poorly funded and understaffed courses. In many cases, students can choose between the M.A., which leans toward the academic, and the M.Phil., which is more of an intermediate degree requiring a few papers and a thesis. Some departments confer a Master of Communication and Journalism (MCJ) degree. Only a few institutions, such as Kerala, Mysore, Poona and Bangalore, offer the Ph.D., mainly because of the lack of professors qualified to supervise doctoral work.[8]

As has already been noted, India is only one of two countries in the region to provide communication training in English, despite the existence of large numbers of newspapers and periodicals published in some 90 Indian languages and dialects, of which the most important are Hindi, Bengali, Urdu, Malayalam, Oriya and Tamil. The English-language press is influential in political circles and is widely read by the educated elite, but the regional-language press, which played an active role in the struggle for independence, has a much higher readership among the increasingly literate non-Anglophone population in the provinces.[9] Some universities, however, have adopted language journalism as a subject, in which the medium of instruction and examination is an Indian language. For example, Saurashtra University in Rajkot uses Gujarati and Kamaraj University teaches in Tamil. Mysore began a language journalism course in 1974, while the Indian Institute of Mass Communication has a graduate diploma in Hindi journalism. The Department of Journalism at Marathwada University claims that its main objective is to prepare students for the Marathi press, and Kashi Vidyapith in Banaras states that the main thrust of the institute will be to "encourage the use of Hindi in the media and assist the media in case of any problem or difficulty in the usage of Hindi."[10]

The university departments of journalism and mass communication have an important role to play in that they are numerous, well distributed throughout the country and inexpensive; but there is little doubt that the Indian Institute of Mass Communication (IIMC), located in New Delhi, is the best equipped, best funded and most prestigious training institution in India. Founded by the government in 1965 as a center for advanced study and communication research, the institute not only runs graduate courses, seminars and lectures in journalism, public relations and advertising but also centralizes information on mass communication education and research and advises central and state governments, as well as foreign institutions, on training structures and strategies.[11]

Over the years, the IIMC has helped to train more than 2,000 graduate students carefully selected from applicants from all over the country. Most of them receive good placement offers even before completing their training, and many have risen to prominent positions in the communication industry. The institute also provides communication training for persons recruited into the Central Information Service and the Indian Foreign Service. Finally, as a UNESCO-designated training center, every year it organizes courses for about 30 mid-level journalists and information officers from various developing countries and members of the non-aligned movement. Many of these now hold positions of responsibility in the information systems of African and Asian countries.

The IIMC, which occupies a new building next to the campus of the Jawaharlal Nehru University in New Delhi, has a staff of 36, including eight professors, five associate professors and three assistant professors. Its facilities include television and sound studios equipped with color cameras, camera control units and a special-effects generator. Other equipment includes projectors, tape recorders, video recorders, 16 English typewriters, seven Hindi typewriters and, a rarity in Indian training centers, two word processors. The institute's library houses over 16,000 volumes on mass communication and receives about 325 periodicals and journals. Although it has not yet been recognized as a university and can thus confer only a diploma and not a degree, the IIMC remains a model center for communication training and is respected throughout the region.

It is to be noted that communication training is given in more nonformal institutions than universities, but the quality of training provided by them is sometimes doubtful, usually because they are understaffed and ill-equipped. Several of these nonformal institutions, however, do offer quality programs. The Bharatiya Vidya Bhavan offers journalism courses in 30 of its 40 centers throughout the country, some of them quite large. The Delhi center, for example, claims to have as many as 1900 trainees, but the Calcutta center, which has no newsroom or typewriters or even laboratory paper, has only 35–40 students.

Another interesting example is the Xavier Institute of Communications, which is part of St. Xavier's College, a Jesuit educational establishment dating back to 1869. This institute, located in Bombay, enrolls about 400 students each year, some of them from the neighboring countries of Pakistan, Bangladesh and Sri Lanka and others from as far away as Tanzania and the Philippines. It offers beginning and advanced courses in journalism, public relations, advertising and film/video production and appears to be quite well equipped for the task. It has a good library and competent staff. According to its director, Xavier is one of the largest nongovernmental media training centers in India.[12]

On the industry side, the Press Institute of India (PII), located in New Delhi, was founded in 1963 by a group of leading newspapers and continues to be funded by contributions from about 30 members. Over the years, the PII has held close to 300 courses attended by well over 3,500 journalists from some 200 newspapers and magazines. Some of the courses last for four to eight weeks. Workshops and seminars, held in different parts of the country, vary from one to five days and are often conducted in both English and the language of the region. Students are usually working journalists sponsored by their employers.[13]

The PII has been active in promoting joint programs with government agencies, professional associations and sister organizations such as the Indian Institute of Mass Communication. It has also run specialized workshops on development journalism and health journalism in conjunction with UNEP (United Nations Environmental Program), UNDP (United Nations Developmental Program) and WHO (World Health Organization). The institute maintains links with press organizations in other parts of the world and has been instrumental in arranging international exchanges through scholarships and fellowships from the Thomson Foundation, the Japanese Newspaper Publishers and Editors Association and a number of American universities, including Harvard and Columbia.

Several newspapers, including the *Times of India*, the *Hindustan Times*, the *Hindu* and the *United News of India*, run their own training schemes. By way of example, the *Times of India* newspaper group began its own intensive nine-month journalism course in 1985 because graduates of university communication programs do not receive enough practical training. The first year was very successful; for the second year, the *Times* received 1,200 applications for 25 places. It is interesting to note that, of the 25 selected, 19 were women. The course consists of four eight-week modules. The first module covers basics of newspaper writing. The second is spent on the workshop newspaper. The third is an internship in a group newspaper, and during the final module students are expected to write an in-depth article suitable for publication. Most of the graduates are hired by the *Times* group, but there is no guarantee of employment.[14]

Finally, in the broadcast area, All India Radio has its own staff training school in New Delhi somewhat similar to the courses run by the BBC in London. India is one of the world's leading producers of motion pictures; and the Film and Television Institute of India in Poona, the largest of its kind in the region, offers a comprehensive range of courses in film-making and television production.[15]

In summary, the communication industry appears to be growing more sensitive to the need for formal training structures and has begun to create its own courses or participate in joint programs organized by professional bodies which is an encouraging sign. At the same time, many university-based programs continue to suffer from lack of resources and facilities and are failing to produce adequately trained professionals. Of late, however, the University Grants Commission has been mandated, under the Special Assistance Program, to create and equip as many as six professional communication training centers in selected universities around the country. It is felt that this may go a long way toward bridging the gap between university programs and industry needs.[16]

Pakistan

Pakistan has the second strongest press system in South Asia, and the penetration of its broadcast media is greater even than that of India. The strongly rooted tradition of British journalism in Pakistan has prompted the media industry to favor strongly on-the-job training and to reject university programs, which suffer from an almost total lack of even the most basic equipment required to teach practical skills.[17] Nonetheless, eight universities and four non-academic institutes now offer some kind of communication education program.

The universities of Punjab, Sind, Gomal, Baluchistan and Bhawalpur offer a two-year course in journalism/mass communication leading to a master's degree. Karachi has both a three-year honors undergraduate program and a two-year master's course. Peshawar offers a one-year diploma and a two-year master's program. Most of these programs trace their origins back to the 1950s, but B.Z University in Multan recently started a one-year journalism diploma course in its department of Political Science and International Relations. By and large, these university programs are patterned after the U.S. model, but they are severely hampered by the lack of faculty, resources and media support enjoyed by their American counterparts.

Among the non-academic institutions, the Information Services Academy in Islamabad is the least professional in that its one-year course, taken by Civil Service recruits entering government information departments, combines communication education with topics such as international affairs, political science and social development. The Pakistan Broadcasting Training Institute and the Pakistan Television Training Institute, both in Islamabad, provide a variety of courses for in-service personnel covering all aspects of broadcast production and programming. The Press Institute of Pakistan offers a range of short courses for professionals, with an emphasis on new developments and technologies. In a related area, the Advertising Association of Pakistan plans to open a training institute for those in the advertising industry.

Without a national communication policy, adequate planning, resources, faculty, equipment and support from the media industry and with the prospect of strong government controls, particularly in the broadcast area, many educators feel that the systematic development of communication training will continue to be unsatisfactory.

Bangladesh

Communication training in Bangladesh is a relatively recent phenomenon, partly because for a long time the growth of journalism was stunted by authoritarian rulers who used the press for political purposes. However, in the early 1960s, a marked increase in the number of newspapers created an urgent demand for training, particularly in the field of print journalism. Some of this demand was satisfied by in-service courses provided by the Press Foundation of Asia (PFA), the International Press Institute (IPI), the Commonwealth Press Union (CPU), the Thomson Foundation and a few other international or regional organizations, but these were available only to those fortunate enough to be able to travel abroad.[18]

In 1962, Dhaka University created the first national training program when it opened a department of journalism offering a one-year degree course. As demand continued to increase, a three-year bachelor's degree was added and later a master's degree. Today, the department trains some 180 undergraduates and about the same number of graduate students in its two-year master's program. The students, 35 percent of whom are women, are selected on the basis of written and oral aptitude tests. Approximately 60 percent of the graduates are absorbed into the communication industry. Others find employment in public relations, publishing or management, where their communication skills are put to good use. Courses are taught by a full-time faculty of about twelve, assisted by adjunct professionals, who make a strong contribution to the practical side of the curriculum; but, like other university programs in the region, the department lacks the technical equipment necessary for effective skills training.

In 1976, the Press Institute of Bangladesh was set up to provide domestic in-service training and orientation courses, with the help of the government, the newspaper industry, PFA, CPU, the Thomson Foundation, UNESCO and the Asian Mass Communication Research and Information Center (AMIC). The institute's full-time instructors, who are all former professionals, teach regular courses in reporting, editing, feature-writing and photojournalism. Specialized courses in political, economic, diplomatic, population, science and environmental reporting are sometimes taught by adjuncts from the newspapers or from some of the regional and international organizations previously mentioned. Compared to the university's department of journalism, the institute is very well equipped, with its own printing press, computers, photo-typesetters, microfilm cameras, video recorders, audiovisual equipment and a large library. Since its creation, it has given advanced training to more than 400 journalists, editors and newspaper managers.

Training for the broadcast media was somewhat neglected until 1980, when the National Institute of Mass Communication (NIMCO) was created with the assistance of UNESCO and AIBD. The institute offers regular courses on broadcast production as well as specialized courses on broadcast news, computer programming, development broadcasting and microwave technology. It also organizes occasional workshops on film-making and cinematography.

Although the press has developed considerably in the last decade, following the end of martial law in 1979, readership is still modest, with a circulation of only 1.5 million for its 60 daily newspapers. In view of the fact that many journalists are still trained on the job, existing formal training facilities appear to be well able to cope with current demand.

Sri Lanka

Over the last decade, the press of Sri Lanka, which is supported by one of the highest literacy levels in the whole region, has undergone tremendous growth, despite or perhaps because of deep social unrest and periods of violent civil war. Today, this multilingual island has a relatively large number of excellent newspapers, weeklies and magazines, published in English, Sinhalese and Tamil. The Sri Lanka Broadcasting Corporation puts out a wide variety of radio programs in these three languages as well as Urdu, Hindi and Arabic. Television programming began in 1979. There is, therefore, a solid demand for trained communicators.

Formal communication training was begun in 1969 at the Junior University, Dehiwela. Although this two-year course was closed down the following year, it provided a model that would be adopted by later training programs.[19] Today, the only fully fledged program is that offered by the Department of Mass Communication at the University of Kelaniya. This program, begun in 1973, offers a two-year general degree course and a three-year honors course, open only to undergraduates having passed their first-year examination at the university. The curriculum covers all aspects of mass communication but leans heavily toward the academic, largely because there is a lack of suitable technical equipment. It should be added, however, that, in order to complete the course, students are obliged to undergo periods of on-the-job training in the media.

The University of Colombo also offers a one-year diploma course in mass media for midcareer journalists in both the print and electronic media. Courses are taught by media experts, critics, lawyers and academics and are conducted in English and Sinhalese. As at Kelaniya, on-the-job training is part of the curriculum. Yet another course, in journalism and writing, is provided by the University of Sri Jayawardhanepura for mid-career media professionals. Taught by the Professor of Sinhala, this one-year course emphasizes creative writing, but the curriculum includes other aspects of journalism.

The Sri Lanka Television Training Institute is a self-contained unit providing all types and levels of training for writers, actors, technicians and other broadcast production staff. Courses, which cover a broad range of topics, are two to four weeks long and are taught by experts from the industry. The institute is particularly well equipped thanks to support from both local and foreign institutions. One of the largest foreign contributors is Friedrich-Ebert-Stiftung of Germany.

There is also a wide variety of smaller communication training schemes run by public bodies such as the Sri Lanka Film Corporation, the Sri Lanka Institute for Development Administration, the Health Education Bureau and the Bank of Ceylon, as well as by private institutions such as the Family Planning Association of Sri Lanka, the Catholic Cinema Organization and the Sri Jinaratana Academy. All in all, the number of sporadic courses is quite high, but only about a dozen institutions provide training with any regularity and consistency.

Nepal

Modern journalism did not emerge in Nepal until the 1950s, when the ruling Rana family was forced to relinquish some of its power and abandon the strictly isolationist policies it had enforced for over a century. Until then, the country's only newspaper was the *Gorkhapatra*. During the 1950s several new titles were founded, mainly by journalists who had worked in neighboring India; but it was not until 1982, when licensing was eased, that newspapers suddenly began to mushroom. In the last ten years, the number of publications has jumped from 90 to about 450, all in the capital or other urban centers. However, some observers believe that, as the situation stabilizes, many publications will have to close down because there are not enough readers or advertising revenues to support them. On the other hand, if some of these publications move to smaller communities with promising readership potentials, Nepal may witness the emergence of a thriving rural press.[20]

Commmunication training has quite naturally followed this development. Today, only three institutions, all of them in Kathmandu, offer courses in journalism and mass communication, and one of those is in danger of being closed because of poor enrollments. The first journalism courses were started at the Ratna Rajya Laxmi campus of Tribhuvan

University in 1976, in response to repeated requests from the journalists' community. Three years later the university created a department of journalism, which now offers a two-year proficiency certificate course and a four-year diploma program. In 1986, the People's Campus, a privately owned campus operating as part of Tribhuvan University, started its own proficiency level course, taught by two part-time instructors from the English-language daily, *The Rising Nepal*. The number of students, never large, has dwindled to about ten, and the program is now in danger of being phased out.

As might be expected, the university programs tend to be academically oriented; although students are taken on visits to media organizations, no full-time internships are required. In 1984, a group of media professionals established the Nepal Press Institute (NPI) to strengthen the practical training of journalists, to conduct mass communication research and to create much-needed teaching materials. The NPI's ten-month program consists of eight months of classroom work and two months in an internship. It also runs specialized short courses, often organized in conjunction with regional and international organizations, especially UNESCO.

Despite their good intentions, the various programs offered by these three institutions are still limited by poor facilities and equipment and a lack of appropriate textbooks in Nepalese. Furthermore, there appears to be a growing apathy toward journalism as a subject of study. Overall enrollments are down. At the Ratna Rajya Laxmi Campus, only 64 students enrolled in 1988, compared to 116 in 1985 and 139 in 1981. At the People's Campus, initial enrollment in 1986 was 18, but this dropped to ten the very next year. During its first year, the NPI had 25 students. Enrollments fell to 21 in 1986 and 20 in 1988. For these reasons, the future of communication training in Nepal does not appear to be very rosy.

Very little information is available about other countries in the region. Kabul University in Afghanistan runs a small journalism program that is no doubt undergoing change after the end of more than ten years of communist rule. In Bhutan, which has only one weekly newspaper with a circulation of 8,500 and a couple of general interest periodicals, there is little need for formal training structures.

SOUTHEAST ASIA

Over the last two decades, communication training has developed enormously in Southeast Asia, particularly in the Philippines, Malaysia, Thailand and Indonesia, which have relatively free press systems, freer, that is to say, than those of Vietnam, Laos, Cambodia and Burma

(Myanmar), in which the mass media are directly controlled by the government. Of all these countries, the Philippines enjoys the greatest freedom and also boasts the largest number of training institutions, several of which enroll students from other countries in the region. Both the Philippines and Malaysia offer doctoral degrees in communication. It is also to be noted that in Malaysia, the Philippines and Thailand there are more women than men enrolled in communication programs. One eminent researcher, Crispin Maslog of the Institute of Development Communication at the University of the Philippines, has even speculated whether this might not be an indication of the degree of modernization of these countries.[21]

The Philippines

Of all the countries in Southeast Asia, the Philippines certainly has the most vigorous system of communication training. At the last count, there were at least 51 schools or departments offering degree programs in journalism or communication, an almost fourfold increase over the thirteen identified in the first survey of communication education in 1971.[22] The earliest program dates back to 1936, when the University of Santo Tomas established a journalism major in the Faculty of Philosophy and Letters. However, most departments were established between the 1960s and the present day. Significantly, much of this growth has been toward the provinces. In 1971, degree programs in journalism and communication were to be found in only two provincial institutions, the School of Journalism and Communication at Silliman and the Department of Agricultural Communication at the College of Agriculture in Los Baños. Today, there are 32 throughout the country, representing 63 percent of all training establishments. Many of them offer programs in rural communication, especially development communication.

One important program, the Institute of Development Communication at the University of the Philippines at Los Baños (UPLB), began life in 1954 as the Office of Extension and Publications at the College of Agriculture. In 1974, when it was renamed the Department of Development Communication, it became the first school to offer a bachelor's degree in development communication. Today, it is one of only two schools to offer a doctoral program. The other, also in the UP system, is the College of Mass Communication in Diliman, founded in 1965.

One phenomenon that is peculiar to the Philippines is the existence of chains of schools. The largest is that of the University of the Philippines (UP), which consists of UP Diliman, UPLB (Communication Arts), UPLB

(Development Communication), UP Baguio, UP Cebus, UP Tacloban and UP Visayas in Iloilo. The Ateneo chain is run by the Society of Jesus and includes Ateneo de Davao, Ateneo de Naga, Ateneo de Manila, Ateneo de Zamboanga and Xavier University in Cagayan de Oro. Another smaller chain is that of the St. Paul religious sisters, consisting of St. Paul Iloilo, St. Paul Manila and St. Paul Quezon City. What will be obvious from this grouping is that not all communication training institutions are state owned, as tends to be the case in other parts of Southeast Asia. Indeed, only 31 percent of them are state colleges or universities. Of the privately owned schools, 26, or slightly more than half of the total, belong to religious orders or sects.

Of the 51 training institutions in the Philippines, 43 offer undergraduate degree programs only. Six schools, Ateneo de Manila, Pamantasan ng Lungsod ng Maynila, Santo Tomas, UPLB, UP Diliman and Philippine Women's University offer both graduate and undergraduate degrees. Two other schools, the Asian Institute of Journalism in Manila and Central Luzon State University in Muñoz, provide master's programs only.

The total number of communication students is estimated to be somewhere between 12,000 and 13,000. The largest enrollments are at the Polytechnic University of the Philippines (approximately 1200), UP Diliman (1,000), Pamantasan ng Lungsod ng Maynila (860) and Philippine Women's University (550).[23] Seventy-six percent of all students are women, a phenomenon that may be explained by the fact that the field has expanded from journalism to public relations, advertising, public information, corporate communication and many other areas.

Generally speaking, instructors in the state-run university programs tend to be better qualified than those in private schools. For example, 11 of the 23 full-time faculty at UPLB's Institute of Development Communication hold Ph.D.s and ten have master's degrees. Seven of the 31 full-time instructors at UP Diliman have doctoral degrees. This proportion falls off sharply in the smaller university programs and private schools, where there is a dearth of educators with higher degrees. As might be expected, faculty in the university programs do more research and carry lower teaching loads. Instructors in some of the private schools teach very heavy loads and are vastly underpaid. Many of them teach only part time. At the same time, state colleges and universities are better equipped than private institutions. The best-equipped schools are UP Diliman, which has film and television production studios as well as its own radio station, and UPLB's Institute of Development Communication, which also has its own radio station, print shop and word processors.

As in other parts of Asia, Philippine communication education is plagued by some familiar problems, including inadequate facilities and equipment, a severe shortage of appropriate instructional materials, a dearth of qualified instructors, a lack of support from the communication industry and the absence of coordination and planning, which has led to the proliferation of substandard programs. In recent years, however, the Philippine Association of Communication Educators (PACE) has begun to address some of these problems.

Non-formal training is also well-developed in the Philippines. Many state universities and some of the better private schools with formal degree programs also offer a wide range of seminars, workshops and summer institutes for professional journalists and senior journalism students. A number of other institutions provide nonformal training programs both regionally and nationally. Two of them, the Philippine Information Agency and the Development Academy of the Philippines, are government sponsored. The others are privately funded by professional associations or religious organizations.

The most influential of these private organizations is the Press Foundation of Asia (PFA), which was set up in Manila in 1967 by a group of Asian publishers and editors. PFA seeks to promote high standards of journalism throughout the region and improve editorial, production and management techniques through practical training programs. Since its creation, PFA has organized well over a hundred workshops and seminars for journalists, more than a fourth of them on development issues. Its popular regional Intensive Course on Population and Development Reporting is supported by the United Nations Fund for Population Activities (UNFPA). Other areas covered have included economics, agriculture, science and technology, the environment, energy and the role of women in development, as well as newspaper management practices, cost control, budgeting and printing. Over the years, more than 2,500 journalists have benefited from these PFA seminars.

Another interesting initiative is to assign two to four journalism students in their junior year to the foundation's newsfeature service, Depthnews, which annually produces some 2,000 features, commentaries and radio scripts mailed to news organizations throughout the region. The interns usually spend their summer vacation at this important agency and are given training in feature writing, desk work and other newswriting assignments.[24]

The Philippine Information Agency (PIA) and the Development Academy of the Philippines (DAP) are both government agencies that offer communication training for government officers. The DAP program is still relatively young, as it was created in 1987, but it has already trained well over 1,000 government workers in communication research and planning, news writing and media relations. Most of its seminars are held at its facilities in Tagatay or Manila, but some of them are organized in the provinces for local government employees. PIA provides training in a very wide range of areas that include communication research and planning, film production, theater production, video and puppetry as well as the usual newswriting, editing and layout skills.

The Philippine Press Institute (PPI) was established in 1964 by a group of publishers, editors and journalists, but was shut down during martial rule between 1972 and 1986. Early training courses focused on in-depth reporting and newspaper editing, but a number of seminars were held for community journalists. More recently, the institute has concentrated on investigative reporting, ethics and press freedom. A parallel organization, Kapisanan ng Mga Brodkaster sa Pilipinas (KBP), offers similar programs in various aspects of broadcasting.

The Communication Foundation for Asia (CFA) is a Catholic organization that has specialized in development communication. It has trained thousands of Filipinos and hundreds of people from all over Asia in the use of various communication techniques for development. Its workshops and seminars cover not only traditional mass communication channels but also such media as puppetry, theater, group communication and comic books. The National Office of Mass Media (NOMM) is another religious organization that coordinates the social communication work of the Catholic Church in the Philippines and organizes communication training for church workers.

In conclusion, it may be said that, while communication training in the Philippines is both vigorous and varied, most of the formal programs suffer from a lack of qualified full-time teachers and inadequate equipment. Furthermore, doubts may be raised about whether current curricula are not too general and too mass-media oriented for the specialized development and community-based needs of the country; and whether the communication industry can absorb the very large numbers of communication graduates being produced by the system.

Malaysia

Because of its cultural and geographic peculiarities, Malaysia has communication structures and training needs that are somewhat different from those of other countries in the region. Malaysia is a federation of 13 states, 11 in Peninsular Malaysia and 2, Sarawak and Sabah, 500 miles to the east in Borneo. Its population of about 17 million is made up of Malays (44 percent), Chinese (36 percent), Indians (10 percent) and a number of other ethnic groups (10 percent). Islam is the official religion, although other religions are practiced. Bahasa Malaysia is the national language, but Radio Television Malaysia (RTM) broadcasts programs in English, Tamil and Mandarin as well as Bahasa Malaysia.[25]

Full-time university training programs did not begin to appear until 1971, but before then a number of non-formal courses were available. In the early 1960s, the Institute Public Relations Malaysia (IPRM) and the Association of Accredited Advertising Agencies (4As) began to offer short courses in their specialized areas. In 1963, the IPI Asian Program, the Asia Foundation, the Malaysian Government and a group of local newspaper companies sponsored a six-month training course in journalism. This project was so successful that, in 1966, the government converted it into the Southeast Asian Press Center (SEAPC), which was to provide valuable support to the new university programs that appeared a few years later. In 1974, SEAPC was renamed the Malaysia Press Institute (MPI).[26]

Broadcast training also began in 1971 at the National Broadcasting Training Center, later renamed Institut Penyiaran Tun Abdul Razak (IPTAR), which provides in-service courses in all areas of broadcast writing, production and engineering. In 1972, the Asian Institute of Broadcasting Development (AIBD), a joint project of UNESCO, the Asia-Pacific Broadcasting Union (ABU) and the government of Malaysia, was set up to train rural broadcasters throughout the region. Housed at IPTAR headquarters, AIBD specializes in the use of radio and television for educational purposes and family planning and has been particularly successful, training some 3,600 broadcasters in the first ten years of its existence.

Early university based programs were met with a great deal of skepticism by professionals and academics alike. Most media professionals, raised in the British tradition of on-the-job training, believed that good journalists are born and not made. Until very recently, graduates with formal training were still a minority in newsrooms, particularly in the non-English language media.[27] At the same time, and this may be another aspect of the British legacy in Malaysia, mass communication generally, and journalism in particular, was not considered to be a suitable university discipline like medicine or law.[28] Fortunately, this attitude is changing, mainly because of the rapid growth of the mass communication industry and the growing need for trained communicators.

The first university courses began in 1971 with the creation of a communication program in the School of Humanities at the University of

Penang, now the Universiti Sains Malaysia (USM). By all accounts, the program, set up to provide a broad-based education in communication that would meet Malaysia's manpower requirements, was apparently initiated with very little planning.[29] However, the first fully fledged School of Mass Communication, launched in 1972 at the Institut Teknologi Mara (ITM), was the result of a serious feasibility study performed by Ralph Kliesch of Ohio University. Initially, the program offered three specialized areas, journalism, public relations and advertising, but broadcasting was added the following year.

Today, seven universities or colleges offer some form of communication training. Apart from ITM and USM, mentioned above, they are Universiti Pertanian Malaysia (UPM), Universiti Kebangsaan Malaysia (UKM), University of Malaya (UM), Universiti Utara Malaysia (UUM) and Mahkota College. The first five institutions offer fairly complete programs in communication, but the offerings of UUM are part of a management concentration, while Mahkota College, which is an extension of Boston University, teaches only two years of communication courses, with the option of completing a bachelor's degree in Boston.

Malaysia does not have a national communication policy, but the Ministry of Education tries to coordinate the programs falling under its jurisdiction in order to avoid duplication of courses and specializations. For this reason, each of the five main universities has adopted a slightly different approach. ITM follows an American model, with four sequences and 134 semester hours spread over three years of full-time study. USM offers mass communication courses in both a Bachelor of Humanities and a Bachelor of Social Science degree. UKM operates on a system of core and electives and confers a Bachelor of Social Science. UPM, an agricultural university, provides a wide range of courses in its Development Communication Department. At UM, communication courses are part of creative writing programs in the Malay and English Studies departments.[30]

The School of Mass Communication at ITM is the largest in the country and offers a program that closely follows the American model, with continous assessment, a semester system and a curriculum that includes liberal studies and professional subjects. With a full-time faculty of 37, it enrolls about 700 day students and 300 evening students, which represents more than half of all communication students in the country. Because of the communication industry's language requirements, 30 percent of coursework is devoted to an intensive study of both English and Bahasa Malaysia. Humanities and social sciences account for a further 30 percent, while the remaining 40 percent covers communication and professional subjects. Another important part of the program is practical training, which takes the form of a five-month internship. In order to complete the school's Diploma of Mass Communication in three years, students are required to take a minimum of 21 credit hours each semester for a total of 130 hours, which is ten hours more than the university programs.

The second largest program is that of UKM, which enrolls about 600 students. USM has 300 students, UM 40 and UPM 30 (graduate students only). Most schools report a preponderance of women students. On occasion, the ratio has been as high as 80 percent women to 20 percent men. Competition to enter all communication programs is severe. For example, at ITM more than 3,000 applications are received every semester for 150 places. All schools require proficiency in both English and the national language, as well as a good high-school certificate. At the private colleges, students are usually those who have not been able to enter a government program.

With regard to graduate studies, UPM, which does not have an undergraduate program, currently offers master's programs in development communication, development journalism, organizational communication and public relations. It also has doctoral programs in organizational communication, development communication and development journalism. UM and UKM both have small graduate programs leading to the M.A. and Ph.D. degrees. ITM does not currently have a graduate program, but it has applied to the Ministry of Education for approval to start both an advanced diploma course, equivalent to an honors degree, and a master's degree to be run in conjunction with an American university.

Most educators feel that technical facilities are barely adequate, but there are considerable variations from one school to another. UPM's Department of Development Communication is apparently the best equipped, probably because it is located in the Center for Extension and Continuing Education, which provides audiovisual services to the whole university. All programs have their own television and radio studios, but these are for practice only as no private broadcasting is allowed. ITM and UKM make use of the extensive facilities of IPTAR and AIBD. Most schools already have or are acquiring computer facilities. ITM, USM and UKM put out their own student newspapers and have their own independent library and resource units. On the whole, while there is always room for improvement, most training establishments appear to be better equipped than their counterparts in some of the other countries in the region.

In 1990, the five leading communication programs had about 95 full-time faculty and 25 technical support staff to train some 1,700 students annually. Of the educators, only 15 have doctorates, although a number of them are pursuing terminal degrees, mostly from American universities, but a few from British institutions. About 65 have master's degrees. The few that hold only a bachelor's are all doing graduate work. Among the specialized training institutes, IPTAR and AIBD are well staffed with experienced broadcast professionals, but MPI and the other smaller institutions have to rely on part-time teachers from both the industry and the universities.

Because of pressure from the communication industry, which is anxious to hire graduates who are ready to start producing on their first day of work, all the university undergraduate programs require media internships ranging from six to 18 weeks. And, of course, the specialized non-formal institutions give particular emphasis to practical training. While employment prospects for communication graduates are currently quite good, growing competition in the job market has led university programs to strengthen the vocational side of their curricula, often at the expense of academic studies. This trend is deplored by many educators, who believe that communication programs should be broad enough to teach graduates to think and to value the public interest. Critics claim that, by over-emphasizing vocational skills that could be rapidly acquired on the job, the universities are producing graduates who are well able to compete on the job market but who have little intellectual depth. This is a criticism that is sometimes leveled at the American system on which many Malaysian programs are modeled.

Thailand

Thailand has a flourishing private press, with dozens of dailies, weeklies and monthlies, published in Thai, Chinese and English. It is forbidden by law to criticize the royal family, but otherwise the press is free to write anything it wants. In order to avoid problems, journalists tend to practice self-censorship. The country also has a number of successful commercial television channels that carry a lot of foreign programming, much of it American, dubbed into Thai.[31]

In this climate, communication training has become extremely popular, so popular that the universities are not able to satisfy demand. Some sources estimate that in the last eight years, the number of communication students has tripled to more than 12,000, while the number of schools offering communication courses has increased to nine. There are several reasons for this, including the enormous popularity of university education among the Thai middle class and the lifting of strict government press controls. There is a great deal of glamour attached to the media, and many students perceive communication studies as a way to prestigious and highly paid jobs. Furthermore, in this developing country, in which 90 percent of the population are farmers, communication is often viewed as a key factor in social and economic development.[32]

Early nondegree courses for working journalists were organized at Chulalongkorn University in the late 1930s and early 1940s but were stopped by World War II. The courses were revived in 1949 but were scrapped four years later. The first degree program in communication and journalism was started in 1953 at the University of Thammasat. The program became the Faculty of Journalism and Mass Communication in 1969. In 1964, Chiang Mai University became the first school in the provinces to offer communication courses. In 1965, Chulalongkorn revived its journalism courses, this time as a degree program in communication, now part of a Faculty of Communication Arts. In 1970, Bangkok University became the first private institution to offer communication training. Finally, in the 1980s, five more universities introduced communication courses, Sukhothai Thammarthirat Open University, Kasetsart University, Kasem Bundit College, the Thai Chamber of Commerce University and Ramkamhaeng University, which is the only institution to offer not a degree program but only minors or electives for students in other faculties. The Thai Chamber of Commerce University, Bangkok University and Kasem Bundit College are privately owned. The others are government funded and are run by the State University Bureau, which plans to open three more university communication departments, all of them in the provinces.[33]

One striking feature of communication training in Thailand is Sukhothai Thammathirat University's open system, somewhat similar to the Open University in Britain. Through television and radio programming, video tapes, audiocassettes and other "distance learning" materials, Sukhothai University is able to reach students all over the country. This system is very popular with working students, who are able to take courses by correspondence without attending a campus. The university organizes proctored examinations at various locations around the country. Enrollments in this open program are very high and have recently been estimated at around 10,000.[34] Ramkamhaeng University also has an open admissions policy, and, like Sukhothai Thammathirat, accepts any student with a high school certificate.

Bankgkok University has the next highest enrollment, with an estimated 1,200 majors. Enrollment at the three most prestigious schools, Chulalongkorn, Thammasat and Chiang Mai, has become extremely competitive. For example, in 1987–88, some 10,000 students competed for

Chulalongkorn's 126 places. Chulalongkorn has the largest faculty and the highest proportion of terminal degrees. Paradoxically, despite its enrollments, Sukhothai Thammathirat has only 14 full-time faculty, none of them with terminal degrees. Chulalongkorn and Thammasat are the only two universities to offer both undergraduate and graduate programs. Thammasat's Faculty of Journalism and Mass Communication offers an M.A. in development communication, communication policy and planning and mass communication. Chulalongkorn's Faculty of Communication Arts has two master's programs, one in mass communication and the other in development communication.

All nine communication schools have at least one television studio and a radio studio, but only four universities, Thammasat, Chulalongkorn, Chiang Mai and Ramkamhaeng, actually broadcast radio programs. Of all the programs, Chulalongkorn is the best equipped and is the only one to have its own printing press, although four of the other schools run laboratory newspapers. Most schools complain of a lack of instructional materials, but a more serious problem appears to be a lack of qualified faculty or a lack of faculty time to prepare, develop and produce appropriate materials.

All undergraduate programs require internships, ranging from a few days to two months and, with one exception, earning one to three credit hours. At Chiang Mai, students take a 300-hour internship for no credit. Most internships are with media organizations and are, therefore, off campus, the only exception being a 30-hour on-campus internship at Sukhothai Thammathirat. On the whole, there is little contact with the communication industry, but three of the major universities, Thammasat, Chulalongkorn and Chiang Mai, have collaborated occasionally with the main professional organizations, in particular the Thai Advertising and Public Relations Association, Reporters Association, Journalists Association, Provincial Journalists Association and Press Development Institute.[35]

All in all, communication education in Thailand continues to grow. Even though almost all training takes place in institutes of higher learning, it tends to have a strong trade-school orientation, particularly in the private universities, which are concerned with preparing students for careers. However, some of the larger universities, like Chulalongkorn, are striving to maintain an even balance between theoretical and practical work.

Indonesia

Indonesia has one of the strongest media systems in Southeast Asia, with over 90 dailies, including 17 in the capital city of Jakarta, a number of rural weeklies and several news magazines, many of which are known for their provocative or satirical articles. Because of low literacy rates, however, and also because the country is formed of more than 3,000 isolated islands spread over some 3,000 miles of ocean, the only true mass medium is radio. Television programming can also be received in the remotest islands thanks to a domestic communications satellite system launched in 1976.[36]

Communication education has developed significantly since the 1950s, when only three schools offered degrees in journalism. Today, 22 institutions provide communication courses throughout the country. They include ten state-owned and two private universities, as well as ten training institutes run by professional organizations, educational associations and foundations. By far the largest of all these institutions is the Institute for Social and Political Sciences (IISIP) in Jakarta, which began life as the Publicistic School of Higher Education in 1953 and which today has a faculty of about 120 and an annual enrollment of 1,200 students.[37]

In the 1960s, as journalists felt the need to improve their education, a number of nondegree courses were begun for those who could not enter the universities. These were expanded over the years in response to rising demand, which could not be met by limited university enrollments. At the same time, major publications such as *Kompas* and *Tempo*, as well as ANTARA, the national news agency, set up their own training schemes. It is interesting to note that early courses often used the term "publicistic," no doubt as a result of Dutch terminology, but that "journalistic" was later adopted because of the strong American influence in communication training.

The ten state universities are spread throughout the country. They are: Universitas Sumatra Utara (USU), Universitas Hasanudin (UNHAS), Universitas Negeri Solo (UNS), Universitas Airlangga (UNAIR), Institut Pertanian Bogor (IPB), Sekolah Tinggi Ilmu Kewartawanan Jakarta (STIK-Jakarta), Universitas Diponegoro (UNDIP), Universitas Gajah Mada (UGM), Institut Ilmu Sosial dan Ilmu Politik (IISIP) and Universitas Indonesia (UI). The two private institutions are Universitas Prof. Dr. Mustopo (UPDM) and Sekolah Tinggi Ilmu Komunikasi Semarang (STIK-Semarang). Of all these schools, only two—IPB and UI—offer a master's degree.

Most schools have inadequate instructional materials and equipment, partly because of limited budgets but also because of lack of maintenance. UPDM and IISIP are fortunate in having a wide range of sophisticated technical equipment, but others have to make do with typewriters and overhead projectors. Almost all the universities have developed internships with local newspapers and radio stations. UNAIR, STIK-Semarang, UNHAS, UPDM and UI run campus newspapers. STIK-Semarang and UNS operate a video and radio lab, while UPDM and STIK-Semarang have photo labs.

Altogether, the universities produce some 400–500 graduates annually, which falls far short of the actual demand for trained communicators, estimated at about 1,000. To meet this demand, ten journalism training institutes, most of them created in the 1970s and 1980s, offer courses designed to teach basic journalistic skills to potential reporters and writers or to improve the skills of media managers or midcareer journalists. The two largest institutes are the Indonesian Journalists Association (P.P. PWI Pusat), founded in 1971, and the Citra Foundation, founded in 1977, each of which has produced over 1,500 graduates since its creation. On the whole, because of their ties to the profession, these training institutes are rather well equipped, and some of them have their own newsroom, computers, printing press and preview room.

Although individual institutions may be less fortunate than others with regard to funding, facilities, equipment, instructional materials and faculty, there do not appear to be any major underlying problems common to them all. In conclusion, communication training in Indonesia is thriving. As the existing schools expand to meet demand, both the Open University and the Indonesian Press Council have plans to launch new communication programs in the near future. Furthermore, the modern facilities of the new Mass Media Training Center in Yogyakarta give some idea of the kind of priority the government is giving to the whole area of communication.

EAST ASIA

The communication training structures of East Asia offer some distinctive differences. Following the 1989 crackdown, training in China has reverted to a communist "public relations" model with a strong emphasis on ideology and social control.[38] In Japan, journalism training still follows a rigid apprenticeship pattern that is part of an elitist approach to higher education and professional recruiting. Korea, on the other hand, has developed a training system that closely parallels that of the United States.

China

China, still the most populous nation in the world, remains an essentially rural society, with 80 percent of its inhabitants living in small villages. The other 20 percent live in large cities, including Beijing, which has a population of about 6 million. These demographic patterns, combined with regional dialects, geographic barriers and a communist rule that has lasted for more than 40 years, make for a unique media system.[39] Furthermore, the complexity of the Chinese language, which produces severe typesetting problems as well as low literacy levels, and the difficulty of distributing print media to outlying areas have resulted in a two-tier media system consisting of the main cities, especially the port cities, and the rural villages.[40]

Despite communist rule, the press acquired a degree of press freedom in the 1980s. However, after the Tiananmen Square uprising, in which Beijing journalists took the side of the protestors and waved banners proclaiming, "Don't Believe Us: We Print Lies," the government reinstated strict controls on the media. A series of purges removed dissident newspaper editors, arrested or transferred supporters of the protest and sent tremors throughout the communication industry, even into the journalism schools.

Historically, the first journalism courses were given at Beijing University in 1918 and consisted of a series of lectures by a couple of journalists, one of whom had studied in the United States. In the 1920s, four journalism departments were opened at St. John's University in Shanghai (1920), Pingmin University in Beijing (1923), Yenching University in Beijing (1924) and Fudan University in Shanghai (1929). The Pingmin program was short-lived, but the other three programs became the foundation of journalism training in China. St. John's and Yenching were both American missionary schools and taught their professional courses in both Chinese and English. Training was curtailed during the Japanese occupation and the war in the Pacific.[41]

After the foundation of the People's Republic in 1949, journalism education was reorganized. Whereas, before 1949, journalism programs had followed the American model, in the 1950s they took their lead from the Soviet Union. It was not long, however, before educators began to criticize Soviet press dogma and call for a system of training that would better reflect Chinese principles of journalism. Such "Rightist" critics fared badly at the hands of the ultra-left wing, and journalism became a "forbidden area" of study or discussion. Newspapers no longer recruited journalists on the strength of their professional qualifications but on the basis of their political credentials. According to a 1983 estimate by the *Chinese Journalism Yearbook*, out of 48,500 editors, reporters, broadcasters and translators working for 1,200 news organizations, 41 percent were college graduates, but only 6 percent were graduates of journalism schools.[42]

In the same year, it was estimated that only about 5,200 journalism students had been trained since the communist take over, but that, in light of the tremendous growth in the number of newspapers and broadcast stations, as many as 90,000 journalism graduates would be needed by the end of the century. By 1987, the number of universities, colleges and institutes offering journalism programs had risen to 33, as compared to 14 in 1983 and only four in 1978. During the 1986–87 academic year, more than 6,000 undergraduates were being taught by more than 600 faculty. Journalism courses have also been integrated into other programs, such as economics, engineering and metallurgy, as well as translation, editing, publishing and foreign languages. Furthermore, apart from formal courses in institutions of higher learning, some 200,000 students are studying some aspect of journalism in night classes or correspondence courses.[43]

The five largest programs are at Fudan University in Shanghai, People's University in Beijing, the Beijing Broadcast College, Xiamen University and Jinan University in Guangzhou.[44] All of these programs except Xiamen offer three-year master's degrees, as does the Academy of Social Sciences in Beijing.[45] The Department of Journalism at Fudan University will be the first to award a Litt. D. degree.[46]

One ambitious new program is the China School of Journalism, launched by Xinhua, the Chinese national news agency, which has long been interested in training recruits for its own news bureaus. Conceived by a veteran agency news executive who had attended Columbia's graduate program and spent some time studying UPI and the AP, the China School of Journalism tends to be more skills oriented than other training institutions. It runs a full-time program for graduates of universities and specialized institutes of higher learning, as well as short courses for midcareer journalists. Its graduate program trains future recruits for its domestic and international services. In 1987, 70 of the agency's established journalists took extended training courses in Canada, Great Britain, Australia and the United States.[47]

The China School of Journalism's approach may well be a model for future journalism training in China. While it espouses an American emphasis on practical work, class discussion, field trips and student publications, it also includes ideological training. However, instead of relearning communist doctrine, students are being taught how to apply Party rules to the stories they are covering. This appears to take a middle road between the hard-line ideological teaching associated with the communist model and the realities of operating media in a modern commercial context. It is difficult to predict how this approach or other approaches may develop in the post-Tiananmen era, but, even with the most repressive controls, the need for trained communicators will remain as urgent as ever.

Japan

Japan has a thriving media industry that is supported by a vibrant economy, sophisticated technologies and high literacy and cultural levels. Daily newspaper circulation is among the highest in the world, with 562 copies per 1,000, while home delivery reaches 97 percent of all households. City dwellers are able to choose from a dozen network channels, whose programming, apart from major movies, is largely "made in Japan." The media industry of this quintessentially mass society is dominated by very large circulation daily newspapers. Indeed, out of 125 dailies, three giants, the *Asahi*, the *Yomiuri* and the *Mainichi*, account for 45 percent of total circulation. Each of these newspapers has as many as 10,000 employees, one-third of whom work in various journalistic capacities. The broadcast media also employ some 16,000 people, including a large proportion of journalists.[48]

The Japanese system of communication education remains relatively unstructured. A few universities offer media studies, but the vast majority of journalists receive on-the-job training. While there is no denying the influence of Western values, Japan has maintained its own very special social structures, based on elitism and group loyalty. In journalism training, these structures have taken the form of a rigid apprenticeship system, ruled by hierarchies and the authority of "seniors." As in other areas of Japanese business, where remnants of the old feudalistic system are still in place, journalists demonstrate lifelong loyalty to the news organization in which they received their training.

The notion of elitism and prestige, on which the whole Japanese educational system is based, flows over into journalism training. Entry into the most prestigious schools is controlled by rigorous competitive examinations. Only the very best succeed. Thus, the graduates of the universities of Tokyo, Waseda, Keio and Kyoto are taken into the most prestigious news organizations, including the Big Three, the *Asahi*, the *Yomiuri* and the *Mainichi*. Typically, these graduates hold degrees in political science, economics or the humanities. Most of them have probably never taken a journalism class. On the other hand, journalists who have received only skills training, outside of the elite schools, are forced to take jobs in smaller, much less prestigious news organizations. This two-tier system produces two types of journalists: highly educated elite professionals and hack writers.

Even after 1945, U.S. influences failed to make much impression on the Japanese system, despite visits from well-meaning American educators and accreditation specialists. In 1926, Professor Hideo Ono started courses on newspaper history at Tokyo University and, on the strength of this, obtained funding from a group of newspaper owners to put together a journalism program. Under Ono's leadership, the university founded a research bureau and expanded the program to take in Japanese press history, principles of journalism, news writing, reporting, photography, advertising and newspaper management. The first two-year course enrolled 50 students. This course has survived as the Institute of Journalism and Communication Studies. Today, with a faculty of 20 and a student enrollment of about 100, the institute offers undergraduate and graduate programs with an emphasis on theoretical media studies rather than practical training.

After the war, three other programs were started. In 1950, Waseda University, a private elitist institution, created an independent department of journalism with a strong political science orientation. Many of its graduates were taken on by the big Tokyo newspapers. Meiji University, another private school, started a one-year evening program that later became a two-year program. But in 1952, the Japanese publishers association criticized these programs, stating that, when compared to American schools, they were still in their infancy.[49] Shortly thereafter, Sophia University, a private religious institution, did set up a program based on the U.S. model, but very few of its graduates actually went into the media. A fourth university, Kansai University in Osaka, offers a three- to four-year undergraduate degree program in its Faculty of Sociology. In summary, the Japanese universities appear to have little interest in producing skilled journalists, no doubt because of the powerful apprenticeship system that is place in the media.

In order to enter the apprenticeship program at one of the five national dailies, candidates have to undergo a three-stage process of written and oral examinations. Only one in 100–150 are accepted. Most of the recruits are from the top four universities. In this way, they are members of the same "university clubs" as other elite groups. The importance of belonging to such clubs cannot be overemphasized. Graduates of other universities are free to apply but stand little chance of succeeding.

Once accepted, the new recruits spend time in all departments of the newspaper, including production. Training systems differ, but the *Yomiuri* program has become a model for other newspapers. Recruits take two hours of lectures in the morning and perform practical assignments during the afternoon, usually under the guidance of senior journalists. The assignments become more numerous and more demanding as the apprenticeship progresses. The socialization process is designed to turn even the most radical elements into docile corporate team players. At the end of the first training period, the probationers are sent to work in one of the group's local newspapers. If they do well there they may be able to work their way back to the main newspaper. Those who succeed tend to be good "corporate men" rather than independent thinkers.

Today, Japanese journalists, who belong to an elite system but who write for an increasingly liberated mass audience, are called upon to play a mediating role between the old feudal traditions and Western influences. As Japanese society continues to change, journalism may find itself facing some difficult challenges, which may well affect the way in which journalists are recruited and trained.

Korea

While Japan and China have developed different systems in response to particular needs, South Korea has wholeheartedly embraced the U.S. model of journalism training. Since the 1970s some 20 four-year undergraduate programs have been created, alongside ten master's programs and eight doctoral programs. American influence has lessened somewhat over the last decade as Korean-trained educators have begun to fill teaching positions in university journalism departments.[50]

Until quite recently, the media of South Korea were hampered by repressive government controls, but since 1988 new press freedoms have encouraged the creation of more than 40 new daily newspapers and countless weeklies. Broadcasting is also well developed with close to 100 percent television penetration. Despite this apparently favorable situation, Korean journalists have found themselves working under adverse conditions.

Newsprint has long been in short supply in Korea. Even before press controls were lifted, the 21 daily newspapers were limited by the Korean Newspaper Publishers' Association to 12 pages. The resulting shortage of space has forced journalists to produce superficial factual reporting rather than in-depth analysis. At the same time, specialized beat reporting is discouraged. Editors routinely rotate beats to avoid professional jealousy or to punish those who fail to perform. Furthermore, journalists are rarely asked to write columns. Most columnists are university professors. On the whole, journalists are perceived to be arrogant and suffer from a poor image. In these circumstances, it is not surprising that journalists have sought to strengthen training.[51]

THE PACIFIC

The Pacific subregion includes Australia, New Zealand and the Pacific Islands, each of which has a somewhat different training system. Australia, long an admirer of the British apprenticeship system, has started to adopt programs that are closer to the American model. New Zealand, with a more stable population and slower growth, remains firmly attached to on-the-job training. The Pacific Islands, once isolated from any kind of formal training, have had access to a variety of training courses organized by the UNESCO-sponsored Pacjourn project.

Australia

Generally speaking, until the 1970s, journalism training in Australia was based on the "copy boy and cadet" system, which was essentially a newspaper institution. Under this system, promising young copy boys were taken on as "cadets." During this cadetship, which usually lasted three years, management was supposed to provide training. Sometimes cadets were lucky enough to be placed under the wing of a kindly senior journalist who would put them on different beats, check their stories and make sure they mastered shorthand and typing. At some newspapers, however, cadets were simply sent out to a business college for a couple of hours a week to learn shorthand. At the end of the cadetship, the fledgling journalists were considered to be trained, provided they had a shorthand speed of 120 words per minute.[52]

This system still exists in certain newspapers, but, although it has produced some excellent journalists, it presents a number of obvious drawbacks. Its focus is narrowly restricted to the priorities, policies and traditions of the news organization in which training is given. It provides strong skills training but fails to offer the analytical and intellectual training required by modern journalists. In response to these shortcomings, the Universities of Melbourne and Queensland started journalism diploma programs in the 1920s, and these lasted into the 1960s. However, these programs were never popular, with either journalists or management. Over a period of 47 years, Queensland awarded only 44 diplomas. Melbourne awarded only 40 diplomas over 40 years.

In the 1960s, following a major educational reform in Australia, a number of colleges of advanced education were created; by the 1970s several of these had introduced journalism programs. Many of them subsequently became freestanding universities. Today some 20 universities, colleges of advanced education and institutes of technology offer courses in mass communication and journalism. As might be expected, most of the university programs are theoretically oriented, while the colleges of higher education and the institutes of technology place more emphasis on practical training. Almost all these programs provide "attachments" in news organizations. Attachments differ from internships in that, because of opposition from the Australian Journalists' Association, students are not allowed to write for publication.

Media managers have generally shown themselves to be cooperative, but, as in many other countries, they would like to see more practical training than theory. Because of such pressures and in the absence of any national accreditation procedure, Australian programs tend to place less emphasis on the liberal arts than do programs in the United States. However, in conclusion, there appears to be little doubt that Australian journalists are turning more to the United States for journalistic models than to Britain, as was the case in the past,[53] which will probably shape the future of communication training in Australia.

New Zealand

There is little to be said about journalism training in New Zealand, where the the old British apprenticeship system is still very much in effect. Typically, recruits are hired out of high school and subjected to on-the-job training. A number of specialized short courses have appeared in recent years, mainly aimed at high-school leavers. One such course, offered by Wellington Polytechnic, is almost exclusively devoted to practical skills.

The Pacific Islands

For a long time, journalists in the Pacific Islands had to go out of the region for training. In 1975, a successful program was started at the University of Papua New Guinea, but this was still a long way from some of the remoter communities. More recently, however, the UNESCO Pacjourn project organized training courses throughout the region, conducting at least one training course every year in each of the 13 participating countries: Belau, Cook Islands, Federated States of Micronesia, Fiji, Kiribati, Marshall Islands, Niue, Papua New Guinea, Solomon Islands, Tonga, Tuvalu, Vanuatu and Western Samoa.

The courses, which were exclusively print oriented, usually lasted two weeks, but they were very flexible. The project coordinator, based in Papua New Guinea, sought to shape courses to suit the needs of individual countries. In addition to in-country courses, Pacjourn also conducted regional and subregional courses, which focused on newsroom management, sub-editing, press law, photojournalism and sports reporting. Finally, Pacjourn organized overseas training courses, study tours and visits to newspapers in other countries.[54] Regrettably, the Pacjourn project had to be terminated in August of 1991 because of a lack of funds. During its three years' existence, however, it successfully trained more than 300 newspaper journalists.

In the 1980s, similar projects, Pacbroad for broadcast training and Pacvideo for video training, were launched by UNESCO with funding from the International Program for the Development of Communication (IPDC) and Friedrich Ebert Stiftung.

NOTES

1. For an excellent overview of press systems in the region, see Anne Cooper Chen and Anju Grover Chaudhary, "Asia and the Pacific," in John C. Merrill, ed., *Global Journalism*, 2d ed. (White Plains, NY: Longman, 1991).

2. Crispin C. Maslog, "Communication and Journalism Training in India, Indonesia, Malaysia, Nepal, The Philippines and Thailand: An Overview," in Crispin C. Maslog, ed., *Communication Education in Asia* (The Philippines: Press Foundation of Asia, 1990), pp. 1–5.

The author is grateful to Professor Maslog for these and other materials about communication training in Asia.

3. Chen and Chaudhary, "Asia and the Pacific," p. 260.

4. R. V. Rajan, "A Paper on India" (Paper presented at a seminar on "Communication Education in the Asia-Pacific: Towards 2000," organized by the Asian Mass Communication Research and Information Centre, Singapore, January 15, 1990).

5. Rajan is particularly critical of poor planning by the educational authorities.

6. Chanchal Sarkar, "Mass Communication and Journalism Education in India," in Maslog, *Communication Education in Asia*, p. 25.

7. Rajan, "A Paper on India."

8. Sarkar, "Mass Communication," pp. 24–25.

9. Chen and Chaudhary, "Asia and the Pacific," pp. 214–215.

10. Sarkar, "Mass Communication," pp. 22–24. Like other data in Maslog, *Communication Education*, this information was gathered as part of a regional survey organized by the Press Foundation of Asia and supported by the Communication Assistance Foundation of The Netherlands.

11. This section on the Indian Institute of Mass Communication draws on Rajan, "A Paper on India" and Sarkar, "Mass Communication."

12. Most of this information comes from the Institute's 1990–1991 brochure.

13. Press Institute of India, *The Story of the Press Institute of India* (New Delhi: Press Institute of India, 1988).

14. Larry Tayor, "Journalism Education at the *Times of India*," *Community College Journalist* 15, no.2 (Spring 1987), p. 3.

15. Chen and Chaudhary, "Asia and the Pacific," p. 261.

16. Rajan, "Communication Education."

17. This section draws on a paper by Sharif Al Mujahid, "Communication Education in Pakistan" (Paper written for the seminar "Communication Education in Asia-Pacific: Towards 2000").

18. Most of the information in this section is taken from a paper written for the "Towards 2000" seminar. The name of the author is unknown.

19. Irvin Weerackody, "The Sri Lanka Situation," written for the "Towards 2000" seminar.

20. Bharat D. Koirala, "Mass Communication and Journalism Education in Nepal," in Maslog, *Communication Education*, pp. 74–78.

21. Maslog, "An Overview," p. 2.

22. This whole section draws on Professor Maslog's article, "Communication Education and Training in the Philippines," in Maslog, *Communication Education*, pp. 79–100.

23. These figures are for 1986–87.

24. Manolo B. Jara (Executive Editor of Depthnews), "Training of Journalists: A PFA Commitment" (Paper presented to an AMIC-MPI Seminar on Communication Training in ASEAN Countries, Kuala Lumpur, October 29–November 2, 1984).

25. Sankaran Ramanathan and Katherine Frith, "Mass Comm Education Young and Growing in Malaysia," *Journalism Educator* 42, no.4 (Winter 1988), p. 10. Ramanathan, a senior lecturer at the Institut Teknologi Mara, has written extensively about communication training in Malaysia.

26. Mohd Hamdan bin Haji Adnan, "Communication Education and Training in Malaysia" (Paper presented to the "Towards 2000" seminar), pp. 4–5.

27. Ramanathan and Frith, "Mass Comm Education," p. 11.

28. Adnan, "Communication Education," p. 1.

29. Ibid., p. 6. This was the impression gained by John Lent, the founding coordinator of the program.

30. Ramanathan and Frith, "Mass Comm Education," pp. 10–11.

31. Chen and Chaudhary, "Asia and the Pacific," pp. 220 and 236.

32. John Warren and Adchara Khotanan, "Communication Education at Thai Universities," *Journalism Educator* 45, no.4 (Winter 1991), pp. 28–33.

33. Wirasak Salayakanond, "Mass Communication and Journalism Education in Thailand," in Maslog, *Communication Education*, pp. 102–104, with some updated information about Kasem Bundit from Warren and Khotanan, "Communication Education."

34. Salayakanond estimated enrollment at around 4,500 in 1987–88. In 1991, Warren and Khotanan put the figure at 10,000.

35. Salayakanond, "Mass Communication," pp. 105–111.

36. Chen and Chaudhary, "Asia and the Pacific," pp. 222–223 and 237–238.

37. Ina Mariana Suparto, "Mass Communication and Journalism Training in Indonesia," in Maslog, *Communication Education*, pp. 37–54.

38. Philip Gaunt, "Developments in Soviet Journalism," *Journalism Quarterly* 64, nos.2–3 (Summer-Autumn 1987), pp. 526–532.

39. Robert Bishop, *Qi Lai! Mobilizing One Billion Chinese: The Chinese Communication System* (Ames: Iowa State University Press, 1989), p. 9.

40. Chen and Chaudhary, "Asia and the Pacific," p. 224.

41. Zhang Jingming and Peng Jianan, "Chinese Journalism Education: Slow Progress since 1918," *Journalism Educator* 41, no.4 (Spring 1986), pp. 11–13.

42. *Chinese Journalism Yearbook* (Beijing: People's Daily Publishing House, 1984), p. 55.

43. Beverly Keever, "Journalism Education Grows by Leaps, Bounds in China," *Journalism Educator* 43, no.1 (Spring 1988), pp. 29–31.

44. Chen and Chaudhary, "Asia and the Pacific," pp. 264–265.

45. Keever, "Journalism Education," p. 30.

46. Zhang and Peng, "Chinese Journalism Education," p. 13.

47. Keever, "Journalism Education," pp. 30–31.

48. Gerd G. Kopper, "Journalistenrolle und Journalistenausbildung in Japan," in Fischer and Roegele, *Ausbildung für Kommunikationsberufe*, pp. 185–196. The whole of this section draws on Kopper's chapter, one of the rare Western sources dealing with communication training in Japan.

49. Nihon Shinbun Kyokai, *The Japanese Press 1952* (Tokyo: Nihon Shinbun Kyokai, 1951), p. 50.

50. Chen and Chaudhary, "Asia and the Pacific," p. 264.

51. Joon-Mann Kang, "Reporters and Their Professional and Occupational Commitment in a Developing Country," *Gazette* 40 (1987), pp. 3–20.

52. Don Woolford, "Australian System Advances Through Third Growth Stage," *Journalism Educator* 34, no.3 (October 1979), pp. 47–51.

53. J. P. Henningham, "Comparisons between Australian and U.S. Broadcast Journalists' Professional Values," *Journal of Broadcasting* 28, no.3 (Summer 1984), p. 331.

54. Personal communication from Peter Henshall, coordinator, Pacjourn Project.

Chapter Eight

Latin America and the Caribbean

This region groups 20 countries in South and Central America and a number of offshore islands, some of them large and well-developed, others quite small and lightly populated. In the past, many of these countries have been plagued by dictatorships, political instability, severe economic problems, galloping inflation, social unrest, mounting foreign debts, drug-related terrorism and tight press controls. For these reasons, journalism and journalism training have been affected by a variety of constraints. In the last few years, however, democratic freedoms have begun to pervade previously authoritarian regimes, and there is now a real hope that journalists will be allowed to play an effective role in furthering newly emerging social objectives. Unfortunately, in the past, journalists in many Latin American countries have been overworked, underpaid and underrated.

LATIN AMERICA

In spite of the problems facing the region, flourishing press systems have emerged, particularly in larger and more prosperous countries such as Brazil, Argentina and Mexico. In many parts of the region, newspapers have traditionally been owned by influential conservative families close to the ruling elite. Broadcasting systems, which are generally more sophisticated than those in other developing regions, are often owned by governments, political parties, religious bodies, unions and universities. Naturally, such affiliations have produced their own constraints and will continue to hamper the development of an independent press, but, as regional cooperation continues to develop and as free-market forces push the media toward a more commercial model, the strength of these constraints will inevitably fade.

Historically, as in other regions of the world, journalism training has moved from the old school of newsroom socialization to formal programs in specialized institutions and university departments. There are some significant differences, however, that have to do with perceptions of journalists' roles, a deeply entrenched antagonism between "professionals" (empíricos) and college graduates (universitarios) and the existence of *colegios*. Some of these differences will become clear during the discussion of training structures in individual countries, but others are common to several countries and should be addressed here.

In spite of the low prestige of the profession, many of the older traditional journalists, particularly in the 1950s, nourished literary ambitions or saw journalism as a springboard to public administration, political office or the diplomatic service. For this reason, assignments covering political or parliamentary affairs were eagerly sought after and journalists were prepared to work in these positions at very low wages. Often, when these ambitions were thwarted, reporters found themselves having to work long hours, to take on a second job for another newspaper or even to sell advertising to their sources. It is not surprising that, in these circumstances, the prestige of the profession sank even lower, often to the satisfaction of the newspaper owners, who could thus continue to pay poor wages.

However, in the 1950s and particularly the 1960s, it became obvious that there was little hope of improving the profession without better training, and a large number of journalism schools and university departments of communication were created throughout the region. In 1950, there were fewer than ten journalism programs in the whole region, but today there are over 200, most of them linked to universities or other institutions of higher learning. Much of this growth has been stimulated and coordinated by the International Center for Advanced Studies in Communication (CIESPAL), which was set up by UNESCO in the early 1960s. Located in Quito, Ecuador, CIESPAL continues to give direction to regional communication initiatives and is considered to be the leading journalism research center in the region. Alongside CIESPAL, a dozen other institutions offer regional courses in practical communication training.

The classic antagonism that exists between newsroom-trained professionals and college graduates throughout the world has taken an unusual twist in Latin America. At one time, most traditional journalists received little or no university training. Those who did take university courses often dropped out after one or two semesters to seek employment. The media owners and managers, on the other hand, usually completed degrees, frequently at prestigious universities either in the United States or Europe. The result was that the professionals often became critics of the establishment, represented by their university-trained employers.

Since the rapid growth of communication programs, however, this situation has been somewhat reversed. Today, the best professional training is to be found in private schools, which are usually quite expensive. Most top administrators and senior editorial staff are graduates of these schools and thus share the same kind of orientation. Furthermore, as the older professionals retire, more and more entry-level recruits are coming into the profession with proper training. This commonality of training, combined with the lifting of certain government controls, is likely to improve the quality of journalism. At the same time, however, university departments of communication, which tend to enroll those who cannot afford to enter the best private schools, are turning out graduates very much attuned to the critical stances of the *dependencia* theorists. In other words, it is the university graduates who are now more critical of the establishment, whereas the professionally trained journalists are being absorbed into a system that increasingly is being driven by commercial rather than ideological and political values.

The situation is further complicated by the existence of *colegios*, to which journalists must belong in order to be able to work. In many cases, their members have to possess degrees from certain recognized schools. The *colegios*, which exist in about a dozen Latin American countries, have been severely criticized by such watchdog bodies as the Inter American Press Association (IAPA), on the grounds that the licensing of journalists threatens the existence of a free press. But, on the whole, Latin American journalists approve of the system because, by restricting entry into the profession, it has the effect of protecting employment and salary levels. Employers, too, have been supportive, initially because of their links with governing elites but also because the system has tended to encourage better training. Despite this support and the recent easing of government restrictions in many countries, the *colegios* obviously remain a potential threat to a truly independent press.[1]

Journalism training in Latin America tends to be rather similar in different countries. Overall, about 75 percent of the schools are associated with universities. The most prestigious schools are private and place greater emphasis on practical skills, while the university programs stress theory and communication studies. In this sense, they follow a familiar pattern that has been explored in some detail in previous chapters. For this reason, instead of attempting to analyze almost identical systems in all the countries of Latin America, the rest of this chapter focuses on four countries that stand out as being different: Mexico, because of its size and influence in the region; Chile, because of the changes that it has undergone; Costa Rica, because of its stability and relatively democratic freedoms; and Cuba, because of its communist ideologies. The chapter finishes with a brief survey of training in the Caribbean.

Mexico

One of the oldest training establishments in Latin America is the journalism school of the Women's University of Mexico in Mexico City, founded in 1936. The school, which is now part of the Faculty of Law and Social Sciences, has done much to open up the profession to women graduates. The influential Carlos Septién García school was founded in 1952, and a number of other schools were opened in the late 1950s and 1960s, many of them in the universities. Today, however, in marked contrast to the trend that has emerged in other parts of the region, the majority of Mexican training programs are private. This is consistent with Mexico's system of higher education, which has a higher proportion of private colleges and universities than many other countries.[2]

In all there are close to 40 institutions offering programs in communication or information, but some of these focus on computer science and informatics. Only 27 provide courses in journalism or mass communication. Of these the four most important are Carlos Septién García, UNAM (Universidad Autónoma de México), which has several branches, Universidad Iberoamericana, which also has more than one campus, and Universidad Kino, all of which offer four-year degree programs. There are also three graduate programs in communication at the Chapingo Postgraduate College, the Universidad Iberoamericana and UNAM in Mexico City. These three programs prepare students for careers in teaching or research.

Other major undergraduate programs include Universidad Autónoma Metropolitana Xochimilco (UAM); Universidad de Monterrey; Universidad del Tepeyac; Universidad Autónoma de Guadalajara; Instituto Tecnológico y de Estudios Superiores de Monterrey; Universidad Anahuac; Universidad de Nuevo León; Universidad Intercontinental and Instituto Tecnológico y de Estudios Superiores de Occidente.

Many of these schools adopted early CIESPAL guidelines, which recommended a curriculum based on 40 percent skills, 20 percent "communication science," 20 percent liberal arts and 20 percent electives, but a number have since modified their programs to match the North American model, which places more emphasis on liberal arts and less on practical skills. However, an examination of the programs of some of the leading schools shows how tightly structured their curricula are.

At Carlos Septién García, students in their first semester are introduced to the basics of communication theory and history as well as spelling, writing and literature. The second semester adds print news, the basics of information gathering, an introduction to radio and television journalism and typing, alongside economics, sociology and more literature. In their third and fourth semesters, students continue writing for the media, take a survey of public relations and advertising, and begin photography. They also have to take courses in psychology, philosophy and communication theory. The third year focuses on different kinds of reporting and writing, goes further into philosophy, takes a detailed look at law, and spends a lot of time on contemporary problems and issues. The seventh semester stresses news analysis, social issues and ethics, while the final semester is devoted to a final thesis and specialized seminars.[3]

At UNAM, the first three semesters are devoted to world economic and social history, Mexican social history, social theory, political economy and methodology. The fourth, fifth and sixth semesters concentrate on the development, structure and management of the mass media, the theory of communication, language and types of journalism. In the two final semesters, students specialize in print journalism, broadcast journalism or research. The first two areas of specialization involve a few workshops in "journalistic practice" or production, but more emphasis is placed on theory and methods.[4]

Universidad Kino also has an eight-semester program that offers introductory workshops on writing, graphic design and photography and advanced courses on "theory and practice" of print and broadcast journalism. But the last two years of the program focus more on social psychology, public opinion, social communication, political and social problems, public administration and media law.[5]

It is clear from the above that many programs place more emphasis on theory than on practice, which from a professional viewpoint is bad enough, but as José Baldivia has observed, in the vast majority of Mexican communication training schools, theoretical subjects are poorly taught, while skills courses are taught theoretically because of the lack of equipment.[6] Baldivia points to a number of other problems, in particular a lack of properly trained teachers. Attempts to use working journalists as educators have not always been successful because of their own lack of education and their inability to teach complex subjects with academic rigor. Furthermore, the abysmal salaries paid to educators have done nothing to raise low teaching standards not only in communication training but in higher education generally. With a few exceptions, the educational level of most communication schools remains deplorably low, partly because there is no serious accreditation process. Schools have their program outlines approved by the Department of Education, but no attempts are made to verify how well or by whom the programs are taught.

Another major problem, according to Baldivia, is the absence of a national policy that would limit the over-proliferation of communication schools. Although no formal studies have been made, the number of graduates who have failed to find employment in their specialized field would suggest that the market is already saturated. As it is, neither the educational authorities nor the universities appear to have any idea what the actual situation is or what future prospects are.

Finally, the principal criticism leveled against the communication schools is that even after four or five years of study, their graduates still cannot write. Furthermore, potential employers in both the electronic and print media are often prejudiced against graduates of the public universities because of their politicization. It is no accident that many news organizations will hire only graduates of private schools.

For these reasons, several newspapers, including the powerful *El Norte* group, have started their own summer training courses, open to bright, young would-be journalists. The trainees typically undergo an intensive period of lectures and workshops on news writing, interviewing, editing, photography and headline writing, combined with actual newspaper assignments. If they do well, they are often taken on as cub reporters.[7]

Chile

The first journalism program in Chile was created by the University of Chile in 1947. Today, the University of Chile offers communication programs at all three of its campuses in Santiago, Valparaiso and Concepción. The first two, which are both located in the Faculty of Social Sciences, focus on communication science. The Concepción program, which is part of the Department of Design, specializes in visual communication. The other public university, Universidad del Norte, has a School of Social Communication. Journalism programs are also offered by two private institutions, Universidad Católica de Chile and the Escuela de Periodismo y Comunicaciones in Concepción.

The split between *empíricos* and *universitarios* has been particularly marked in Chile, which has been plagued by political upheavals and repressive press controls over much of the last two decades. During the Allende and Pinochet regimes, some of the schools were closed down, but since 1988 press freedoms have been restored and the communication schools reopened. Perhaps for these reasons, the traditions of the *empíricos* have survived longer than in other parts of Latin America. It is also true that university programs are out of touch with the realities of the journalistic profession.[8]

Whatever the reasons, the fact remains that most journalists in positions of importance have undergone some kind of journalism training, partial or complete, but that they have also been shaped by the older professionals who were their teachers. It has also been argued that in pre-Allende days, when Article 10 of the Constitution guaranteed press freedoms, the "empirical" journalists had a greater critical sense than journalists trained later in the universities.[9] When the first university programs were begun in the 1950s, the notion of "communication" did not appear anywhere in the curricula, which were firmly based on newsroom practices. Indeed, "theory" was seen as a betrayal of journalism. But, over the years, as the influence of the *empíricos* has diminished, university programs have moved more toward communication studies as part of the social sciences.

Today, even the private schools place less emphasis on skills training. For example, the curriculum of the Catholic University, which is generally considered to be the most professional school in the country, is heavily oriented toward theory. The program, which is divided into three cycles, an introductory cycle, a transitional cycle and a terminal cycle, lasting four to five years, contains nine concentrations. Only one of them focuses on grammar and news writing and this is limited to the first four semesters. By far the largest concentration, which runs right through the program, is devoted to current affairs and "information workshops." Other major concentrations cover social science, theory of communication and public opinion; great ideas of the Western world; contemporary history, economic thought and comparative political systems; and philosophy, ethics, law and communication policies. There is also a small concentration in visual expression and photojournalism, as well as a research concentration.[10]

In conclusion, as the *empíricos* gradually retire from the work force, the universities will continue to educate most communicators. However, because of the intellectualism attached to their academic vocation, the universities cannot hope to produce trained professionals ready to function. What they can do, however, is provide their graduates with the tools to train themselves, somewhat like doctors and lawyers, who, once they have completed their studies, still need to acquire professional experience. Many graduates are reluctant to accept this, but perhaps one of the more constructive initiatives the *colegio* can take will be to support and reinforce this process.[11]

Costa Rica

Costa Rica is a small, stable and relatively well-developed country in Central America and, insofar as there has never been more than one school of journalism in Costa Rica, the history of journalism training is synonymous with that of the Escuela de Periodismo or, as it became known later, the Escuela de Ciencias de la Comunicación Colectiva (School of Collective Communication Sciences). The school, which was founded in September 1968 by the University Council of the University of Costa Rica, started its first courses in the following year.

It is significant that, at its creation, the school offered two parallel programs, one for the *empíricos* or working professionals and the other for regular students. The professional program, known as "the emergency plan," was intended to provide working journalists with an opportunity to acquire some kind of systematic training in communication at a time when the College of Journalists was being formed. The plan was not a great success. Out of the 25 who enrolled in the first two-year program, only 2 graduated, and in the following years only five more students, out of a total of 80, succeeded in graduating. The first regular program, which followed the guidelines of CIESPAL, was divided into three areas: communication sciences; professional techniques and practices; and humanities.[12] Subsequently, the program was revised to include two parallel tracks: journalism and communication. The professional journalism track is based on a system of workshops in 15 of the degree program's 26 areas. The other 11 areas include such theoretical subjects as journalism history and law, introductory statistics and research methods and the sociology and psychology of communication. The communication track covers the "psychosocial analysis" of the media, semiology, mathematics and statistics, as well as communication theory, interpersonal communication and the "epistemology of communication."[13] More recently, emphases in advertising and public relations were added. Enrollments have grown steadily over the years, but in 1979 enrollment was limited to 70 in journalism, 40 in communication, 50 in public relations and 40 in advertising.

Costa Rica's press system is generally considered to be one of the freest in the region, but journalism is regulated by a strong *Colegio de Periodista*. Only members of the College are allowed to work as journalists and only graduates of the School of Journalism are allowed to be members, although a number of older professionals were grandfathered in when the College was created in 1969. It is evident that both the College and the School of Journalism have an important combined role to play in regulating the profession. This role has come under some criticism in the past, but many people in the profession believe that it has done a lot to improve the level of journalism in the country.

Cuba

Prior to the 1959 revolution, Cuba had a network of six professionally oriented journalism schools and a powerful National College of Journalists that not only regulated entry into the profession but also dictated the number of students that could be enrolled in journalism programs. The first school, the Marquez Stirling School, was opened in Havana in 1942. Subsequently, five other schools, modeled after the Havana school, were opened in the provincial capitals, Santiago de Cuba, Santa Clara, Mantanzas, Camagüey and Pinar del Rio. In 1955, a Higher Institute of Journalism was created by the University of Havana to provide specialized training in social and historical studies for graduates of the journalism schools.[14]

All this was swept away during the Revolution. At the same time, many journalists fled the country or simply left the profession. The media were taken over by the government and, as in most former communist countries, journalists became "ideological workers." As a result, ideology, in particular Soviet ideology, has become an important part of journalism training, but North American influences have remained strong in the more technical areas, such as writing, editing and layout. Today, journalism training is provided by the Union of Cuban Journalists (UPEC), two universities and a few on-the-job schemes.[15]

Since its creation in 1963, UPEC has set out to improve the ideological, cultural and technical training of its approximately 2,700 members. It organizes short training courses and correspondence courses in various areas of journalism, creates training materials, runs language courses for journalists and publishes a number of trade magazines. It has also developed training courses for a 10,000-strong network of amateur journalists throughout the country and set up a Center for Mass Media Studies. In the mid-1970s, UPEC created an International Center for Journalist Training, which offers occasional basic training courses for young journalists from developing countries and regular seminars for established Latin American journalists on such topics as North American imperialism. These seminars have been popular, attracting 20 to 30 participants each year. Finally, UPEC has sent distinguished Cuban journalists to lecture and teach occasional courses in such countries as Ethiopia, Mozambique, Nicaragua and Grenada.

The University of Havana and the University of Oriente also run formal journalism training programs at both their main and branch campuses, enrolling a total of about 500 students every year. Since it was founded in 1963, the Havana school's five-year program has trained over 3,000 communication specialists, many of them from the Soviet Union, Eastern Europe, North Korea, Vietnam and parts of Africa and Latin America. The introductory cycles of the program combine basic general subjects with specific writing and production courses. In the final cycle, students are able to choose a specialization. Writing courses are taught by media professionals either on a part-time or full-time basis. Other courses are taught by full-time academic faculty, most of whom have master's degrees from Cuban universities. In the past, teaching materials have often been translations of Soviet or North American textbooks, but in recent years a number of domestically produced books have appeared.

After graduating and completing two years of compulsory social service, students are placed in jobs by the party's Central Planning Board, which takes into account not only local industry needs but also each student's place of residence and academic record. A degree in journalism is not a prerequisite for employment as a journalist and it is still possible for aspiring journalists to receive on-the-job training, particularly in certain technical areas of broadcasting or filmmaking. In practice, however, most employers prefer candidates with appropriate degrees.

At the time of this writing, the political future of Cuba remains uncertain. If, like the countries of Eastern and Central Europe, it abandons Communism and moves toward a free-market economy, it seems highly likely that it will quickly revert to the unfettered commercial media system that existed in pre-Castro days.

THE CARIBBEAN

Most of the island economies of the Caribbean are too small to support individual communication training programs. However, the Caribbean Institute of Mass Communication (CARIMAC) at the University of the West Indies in Jamaica offers a one-year diploma course and a three-year degree program in print and broadcast journalism that have been attended by students from all over the region. The institute's month-long summer course is also well attended. Created in 1974 by the Government of Jamaica, with the assistance of UNESCO, the Friedrich-Ebert-Stiftung and USAID, CARIMAC organizes regional conferences, seminars and workshops in various countries of the Caribbean Community (CARICOM) and assists governmental and nongovernmental agencies throughout the region in the systematic use of communication methods and technology for development purposes.[16]

From the start, it was decided that CARIMAC's program should meet a variety of needs. It should have a sound theoretical base as well as a foundation in the Caribbean environment and should, therefore, include courses in the social sciences, communications and Caribbean studies. It should also combine theoretical and practical training in the mass media, with an emphasis on writing, interviewing and production. Finally, the program should cater to persons in different fields of communication and should address training needs at different levels both intramurally and extramurally. To date, the institute has trained over 300 diploma students and 200 degree students, many of whom hold senior communication positions in every member country of CARICOM.

In order to qualify for admission to the diploma course, candidates must have either a degree or the equivalent as well as at least three years' experience in the mass media. They also have to provide samples of their professional work. After a year of study, students have to pass examinations in the five following areas:

- History, politics and culture of the Caribbean
- Principles of sociology and economics
- Communication and society
- Media and language
- Communication techniques

In order to be admitted to the degree program, candidates have to achieve a high score on a general knowledge test given during registration week. There are three degree options, communication with language and literature, communication with social sciences, and a more general degree in communication, social sciences, language and literature.

In conclusion, while CARIMAC is certainly doing all it can to stem the tide, there is still a growing need for trained communicators throughout the region. One of the options being studied by UNESCO and other international agencies is that of training trainers to handle continuing education within media organizations.

NOTES

1. Bruce Malcolm, *To License a Journalist: A Landmark Decision in the Schmidt Case* (New York: Freedom House, 1986).

2. This section draws on José Baldivia, Mario Planet, Javier Solís, and Tomás Guerra Rivas, *La Formación de los Periodistas en América Latina: México, Chile, Costa Rica* (Mexico: CEESTEM/Editorial Nueva Imagen, 1981).

3. Taken from the school's "plan de estudios," sent to the author.

4. Taken from UNAM's "Plan de estudios de la licenciatura en ciencias de la comunicación," sent to the author.

5. Taken from Universidad Kino's "Licenciado en Periodismo" brochure, sent to the author.

6. Baldivia in Baldivia et al., *La Formación de los Periodistas*, pp. 82–83.

7. Ray Newton, "J-Education, Mexican Style," *Journalism Educator* 23 (October 1972), pp. 16–17.

8. Mario Planet in Baldivia et al., *La Formación de los Periodistas*, p. 189.

9. Ibid., p. 202.

10. Taken from the university's degree program in "social information," sent to the author.

11. Planet in Baldivia et al., *La Formación de los Periodistas*, p. 235.

12. Javier Solís and Tomás Guerra in Baldivia et al., *La Formación de los Periodistas*, pp. 331–335.

13. Ibid., p. 348.

14. Juan S. Valmaggia, "Latin America," in UNESCO, *The Training of Journalists: A World-wide Study on the Training of Personnel for the Mass Media* (Paris: UNESCO, 1958), pp. 128–130.

15. John A. Lent, "Journalism Training in Cuba Emphasizes Politics, Ideology," *Journalism Educator* 39, no.3 (Autumn 1984), pp. 12–15.

16. The University of the West Indies, *Caribbean Institute of Mass Communication* (Mona, Jamaica: UWI, 1988).

Chapter Nine

Africa

Communication training in Africa is beset by a number of problems, some of which are peculiar to the region and some of which are shared by other developing areas of the world. Mass communication is a recent phenomenon in Africa and is less developed than in most other regions, but it continues to grow, creating an increasing demand for trained communicators. Because of a general lack of resources, both financial and human, more than half the countries in the region lack adequate national training facilities. Many of the institutions that do exist suffer from a chronic shortage of qualified educators, technical equipment and suitable teaching materials. Low literacy rates, low levels of general education and a staggering diversity of languages and cultural traditions further complicate the process of communication and call for specialized training, which is not usually available. Foreign influences have been strong and, while most assistance programs have been well-intentioned, some of them may have hindered the growth of self-reliance. The mistrust of formal journalism training, left over from colonial days, still flourishes, particularly where university programs are concerned. Despite these problems, considerable strides have been made in developing regional training initiatives and in strengthening the programs offered by some of the older training centers.

Historically, formal communication training dates from the late 1950s and early 1960s, when many African states acquired independence from former colonial powers. Before that time, most newspapers, with a few exceptions in West Africa, were produced by and for the white settlers. Training, such as it was, was given on the job. In Nigeria a few African journalists were trained in this way, but they were rarely entrusted with anything but the most elementary tasks. The French, too, sent a few Africans back to France for training, but there they learned a high level of literary journalism that was quite unsuitable for African audiences. As a result, when independence came, most African countries suddenly found themselves without trained communicators. In many cases, they were forced to call upon Europeans to run their media, at least until they could develop their own training schemes.[1]

But, where to start? Frank Barton, a pioneer of journalism training in Africa in the 1960s, once observed, "The real African revolution only *began* with independence."[2] The initiative with which Barton was associated, sponsored by the International Press Institute (IPI), was one of several crash programs provided by organizations such as UNESCO, the International Federation of Journalists in Brussels, the International Organization of Journalists in Prague, the American Press Institute, the African American Institute in the United States and the Thomson Foundation in the United Kingdom. The IPI program, started in 1963 by Tom Hopkinson, a former editor of *Picture Post* and editor-in-chief of *Drum* magazine, offered six-month training courses in both Nairobi in Kenya and Lagos in Nigeria. Over the next five years, these courses, funded by the Ford Foundation of the United States, successfully trained 311 journalists from 18 African countries.

Writing about the IPI program in 1969, Frank Barton described some of the difficulties that had to be overcome.[3] To begin with, IPI's role in Africa was not, as in Asia, to assist in the modernization of the press but rather to assist in the creation of the press and the idea of newspapers as part of society. Indeed, at that time, the few newspapers that did exist were located in major centers and, more often than not, were staffed by expatriates. Furthermore, when independence arrived, Africa had only a handful of literates capable of being trained as journalists. The most urgent need was to help the few existing journalists to improve their skills, but Africans generally were suspicious of the press, which was often seen as the continued reflection of Europe or of authority. In many cases, too, African ideas of press freedom ran contrary to those held by IPI.[4] The press was often an instrument of official government policy and, although the notion of development journalism had not yet fully emerged, African journalists often found themselves torn between their professional and their national loyalties. Finally, even at this early stage, there was already much resentment about foreign coverage of African affairs.

Despite these difficulties, the IPI program went a long way toward bridging the gap between independence and the creation of more permanent training facilities. Successful programs were also run by UNESCO in Dakar, Senegal, and Kampala, Uganda, and by the IOJ in Guinea, Mali and Ghana. Other foreign organizations offering courses in Africa, apart from those already mentioned, have included the British Council, the Canadian International Development Agency, Deutsche Welle, Friedrich-Ebert-Stiftung, and the French Institut National de la Communication Audiovisuelle.

Most of the initiatives undertaken in this way were motivated by a genuine desire to improve African journalism, but other motivations, of a political and commercial nature, were not always absent. Also, even when motives were pure, the training that was dispensed was inevitably based on what the sponsors of the different programs considered to be "the right kind" of journalism, which, in many cases, did not correspond to African needs and realities. In this respect, the least sensitive programs were those that required trainees to travel to foreign centers. Western sponsors soon recognized this, but some of the socialist African countries continued to send journalists to the Soviet Union and China for obvious ideological reasons. All in all, despite their shortcomings, these various initiatives quickly produced a solid core of trained communicators.

At about the same time, a number of permanent training facilities were opened, mainly in Ghana, Nigeria and Kenya. They include the Kenya Institute of Mass Communication, the Nairobi School of Journalism, the All Africa Conference of Churches Communication Training Center in Nairobi, the Nigerian Institute of Journalism, the Ghana Institute of Journalism and the Ghana National Film and Television Institute. Although they were created in response to national training needs, they have attracted students from other countries and, in this way, function as regional training centers for English-speaking Africa. Other regional programs have been created for French-speaking journalists at the Ecole Supérieure de Sciences et Techniques de l'Information (ESSTI) in Yaoundé, Cameroon, the Centre d'Etudes des Sciences et Techniques de l'Information (CESTI) in Dakar, Senegal, the Institut des Sciences et Techniques de l'Information (ISTI) in Zaire and the Centre Interafricain d'Etudes en Radio Rurale de Ouagadougou (CIERRO) in Burkina Faso.[5]

For many years, despite the existence of regional organizations, most of them created with the assistance of UNESCO, national programs and individual schools suffered from a lack of coordination conducive to the development of appropriate curricula, teaching materials and research. In 1976, African communication trainers met in Nairobi to set up the African

Council on Communication Education (ACCE), a unique nonprofit non-governmental organization, whose main objectives are:

• to promote communication training and development through local, regional and continental workshops and consultations
• to assist in curriculum development
• to assess common training needs and develop ways of meeting them
• to evolve a system of accreditation
• to encourage research and promote the collection and dissemination of information on communication training issues[6]

ACCE recently founded the Institute for Communication Development and Research, which seeks to provide communications specialists with the means to improve their skills and increase their understanding of communication processes and the role of their specific media. ACCE also publishes a research journal, *Africa Media Review*, a quarterly newsletter, *Africom*, and periodic reports in its *Africa Media Monograph Series*. The organization groups about 70 communication schools and training institutions from over 30 African states.

The rest of this chapter will review some of the major communication programs in sub-Saharan Africa. Training facilities in the Maghrebin countries will be covered in a later chapter on North Africa and the Middle East.

WEST AFRICA

West Africa has produced some of the strongest press systems on the African continent, partly because of powerful colonial influences but also because of such political journalists as Kwame Nkrumah of Ghana, Nnamdi Azikiwe of Nigeria, Félix Houphouët-Boigny of the Ivory Coast and Léopold Senghor of Senegal, who used newspapers as organs of dissent and revolution and who saw journalism as a way of achieving African independence.

Nigeria

As one of the most developed and heavily populated countries on the continent, Nigeria has the largest number of newspapers and one of the most sophisticated broadcasting systems in sub-Saharan Africa. It is not surprising that, as a result, it also has the largest number of training facilities, a total of over 40, offering programs not only in print journalism and broadcast production but also in speech communication, communication sociology, language and communication arts and theater arts. In general terms, there are four types of training, provided by the universities, the polytechnics, a few specialized national institutes and professionally oriented in-house courses.[7]

The oldest communication program in the country is the communication sociology course at the University of Ibadan, dating back to 1949. However, the oldest journalism program is that of University of Nigeria-Nsukka's Department of Mass Communication, which began life in 1962 as the Jackson College of Journalism and which today offers a two-year bachelor's degree and a four-year master's degree in print journalism, radio journalism, photojournalism or media management. The Department of Mass Communication at the University of Lagos, created in 1967, also provides undergraduate and graduate training and recently added a Ph.D. program. Both the University of Maiduguri and Bayero University in Kano offer three-year degree courses in journalism as well as short courses for working journalists. The degree programs typically offer liberal studies and skills in a 70:30 percent ratio. Other Nigerian universities, Calabar, Cross River State, Ibadan, Ilorin, Jos and Ahmadu Bello, offer degree programs in various communication subjects.[8]

Ten polytechnics, strategically located around the country, offer two- or four-year courses leading to the National Diploma or Higher National Diploma in journalism or mass communication. Over the years, the polytechnics have trained large numbers of journalists, mainly junior reporters or sub-editors. Academic standards are quite high, but, generally speaking, the polytechnics are considered to be less prestigious than the universities, Nsukka and Lagos in particular.

The Nigerian Institute of Journalism (NIJ), modeled after the Ghana Institute of Journalism, was founded in 1971 by the *Nigerian Daily Times* and other private newspaper groups. It organizes three-month short courses and one-month seminars on editing, writing and reporting, attended mainly by working journalists on release from news organizations in the print and broadcast media. The NIJ also runs a full-time two-year program for high school graduates, leading to a diploma. Because of its close connections with leading newspapers, the NIJ enjoys considerable prestige in the industry. A number of other institutes, the Federal Institute of Public Information, the Institute of Management and Communication, the Institute of Management and Technology, the Institute of Mass Communication Technology and the Institute of Technology, offer various diploma or certificate programs in journalism, mass communication, public information, advertising and public relations.

Finally, in the field of broadcasting, the Television College at Jos trains all technical and editorial personnel employed by the Nigerian Television Authority. This is a large, well-run facility with separate departments of Design, Engineering, Production, General Studies and Television Journalism, offering both short courses and certificate- and diploma-level programs. The Federal Radio Corporation of Nigeria runs a Division of National Training and Manpower Development for its own radio personnel. The universities of Lagos and Nigeria-Nsukka also provide some radio training, but, although they have well-equipped studios, they are not allowed to broadcast off campus.

With regard to faculty, there have been some major changes over the last two decades, particularly at the major universities. In the 1970s, the universities had to rely heavily on UNESCO consultants or media professionals, but today about 95 percent of the faculty employed by Lagos and Nigeria-Nsukka are well-qualified scholars with, however, little professional experience. In response to criticism from the industry, a few scholars now spend sabbaticals in the media. At the polytechnics, the proportion of professionals is much higher, but heads of departments are usually academicians. At the NIJ and other specialized institutes, faculty are almost exclusively professionals.

All in all, the educational level of professional communicators has risen considerably. Up to the middle of the 1980s, the media expanded rapidly and there was a great demand for trained communicators, but since then demand has stabilized and, today, even well-qualified M.A.s and Ph.D.s may have trouble finding jobs. The availability of new job openings is limited by the relatively small number of media centers in the country. However, the Ministry of Information continues to absorb quite a lot of journalists into its public information services.

As in many other countries, the universities have been criticized for placing too much emphasis on theory and not enough on practical skills. Academics are also accused of doing research that is not relevant to African priorities and of not staying in touch with the profession. However, academics and not a few assignment editors argue that journalists need more general knowledge; otherwise, they have no idea of what story to work on or what the implications of a story are.

Ghana

Ghana became the first African state to achieve independence in 1957, partly because of the revolutionary efforts of a newspaper editor, Kwame Nkrumah, who later became president of his country. Ghana also has a history of journalism going back to the 1820s and one of the first news-papers to be edited by an African, the *Accra Herald*, founded in 1858. It is fitting, then, that Ghana should have been home to the first training institute in black Africa, the Ghana Institute of Journalism, which was founded by Nkrumah in 1959 as part of the Accra Technical Institute.[9] Today, the institute offers a two-year diploma for day students and a three-year diploma for evening students, as well as a yearly one-month refresher course in journalism. As might be expected in a school modeled on British traditions, the courses are heavily skills oriented.

The School of Communication Studies at the University of Ghana in Legon, created in 1973, offers a one-year graduate diploma and a two-year master's degree, both of which are theory-oriented. The school accepts both university graduates intent on pursuing an advanced degree and experienced professional journalists seeking to acquire research skills. The National Film and Television Institute, founded in 1978, offers practical and theoretical courses in interpersonal communication, communication and development, communication for rural development, broadcasting and film training.[10] Over the years, this institute has provided training to students from all over West Africa.

Senegal

The capital of Senegal, Dakar, at one time known as "the African Left Bank," was long the outpost of French culture in French West Africa and as such supported a flourishing press, originally aimed at French expatri-ates but later adopted by such outstanding African intellectuals as Léopold Senghor. The regional importance of the city was confirmed in 1970 with the creation of the Centre d'Etudes des Sciences et Techniques de l'Information (CESTI) at the University of Dakar, which has attracted students from many French-speaking countries, including Benin, Burkina Faso, Ivory Coast, Mali, Mauritania and Niger. It now offers a three-year degree program in communication and research.

Another regional center is the Centre Régional de Recherche et de Documentation Pour le Développement Culturel (CREDEC), also in Dakar, which specializes in development communication. This is a small facility, but it offers courses in a wide variety of fields, including press, film, the book industry, broadcasting, economics of communication, com-munication and development, intercultural communication, communica-tion media, and communication for rural development. It also produces bulletins, books, reports and the *Journal de CREDEC*.

Finally, the Panafrican News Agency (PANA), an intergovernmental organization located in Dakar, sponsors training workshops on news agency journalism.

Burkina Faso

Burkina Faso, with three large facilities located in Ouagadougou, has also served as a regional training center for communication and development. CIERRO, which has already been mentioned, specializes in the use of community media, especially radio, for rural development. The Institut Africain d'Education Cinématographique specializes in film, but also offers practical courses in the print media, broadcasting and audiovisual instruction, as well as theoretical courses in intercultural communication, economics of communication, community media and communication and development. The third facility, the Centre de Formation Professionnelle de l'Information, stresses both mass and interpersonal communication techniques for rural development. All three facilities were created in the 1970s.

Ivory Coast

The University of Abidjan has two departments involved in communication training. The Department of Communication Science offers a four-year undergraduate program and a two-year graduate program. The Centre d'Enseignement et de Recherche Audio-Visuels (CERAV) specializes in media education, telecommunication informatics, audiovisual instruction, video and various other aspects of communication. Its research is published in periodical journals and occasional reports.

Cameroun

The Advanced School of Information Sciences and Techniques (ESSTI) in Yaoundé has been an important regional center for French-speaking Africa since 1982. The facility was created with financial aid from France and Canada and with technical assistance from UNESCO. It has also received support from a number of African countries that have sent students for training. In the past, some foreign students were given free tuition and lodging, but financial restraints have forced ESSTI to reduce enrollment from outside the country. With a full-time faculty of nine, the school offers three main programs: Division I for information technicians; Division II for nonspecialist journalists; and Division III for specialist journalists. The school also publishes a number of journals including *Esti-Info*, *Esti-Forum*, *Esti-Biblio* and *Bulletin* as well as annual reports and dissertations.

Elsewhere in West Africa, the University of Liberia offers a four-year undergraduate degree program in mass communication; the All African Conference of Churches organizes courses on Christian communication, community media and communication development in Lome, Togo; and the Faculty of Health Sciences in Cotonou, Benin, runs a unit specializing in audiovisual communication applications.

EAST AFRICA

Under British domination, East Africa enjoyed a respectable selection of newspapers, mainly confined to the urban centers, mainly published in English and mainly but not exclusively reserved for the white settlers. Since independence, Kenya's economy has developed along Western lines and has produced one of the freest press systems on the African continent. Uganda has been governed by a succession of authoritarian regimes, either military or civilian, and Tanzania has failed to prosper under its socialist rule. The training communication facilities that are available are a reflection of the relative freedom and prosperity of each country.

Kenya

As an important economic and cultural center, Kenya's capital, Nairobi, is home to a number of regional or continental organizations. ACCE, which has already been mentioned on several occasions, groups some 70 communication schools and over 200 communication researchers, scholars and media practitioners in about 33 African countries. Its main function is one of coordination, but it does run short-term workshops and seminars in such areas as media management, communication and rural development, women in the media, rural journalism and communication policy and planning for development. Those taking part in the workshops are usually journalists and communication educators.[11]

The University of Nairobi's School of Journalism, founded in 1970, used to offer a two-year undergraduate diploma but now provides only a one-year graduate program. Its research activities have focused on communication and development and rural journalism. The Kenya Institute of Mass Communication began life as a broadcast engineering school in 1961, but, since 1968, it has added courses in broadcast production, film, audiovisual instruction and communication technology. Its two-year program leads to a diploma in mass communication.

Nairobi is also home to two Christian communication training organizations. The All Africa Conference of Churches (AACC) Communication Training Center, founded in 1963, offers two- and three-month courses in radio production, audiovisual instruction and technical training. The Department of Communications of Daystar University College runs both a BA and an MA program in Christian Communication. Daystar has been particularly active in developing its own specialized teaching materials.[12]

Finally, the Centre for African Family Studies runs four- and five-week courses in family-planning communication in both French and English, and a smaller institution, AMECEA Communications, founded in 1968, provides training in organizational communication, mass media, film and audience research.

Tanzania

The main training facility, overseen by the Ministry of Information and Broadcasting, is the Tanzania School of Journalism in Dar-es-Salaam, which runs a two-year program with courses in newspaper writing, reporting and editing, broadcast news and audiovisual instruction. As in other institutions of higher learning in Tanzania, students must be members of the Revolutionary Party and must have completed their national service.[13] Skills courses are taught by a core of full-time faculty, while political economy, public relations and law are taught by part-time adjunct faculty. After finishing their two-year program, students are obliged to complete a six-month internship.[14]

There is a strong demand for trained journalists, particularly from the Tanzanian news agency, SHIHATA, which was set up in July, 1976. However, for political reasons, SHIHATA will not employ newsmen and cameramen who are highly trained but who do not accept the Party policy. According to the agency director, Lawrence Mnubi, "a good SHIHATA worker should understand that he is a Party and Government functionary."[15]

The Nyegezi Social Training Center in Mwanza also has a journalism department offering a two-year diploma course with an emphasis on both theory and practice. This facility, started in 1963, can handle some 20 students with a full-time faculty of four. Over the years, it has trained students from Tanzania, Uganda, Kenya, Malawi and Sudan.

Two smaller facilities, the Lutheran Radio Center in Moshi and Tanzania Information Services in Dar-es-Salaam, offer courses in public relations, communication for rural development, interpersonal communication and intercultural communication.

Uganda

After decades of authoritarian rule and government control, Uganda's media system has remained very limited, with one of the lowest newspaper circulations in the world. Its sole training facility is the Uganda School of Journalism in Lugogo, run by the Institute for Public Administration. The school, which has a faculty of eight, offers a nine-month diploma course in journalism open to students with two years' experience in a news organization and a high school diploma.

CENTRAL AND SOUTHERN AFRICA

The two main centers for communication training in this subregion of Africa are Zambia, for English-speaking countries, and Zaire, for French-speaking countries.

Zambia

The Africa Literature Center in Kitwe has one of the oldest journalism programs on the continent. This church-related program, begun in 1959, includes a one-year diploma and a certificate in journalism as well as annual short courses for working journalists. Despite its religious orientation, the program is well respected. However, the two main facilities in the country are the Journalism Department of the Evelyn Hone College, which offers a three-year diploma with a strong emphasis on practical skills, and the University of Zambia's Department of Mass Communication, which runs a four-year undergraduate degree program. The Zambia Institute of Mass Communication (Zamcom) also runs journalism courses for students with a high-school diploma or three years' professional experience.

Zaire

As has already been mentioned, the Institut des Sciences et Techniques de l'Information (ISTI), which is part of the national university in Kinshasa, serves as a regional training center for French-speaking countries in the region and has attracted students from Benin, Burundi, Chad,

Central African Republic, Rwanda and Togo. It offers bachelor's, master's and doctoral degrees in both print and electronic journalism.

Otherwise, Zaire has a large broadcast training school, the Studio-Ecole de la Voix du Zaire, run by the national broadcasting organization, which offers two-year courses in mass media, broadcasting, film, audiovisual instruction and communication technology. The Union Panafricaine des Télécommunications also runs a few courses in telecommunications, but its main function is research.

Elsewhere in the region, both Burundi and Mozambique have national journalism schools. Swaziland has a Center for Development Communications in Mbabane specializing in basic and advanced radio writing and production. Finally, in Zimbabwe, the Christian College of Southern Africa (CCOSA) in Harare offers a four-year degree program in mass communication, news editing, graphic design, interpersonal communication and photojournalism. The Harare Polytechnic also offers a two-year diploma and a one-year National Diploma in mass communication as well as short courses and workshops for working journalists and media trainers.[16]

SOUTH AFRICA

South Africa has tended to follow the British apprenticeship system, but as journalism developed after World War II, the Argus Group created the Argus Cadet School of Journalism to train recruits for its newspapers. Training involved a five-month attachment at the *Cape Argus* in Cape Town. The program was later moved to Johannesburg. Another group, South African Associated Newspapers, ran a similar program. In the late 1960s, the University of Potchefstroom started a four-year undergraduate program, a one-year graduate diploma and a master's in communications and journalism. Shortly thereafter the University of South Africa in Pretoria, Rhodes University in Grahamstown and Rand Afrikaans University in Johannesburg also began degree programs in journalism. Finally, in the 1970s, a Department of Communication was created at the University of Orange Free State in Bloemfontein.[17]

CONCLUSIONS

Communication training in Africa faces a number of problems that are common to all developing regions of the world. It is plagued with the same lack of resources: money, trained educators, technology, textbooks and other teaching materials. But, more than in other regions, training has been affected directly and indirectly by economic problems, language difficulties and persistent postcolonial influences.

Obviously, the struggling economies and, in some cases, extreme poverty of many African nations have had a direct effect on training by failing to provide money to put into programs, facilities and qualified teachers. But economic conditions have also had some indirect effects. In their quest for economic development, many countries have had to resort to centralized planning and strong government controls of all public institutions, including the media. The resulting press systems have created a need for specific types of communicators and specific types of training, quite unlike those to be found in the Western nations that have provided the training models frequently used in Africa. This has produced some serious tensions between journalists and governments and between governments and news organizations.

As in other parts of the world, mobilization of the population is seen as essential to development, and the mass media have a crucial role to play in educating, informing, persuading and organizing the people.[18] The notion of developmental journalism has been much debated, but it does appear in many African training programs in the form of courses on "communication and development," "communication for rural development" and "community media." But, here again, there are some serious conflicts between development issues and the economics of modern media management, just as there are conflicts betwen developmental journalism and basic press freedoms. These problems, which are fundamental to training approaches, are unlikely to be resolved until economic conditions improve.

The continued influence of former colonial ties appears to be stronger in Africa than in other regions of the world, partly because independence came later but also because the lack of economic development has prevented individual African nations from finding their own identities. As one Nigerian educator has pointed out, some of Africa's pioneer mass communication trainers stepped into the departing "whiteman" shoes without the slightest intention of changing. In some instances, they are more orthodox than their former colonial masters.[19] The same commentator stresses the importance of mass communication training for self-reliance, which, among other things, presupposes less dependence on advanced industrial states, especially former colonial powers.

Dependence can take the form of social, cultural, political and economic influences. With regard to communication and communication training, dependence can be the prevalence of foreign-generated news in the African media, which can be interpreted as a tacit admission of the inadequacy of African journalism.[20] The ramifications of this kind of dependence are far-reaching. One response has been a search for an African identity, distinct from European influences. Afrocentricity, which has emerged as an alternative to Eurocentricity, may be a valid concept within the confines of the African continent and may, indeed, serve to redefine African culture and communication, but it is not a valid concept when it comes to communicating with the outside world.[21]

Finally, despite the admirable efforts of ACCE, the standardization and accreditation of training programs remain problematical as long as different concepts of communication, born of different colonial influences, continue to exist. However, as communication needs change, as the reflection of strengthening economies, some of these differences are likely to disappear.

NOTES

1. L. John Martin, "Africa," in John C. Merrill, ed., *Global Journalism*, 2d ed. (White Plains, NY: Longman, 1991), pp. 199–200.

2. Frank Barton, *African Assignment: The Story of IPI's Six-Year Training Program in Tropical Africa* (Zurich: International Press Institute, 1969), p. 5.

3. Ibid., pp. 7–30.

4. Ibid., pp. 34–38.

5. UNESCO, *Perspectives for Regional and International Cooperation*, Conference Document CII-91/CONF CC-609 (Paris: UNESCO, April 30, 1991).

6. ACCE, *African Council on Communication Education*, a membership flier (Nairobi: ACCE, n.d.).

7. The author is indebted to Professor Folu Ogundimu of Michigan State University, who provided much of the background information presented in this section.

8. African Council on Communication Education, *A Directory of Communication Training Institutions in Africa* (Nairobi: ACCE, 1988), pp. 16–35.

9. Martin, "Africa," p. 200.

10. ACCE, *A Directory*, p. 12.

11. Personal communication from Dr. S. T. Kwame Boafo, Executive Coordinator of ACCE, January 8, 1991.

12. ACCE, *A Directory*, p. 60.

13. Martin, "Africa," p. 201.

14. Tanzania School of Journalism, *New Trends in Journalism Education and Practice in Tanzania* (Dar-es-Salaam: Ministry of Information, 1980), p. 30.

15. Ibid., p. 81.

16. ACCE, *A Directory*, p. 48.

17. Martin, "Africa," p. 202.

18. Chen C. Chimutengwende, "The Role of Communications Training and Technology in African Development," in George Gerbner and Marsha Siefert, eds., *World Communication: A Handbook* (White Plains, NY: Longman, 1984), p. 362.

19. Jerry Komia Domatob, "Communication Training for Self-reliance in Black Africa: Challenges and Strategies," *Gazette* 40 (1987), p. 174.

20. Onuma O. Oreh, "Developmental Journalism and Press Freedom: An African Viewpoint," *Gazette* 24 (1978), p. 38.

21. Usman Jimada, "Nigerian Media Training: An Alternative Model," in Mohammad Nur Alkali, Jerry Domatob, Yahaya Abubakar and Abubakar Jika, eds., *Mass Communication: A Book of Readings* (Enugu, Nigeria: Delta Publications, 1988), pp. 155–157.

Chapter Ten

North Africa and the Middle East

This is a difficult area to define. The regional grouping used by UNESCO, "the Arab States," covers most of the area and has the advantage of representing a certain uniformity of religion, culture and language. However, the Middle East is generally considered to include a number of non-Arab nations, such as Iran, Israel and Turkey, the last being particularly hard to place, as it lies between Asia and Europe. Consequently, for the purposes of this study, the region is divided into the Middle East, which includes both Arab and non-Arab states, and North Africa, which includes the former French possessions, Algeria, Tunisia and Morocco, and Egypt, Libya and the Sudan.

Virtually all countries in the region are part of the developing world, but the presence of oil makes for a wide variety of income levels. Media systems reflect this economic diversity but are also affected by differences in political, social, educational and cultural structures. Religion is a particularly strong influence in some countries. On the whole, there is no great shortage of training facilities in the region, but there is a chronic shortage of properly qualified educators and appropriate teaching materials, particularly in the Arab countries. At some time in the past, the training programs of most countries in the region have been strongly influenced either by French or by American and British educational traditions. More recently, powerful nationalist and Islamic tendencies have also begun to have an effect.

William Rugh's comparative framework for the analysis of press systems in the Arab world is still valid and could be extended to other countries in the region.[1] Rugh divided countries into three types. Traditional countries, with a long history of conservative rule, often in the hands of a powerful family or royal dynasty, tend to have what Rugh calls a "loyalist" press. Examples of this are Jordan, Saudi Arabia and most of the Emirates. Leftist or revolutionary countries, such as Algeria or Yemen, have a "mobilization" press. Stabler democracies, such as Israel or Turkey, have a "diverse" press. It could be argued that some of the more fanatical Muslim regimes form a separate group, but their emphasis on strict ideology and national mobilization places them among the revolutionary countries.

With the exception of the few "diverse" systems, almost all the countries in the region have some kind of state control, in the form of direct government intervention, self-censorship, "official" news briefings or national news agencies. This may not directly affect training, which is more technical than ideological, but it does affect the way in which journalism is practiced and the kind of esteem in which journalists are held.

NORTH AFRICA

There is generally more information available about communication training in North Africa than in the Middle East, perhaps because the countries of North Africa tend to maintain closer ties with Europe.

Tunisia

Tunisia has one of the most complete training systems in the region. The Institute of Press and Information Sciences at the University of Tunis, founded in 1967, offers a four-year undergraduate program. With a faculty of 40, this facility is able to educate large numbers of students, but its emphasis is largely theoretical.

A more professional orientation is provided by the African Advanced Training Center for Journalists and Communicators, which is overseen by the Ministry of Culture and Information. The center has been in operation since 1983 and has trained well over 2,000 students, many of them from other French-speaking African countries. All the center's offerings are specialized short courses for working journalists. The director of the center insists on the professional nature of its courses, many of which are taught by specialists from France, Germany and the United States.[2]

Courses are often subsidized by the cultural service of the French Embassy, the Friedrich Naumann Foundation and the United States Information Agency. The center also organizes occasional courses for the Tunisian African Press Agency (TAPA).

Algeria

If Tunisia has the largest program, Algeria has the oldest, the Institute of Information Sciences and Communication at the University of Algiers, founded in 1965. By all accounts, this program is underfunded and has been criticized for its lack of practical training and equipment,[3] but it still enrolls some 800 undergraduate students and 60 graduate students. The National Institute of Higher Journalism, also in Algiers, provides a more professional approach, but it too suffers from a lack of adequate funding. Finally, the National Audiovisual Center at the University of Constantine provides both practical and theoretical courses in audiovisual applications.

Egypt

Egypt has several communication programs. The largest is that of Cairo University, which, incidentally, is the only institution in the region to offer a doctoral degree in communication. As in other universities, courses tend to be theoretical. However, the Department of Journalism and Mass Communication at the American University in Cairo, which is headed by a former U.S. journalist, James J. Napoli, is much more professionally oriented. As Napoli has written, this sometimes leads to problems.[4] The courses taught emphasize Western values and Western ways of reporting, which are based on libertarian principles. But, even though a multiparty system has emerged, Egypt is still a strongly authoritarian regime that does not condone criticism from the opposition press. Students inculcated with Western ideas about what constitutes news and how it should be written may be viewed as subversive when they enter the Egyptian media.

Other training facilities in Egypt include the Egyptian broadcasting authority's Radio and Television Training Center, and International Information and Communication Consultants, which specializes in audience research, public relations and communication for development.

Elsewhere in the region, Morocco, Sudan and Libya all have national training programs. The Higher Institute of Journalism in Rabat, which has a faculty of 13, provides training in mass media, film, communication technology and communication law. The National Mass Communication Training Center in Khartoum offers six-month courses in journalism, public opinion, public relations, communication law and communication and development for information officers who have worked for at least two years in mass communication positions. The Omdurman Islamic University in Khartoum also has a Department of Journalism and Communication. Finally, the University of Libya in Bengasi offers an undergraduate degree in mass communication. Bengasi is also home to the Arab Association of Communication Teaching and Training Institutes, which was created in 1976. In the past, this association has been seriously hampered by lack of funds, but, potentially, it has a key role to play in standardizing curricula, textbooks and teaching aids and in coordinating the efforts of training institutions throughout the Arab world.

THE MIDDLE EAST

UNESCO has identified some 23 academic programs and 31 professional training facilities throughout the Arab region, which includes the North African countries covered in the previous section.[5] But little current information is available about training in Afghanistan, Lebanon, Iran, Iraq and other Gulf states that have been disrupted by war, civil unrest or other problems. Response to survey questionnaires and other requests for information has been particularly poor from this region.

The Gulf States

Many of the oil-rich Gulf states, which have low levels of literacy, have turned to the West for sophisticated broadcasting systems. Broadcasting is an excellent way of communicating with large masses of people spread over wide areas. In authoritarian press systems such as those in the Gulf, in which information is limited and mainly of an official, educational or religious nature, the demand for trained journalists is less urgent than the need for qualified technical personnel. For many years, the training of engineering and production staff took place in the West, usually in those countries that had supplied broadcasting equipment. In the last ten years, however, the Arab States Broadcasting Union (ASBU) Radio and Television Training Center in Damascus, Syria, has provided courses for more than 2,000 trainees from all over the region. To a lesser extent, the Egyptian Radio and Television Training Center has also trained specialists from the Gulf states.

Despite the importance of broadcasting as a means of mass communication, particularly for religious purposes, there is still a growing demand for trained journalists by newspapers, magazines, news agencies and government news services; and today there are degree programs in journalism throughout the region. Syria has a degree program as well as a two-year diploma course. Journalism is taught at three universities in Saudi Arabia. Lebanon has two schools. Jordan has a degree program at Yarmouk University and a two-year program at the University of Jordan in Amman. Iran's schools have almost certainly been affected by the process of Islamization. Iraq had a department of journalism at Baghdad University, which may still be functioning. Kuwait and Qatar were considering starting journalism programs before the Gulf war.[6]

Turkey

Turkey is one of the largest and most developed nations in the Middle East and, since the Gulf war and the break-up of the Soviet Union, it is destined to become an increasingly influential force in the region. Because of a relatively high literacy rate, Turkey also has one of the strongest print media systems in the region, with 38 dailies, including the influential *Cumhuriyet*.

Istanbul University started a two-year journalism program in 1951, but the first facility to offer a degree program was the University of Ankara's School of Journalism and Broadcasting, which was created in 1965 by UNESCO, the Ankara Journalists' Association and the Journalists' Union. The school now has three distinct departments specializing in journalism, broadcasting and advertising/public relations.[7] Four-year undergraduate degree programs are also offered by four other schools of journalism at Istanbul University, Marmara University, Ege University and Gazi University. All five schools offer master's degrees, but only Ankara and Istanbul have doctoral programs. Anadolu University in Eskisehir runs a communication program, and the Mima Sinan University in Istanbul houses an Institute for Film and Cinema.

Altogether, these schools enroll about 600 students every year, but this far exceeds demand. Only the best graduates find jobs in the communication industry. Media professionals often complain that university journalism graduates are not adequately trained to meet the needs of the profession. As all the universities offering journalism programs are "equal opportunity public institutions," students are selected by a central entrance examination. A high-school diploma is required. Students come from all socioeconomic backgrounds, as journalism is generally considered to be a fairly prestigious occupation.

NOTES

1. William Rugh, *The Arab Press* (Syracuse, NY: Syracuse University Press, 1979), pp. 28–29.

2. Personal communication from Mr. Ridha Najar, director of the center, December 27, 1990.

3. Mohamed Kirat, "The Algerian News People" (Ph.D. diss., Indiana University, 1987.

4. James J. Napoli, "In Egypt, Learning U.S. Journalism Can Look Subversive," *Journalism Educator* 41, no.2 (Summer 1986), pp. 31–34.

5. UNESCO, *Perspectives for Regional and International Cooperation*, Conference Document CII-91/CONF CC-609 (Paris: UNESCO, April 30, 1991), p. 10.

6. Christine Ogan, "Middle East and North Africa," in John C. Merrill, ed., *Global Journalism*, 2d ed. (White Plains, NY: Longman, 1991), p. 145.

7. Personal communication from Professor Oya Tokgöz, Director of the School of Journalism and Broadcasting, University of Ankara, January 17, 1991.

Chapter Eleven

Challenges and Prospects

The challenges facing communication training are many and varied, but they tend to fall into two main clusters. In the developing world, they are usually related to a general lack of resources or to varying degrees of government control. In the industrialized countries, a new set of challenges are appearing as the result of technological change. Because of these challenges, training is still developing in different ways, but long-term prospects point toward the gradual homogenization of both journalism and journalism training.

CHALLENGES FOR THE DEVELOPING WORLD

There are wide variations in population, economic wealth, education and literacy within the Third World, but the single most important common characteristic that emerges from any analysis of communication training in developing countries is the inadequacy of resources, both material and human. As was shown in previous chapters, most training programs, even in the wealthier developing nations, suffer from a chronic shortage of appropriate teaching materials and qualified educators. A few countries have begun to produce their own textbooks in local languages, but that requires financial resources that are all too often lacking. Many teachers have to resort to adapting or translating materials from outdated American or European textbooks, which are rarely suitable for local needs.

Also, with the exception of some of the oil-rich Arab states, most institutions lack the funding to build adequate facilities and purchase the technical equipment needed to provide the right kind of professional training, not only in broadcasting but also in print journalism. Some schools have to make do with a few manual typewriters. It is unusual to find the full range of computers, layout screens and other photographic or electronic equipment used in modern newspapers. Networked computer labs are rare. Even when resources are available to buy equipment, there is still the problem of maintenance and spare parts. In these circumstances, it is easy to understand why professionals are often critical of training programs, particularly in universities, and why internships are essential.

Some developing nations have partially solved the problem of producing qualified personnel for the electronic media by running training programs in national broadcasting organizations, which are usually owned and firmly controlled by the state. In any case, given the importance attached to broadcasting as a means of educating and informing the masses and of building unity for development, funding is sometimes more readily available for equipping broadcast training facilities than for print journalism programs. Newspapers have traditionally been more critical of governments than state-run broadcasting networks have been, even in those countries that have strong press controls.

The shortage of qualified educators is another major problem, but one that is evolving. Early training courses were often taught by expatriate professionals, a situation that was unsatisfactory on several counts. As expatriates, they were sometimes insensitive to local priorities, particularly in a post-independence context. As former professionals, they were usually far more concerned with skills than with the need for analysis and an understanding of issues. At a later stage, courses were taken over by indigenous teachers, but they had received their training either overseas or at the hands of expatriates. More recently, a new generation of indigenous, locally trained educators has moved to the forefront, particularly in the universities. They often lack professional experience and are sometimes criticized for being too theoretical. As a result, a growing number of them are spending release time working in the industry. Some of the best programs combine theoretical courses taught by university-trained faculty with practical skills courses taught by adjunct professionals. Currently, the situation is evolving in the right direction, but it may be a long time before locally trained, indigenous educators with both practical experience and theoretical knowledge become available.

Another consequence of the lack of resources is the difficulty of coordinating programs, standardizing curricula and organizing accreditation procedures, all of which are necessary to raise the standards of training given. The situation is further complicated by the fact that, in many developing countries as in quite a few industrialized nations, state university programs exist alongside private universities and professional institutes of journalism. The antagonism that exists among these various types of institution is not conducive to coordination. Despite these problems, coordinating and accrediting bodies are appearing in a growing number of countries.

Some form of government control tends to be the norm in many parts of the developing world, although there are notable exceptions. Press controls inevitably affect the way in which journalists gather, select and process information as well as the way in which they are trained. Journalists who function as government information officers require training very different from that of those who function as government watchdogs. Indirectly, press controls also influence the quality of students recruited into training programs. In countries in which journalists are considered to be government employees, or "flacks," the profession is unlikely to attract the best and the brightest students or the most qualified teachers. In such systems, courses on ethics, professional standards, investigative reporting, press history and different aspects of communication theory have no place in the curriculum. This means that journalists are only partially trained and would find it difficult to function if press freedoms were suddenly reinstated. This problem, common to many developing countries, is one that is shared by journalists of the new democracies of Eastern and Central Europe.

However, despite the daunting array of challenges facing the developing world, progress is slowly being made. In all but the poorest countries, programs are improving, more qualified educators are being produced and more resources are being allocated to training. More importantly, perhaps, transborder information flows and the spread of such technologies as videocassettes and fax are making it increasingly difficult to impose tight press controls. Self-censorship is still common, but, on the whole, journalists are being given more responsibility and, as a result, the prestige of the profession is slowly rising.

CHALLENGES FOR THE INDUSTRIALIZED NATIONS

The challenges facing communication training in the industrialized nations have less to do with resources, although there can never be enough money spent on education. Nor do they have to do with press controls, although government intervention is a reality in more than one advanced country. These challenges have more to do with such factors as new technologies and changes in patterns of media ownership.

In those countries that can afford it, new technologies are having an enormous impact on communication. Computers, electronic databases and interactive networks, linked to communication satellites, fiber optic cables and other delivery systems, have revolutionized the way in which individuals, corporations, governments and the media gather, process and disseminate information. In this general context, training for professional communicators is becoming much more specialized and educators are finding it difficult to keep up with new developments. Programs are scrambling to adapt their curricula, but equipment is costly and there is a shortage of teachers with suitable knowledge of the new technologies.

There are other problems associated with new technologies, beyond the need for equipment and trained educators. The convergence of communication technologies is such that the lines of demarcation between the traditional media are becoming blurred. Increasingly, the "printed" word is being created, manipulated and moved, often over large distances, without ever touching paper. In Western Europe, videotex and teletext applications are now a reality. The satellite transmission of newspaper content to remote printing plants poses the question of whether newspapers are not becoming an electronic medium. The delivery of electronic newspapers to terminals in individual homes is technically possible if unlikely in the immediate future.

Even on a more mundane level, the use of electronic news management systems, on-line databases, electronic pagemakers and automatic typesetting has introduced a whole range of new skills that journalists must learn. At the same time, some traditional journalistic skills are no longer needed. As a result, the training of modern journalists will require less emphasis on practical skills and more emphasis on technology, knowledge of specialized issues and analytical thinking.

Another factor affecting training is competition. Group ownership of newspapers has virtually eliminated competition within individual markets, but competition with other media has intensified. One of the main results of this has been a move away from straight news to news as entertainment. In order to be successful, news formats now have to resort to "happy talk" or to distinctive layouts, extravagant color and the pictorial representation of factual information. There is increasing emphasis on the amusing, the bright and the bizarre.

Finally, areas such as public relations, advertising, public affairs, community relations and corporate communication are growing more rapidly than traditional journalism, and these are the areas in which students seek training. There will always be a place for straight journalism and trade-school-type journalism training, particularly for small local newspapers, but inevitably communication training is going to have to change if it is to meet the challenges discussed above. The move toward integrated communication programs is one that traditional journalism schools resist, but it is one that reflects the realities of the communication industry.

PROSPECTS

To be gloomy, it would be easy to believe that the gap between North and South will continue to widen. With this scenario, limited resources will continue to hamper the development of Third World communication training programs. Regional initiatives will provide some direction and will certainly help to further coordination, standardization and accreditation. Without adequate funding, however, a two-tier system is likely to emerge, not only between the developing countries and the industrialized nations but also within the Third World itself. The lower tier will continue to struggle with the basic training needs of underfunded and ill-equipped press systems. The upper tier will develop innovative new approaches to training in the high-tech environment of modern communication.

A more optimistic but improbable scenario would involve a narrowing of the gap between North and South. Although this is unlikely to occur within the foreseeable future, the economies of certain developing nations are indeed improving while those of several industrialized nations are declining. More realistically, regional and international assistance programs will gradually raise the level of communication in the developing world. As this occurs, press philosophies, communication systems and training needs will grow closer together, and the homogenization of journalism already apparent in the countries of the West will spread to the developing countries. It could be debated whether such an outcome is desirable, let alone possible, but for the moment communication training in every region of the world will continue to vary and will continue to face different challenges.

Appendix

Directory of Training Institutions

NORTH AMERICA

Canada

College of Communication
Canadian Broadcasting
 Corporation (CBC)
1500 Bronson Avenue
Ottawa, Ontario K1G 3J5

Department of Journalism and
 Public Communication
UQAM, CP 8888
Montréal, Quebec H3C 2P8

Department of Journalism and
 Broadcasting
Université Laval
Cité Universitaire
Quebec GIK 7P4

Department of Journalism
Pavillon Marie Victorin
Université de Montréal
90 Rue Vincent d'Indy
Montréal, Quebec HC3 3J7

Department of Communication
Université de Montréal
B.P. 6128 Université de
 Montréal Succursale 'A'
Montréal, Quebec H3C 3J7

School of Communication Studies
University of Calgary
2500 University Drive NW
Calgary, Alberta T2N IN4

Graduate Program in Communication
McGill University
3465 Peel Street
Montréal, Quebec   H3A 1W7

Graduate School of Journalism
Communication Studies
Simon Fraser University
Burnaby, British Columbia V5A IS6

School of Journalism
Carleton University
Ottawa, Ontario KIS 5B6

Information and Communication
   Programme
University of Moncton
Moncton, New Brunswick E1A 3E9

Department of Communications
Trinity Western University
7600 Glover Road
Langley, British Columbia V3A 6H4

Department of Public Relations
Mount Saint Vincent University
166 Bedford Highway
Halifax, Nova Scotia B3M 2J6

School of Journalism
Ryerson Polytechnical Institute
Toronto, Ontario M5B 1E8

Journalism Department
St. Clair College of Applied Arts
   & Technology
Windsor, Ontario N9A 6S4

Department of Communication
University of Ottawa
554 King Road
Ottawa, Ontario K1N 6N5

Graduate School of Journalism
University of Western Ontario
London, Ontario N6A 5B7

Department of Communication
   Studies
University of Windsor
Windsor, Ontario N8X 1P9

Department of Journalism
Concordia University
7141 Sherbrooke Street West
Montréal, Quebec H4B 1R6

School of Journalism &
   Communication
University of Regina
Regina, Saskatchewan S4S 0A2

United States of America

Department of Communications
University of Alabama
Tuscaloosa, AL 35487-0172

Department of Journalism
University of Alaska-Anchorage
Anchorage, AK 99508

Department of Journalism &
   Broadcasting
University of Alaska-Fairbanks
Fairbanks, AK 99775-0940

Walter Cronkite School of
    Journalism &
    Telecommunications
Arizona State University
Tempe, AZ 85287-1305

Department of Journalism
University of Arizona
Tucson, AZ 85721

Department of Journalism
University of Arkansas
Fayetteville, AR 72701

Department of Journalism
University of Arkansas-Little Rock
Little Rock, AR 72204

College of Communications
Arkansas State University
State University, AR 72467

Department of Journalism
Humboldt State University
Arcata, CA 95521

Graduate School of Journalism
University of California-Berkeley
Berkeley, CA 94720

Department of Journalism
California State University-Fresno
Fresno, CA 93740-0010

Department of Communications
California State University-Fullerton
Fullerton, CA 92634

Department of Journalism
California State University
    Long Beach
Long Beach, CA 90840

Department of Journalism
California State University
    Northridge
Northridge, CA 91330

Department of Journalism
San Diego State University
San Diego, CA 92182
Department of Journalism
San Francisco State University
San Francisco, CA 94132

Department of Journalism &
    Mass Communication
San Jose State University
San Jose, CA 95192

School of Journalism
University of Southern California
University Park, CA 90089-1695

School of Journalism &
    Mass Communication
University of Colorado
Boulder, CO 80309

Department of Technical Journalism
Colorado State University
Fort Collins, CO 80523

Department of Journalism
Howard University
Washington, DC 20059

College of Journalism &
    Communications
University of Florida
Gainesville, FL 32611-2084

School of Journalism, Media &
    Graphic Arts
Florida A & M University
Tallahassee, FL 32307

Department of Mass Communication
University of South Florida
Tampa, FL 33620

Communication Arts
University of West Florida
Pensacola, FL 32514

Henry W. Grady College of
    Journalism & Mass
    Communication
University of Georgia
Athens, GA 30602

Department of Journalism
University of Hawaii-Manoa
Honolulu, HI 96822

School of Journalism
Southern Illinois University
Carbondale, IL 62901

Department of Journalism
Eastern Illinois University
Charleston, IL 61920

Department of Journalism
Northern Illinois University
DeKalb, IL 60115

Medill School of Journalism
Northwestern University
Evanston, IL 60208-2101

College of Communications
University of Illinois
Urbana, IL 61801

School of Journalism
Indiana University
Bloomington, IN 47405

Department of Journalism
Ball State University
Muncie, IN 47306

Department of Journalism and
    Mass Communication
Iowa State University
Ames, IA 50011

School of Journalism &
    Mass Communication
Drake University
Des Moines, IA 50311

School of Journalism &
    Mass Communication
University of Iowa
Iowa City, IA 52242

William Allen White School of
    Journalism &
    Mass Communication
University of Kansas
Lawrence, KS 66045

A. Q. Miller School of Journalism
    & Mass Communications
Kansas State University
Manhattan, KS 66506-1501

Department of Journalism
Western Kentucky University
Bowling Green, KY 42101

School of Journalism
University of Kentucky
Lexington, KY 40506-0042

Department of Journalism &
    Radio-TV
Murray State University
Murray, KY 42071
Manship School of Journalism
Louisiana State University
Baton Rouge, LA 70803-7202

College of Journalism
University of Maryland
College Park, MD 20742

School of Journalism
Michigan State University
East Lansing, MI 48824-1212

School of Journalism and
    Mass Communication
University of Minnesota
Minneapolis, MN 5455-0418

Department of Mass
    Communications
St. Cloud State University
St. Cloud, MN 56301

Department of Journalism
University of Southern Mississippi
Hattiesburg, MS 39406-5158

Department of Mass
    Communications
Jackson State University
Jackson, MS 39217

Department of Journalism
University of Mississippi
University, MS 38677

School of Journalism
University of Missouri
Columbia, MO 65205

School of Journalism
University of Montana
Missoula, MT 59812

College of Journalism
University of Nebraska-Lincoln
Lincoln, NE 68588-0127

E.W. Scripps School of Journalism
Ohio University
Athens, OH 45701

Reynolds School of Journalism
University of Nevada-Reno
Reno, NV 89557-0040

Department of Journalism
Bowling Green State University
Bowling Green, OH 43403

Department of Journalism
University of New Mexico
Albuquerque, NM 87131

School of Journalism
Ohio State University
Columbus, OH 43210

Graduate School of Journalism
Columbia University
New York, NY 10027

School of Journalism &
    Mass Communication
Kent State University
Kent, OH 44242

Department of Journalism &
    Mass Communication
New York University
New York, NY 10003

H. H. Herbert School of Journalism
    & Mass Communication
University of Oklahoma
Norman, OK 73019

S. I. Newhouse School of
    Public Communications
Syracuse University
Syracuse, NY 13244-2100

School of Journalism &
    Broadcasting
Oklahoma State University
Stillwater, OK 74078-0195

School of Journalism &
    Mass Communications
University of North Carolina
Chapel Hill, NC 27599-3365

Department of Journalism
Oregon State University
Corvallis, OR 97331

School of Communication
University of North Dakota
Grand Forks, ND 58202

School of Journalism
University of Oregon
Eugene, OR 97403-1275

School of Communications
Pennsylvania State University
Philadelphia, PA 16802

Department of Journalism
Temple University
Philadelphia, PA 19122

College of Journalism
    & Mass Communications
University of South Carolina
Columbia, SC 29208

Department of Mass Communication
South Dakota State University
Brookings, SD 57007-0596

Department of Communication
East Tennessee State University
Johnson City, TN 37614

School of Journalism
University of Tennessee
Knoxville, TN 37996

Journalism Department
Memphis State University
Memphis, TN 38152

School of Mass Communication
Middle Tennessee State University
Murfreesboro, TN 37132

Department of Journalism
University of Texas-Austin
Austin, TX 78712

Department of Journalism
Texas A & M University
College Station, TX 76019

Department of Journalism
University of North Texas
Denton, TX 76201

Department of Journalism
Texas Christian University
Fort Worth, TX 76129

School of Mass Communications
Texas Tech University
Lubbock, TX 79409-3082

Department of Communications
Brigham Young University
Provo, UT 84602

Department of Communication
University of Utah
Salt Lake City, UT 84112

Department of Journalism &
    Mass Communications
Washington and Lee University
Lexington, VA 24450

School of Mass Communication
Virginia Commonwealth University
Richmond, VA 23284-2034

School of Communications
University of Washington
Seattle, WA 98195

College of Communication
Marquette University
Milwaukee, WI 53233

School of Journalism &
    Mass Communication
University of Wisconsin-Madison
Madison, WI 53706

Department of Journalism
University of Wisconsin-Oshkosh
Oshkosh, WI 54901-8696

Department of Journalism
University of Wisconsin-River Falls
River Falls, WI 54022

Perley Isaac Reed School of Journalism
West Virginia University
Morgantown, WV 26506-6010

The above list contains only those schools or departments accredited by the Accrediting Council on Education in Journalism and Mass Communication.

AEJMC
1621 College Street
University of South Carolina
Columbia, SC 29208-0251
(803) 777-2005

The Association for Education in Journalism and Mass Communication (AEJMC) lists 410 member institutions. The Speech Communication Association (SCA) lists about 750 member institutions. Both organizations supply complete lists upon request.

SCA
5105 Backlick Road, Bldg. E
Annandale, VA 22003
(703) 750-0533

WESTERN EUROPE

Austria

Department of Mass Communication
University of Salzburg
Residentzpaltz 1
5020 Salzburg

Department of Communication
University of Vienna
Dr. Karl Lueger-Ring 1
1010 Vienna

Katolische Medienakademie
Singer Strasse 7
Stg. 4
1010 Vienna

Belgium

Centre d'Etudes des Techniques de
    Diffusion
Université Libre de Bruxelles
44, avenue Jeanne
Brussels 5

Département de Communication
Faculté de Droit
Université de Gand
Universiteitstraat 8
9000 Gand

Association Catholique
    Internationale pour la Radio et
    la Television (UNDA)
12, rue de l'Orme
1040 Brussels

Centrum voor
    Communicatiewetenschappen
Katholieke Universiteit Leuven
Evanstraat 2A
3000 Leuven

Institut d' Etudes Supérieures en
    Communication Sociale
Université de Mons
20, place du Parc
7000 Mons

Le Département de Communication
    Sociale
Université de Louvain
14, ruelle de la Lanterne Magique
1348 Louvain-la-Neuve

Sectie Communicatiewetenschap
Faculteit der Letteren en
    Wijsbegeerte
Vrije Universiteit
Pleilaan 2
1050 Brussels

Institut National Superieur des Arts
    du Spectacle (INSAS)
8, rue Thérésienne
1000 Brussels

Départment de Communication
Université de Liège
7, place du 20-Août
4000 Liège

Seminaire de la Presse et des
    Grands Moyens
    de Communication
Université de Gand
Universiteitstraat 14.
9000 Gand

nstitut Belge d'Information et
    de Documentation
3 Rue Montoyer
1040 Brussels

Denmark

Danmarks Journalisthøjskole
Olof Palmes Alle 11
8200 Aarhus

Department of Communication
University of Aarhus
Ndr. Ringgade
8000 Aarhus

Department of Communication
University of Copenhagen
Frue Plads/Noerregade 10
POB 2177
1017 Copenhagen

Department of Communication
University of Odense
Campusvej 55
5230 Odense

Department of Communication
Aalborg University Center
POB 159
Langagervej 2
9100 Aalborg

Deparment of Communication
Roskilde University Center
POB 260
Marbjergvej 35
4000 Roskilde

Finland

Department of Communication
University of Helsinki
00100 Helsinki

Institute of Journalism &
    Mass Communication
University of Tampere
POB 607
33101 Tampere 10

France

Institut Français de Presse
83 bis, rue Notre Dame des Champs
75006 Paris

Direction de la Formation
    Professionnelle
4, avenue de l'Europe
94360 Brie-sur-Marne

Centre de Formation des
   Journalistes (CFJ)
33, rue du Louvre
75002 Paris

Ecole Supérieure de Journalisme
   (ESJ)
50, rue Granthier de Chatillon
59000 Lille

Centre Universitaire
   d'Enseignement de Journalisme
Université de Strasbourg III
10, rue Schiller
67 Strasbourg

Département Carrières de l'Information
Institut Universitaire de Technologie
Université de Bordeaux III
33405 Talence

Centre de Formation
29, rue de Vanne
92120 Montrouge

Centre Transméditerranéen de la
   Communication
Université d'Aix-Marseille II
Jardins de Pharo
58, blvd. Charles Livon
13007 Marseille

Germany

Institut für Medienwissenschaft
   und Literatursoziologie
Technische Universität Berlin
Ernst-Reuter-Platz 7
1000 Berlin 10

Institut für Publizistik
Freie Universität Berlin
Hagenstrasse 56
1000 Berlin 33

Universität Goettingen
Humboldtallee 38
3400 Goettingen

Sektion für Publizistik und
   Kommunikation
Universität Bochum
4630 Bochum

Institüt für Journalistik
Universität Gottingen
Nikolausberger Weg 5c
34 Gottingen

Karl-Marx-Universität
Karl-Marx-Platz 9
7010 Leipzig

Institut für Publizistik
Karolinenplatz 3
8000 Munich 2

Akademie für Journalistik
Deutsche Welle
P.O.B. 100444
Räderbergguertel 50
5000 Köln

Institut für
  Kommunikationswissenschaft
Universität Köln
Leyholdstrasse 62
5000 Köln 51

Deutsche Journalistenschule
Altheimer Eck 3
8000 Munich 2

Greece

University of Athens
Odos Panesepistimiou 30
10679 Athens

Pantios University of Social &
  Political Sciences
Leoforos A. Syngrou 136
17671 Athens

Ireland

School of Journalism
College of Commerce-Rathmines
Rathmines

School of Communications
Dublin City University
Dublin

Graduate Center for Journalism
University College-Galway
Galway

Italy

LUISS Universita
Via Pola 12
00198 Rome

Corso propedeutico alle
  Professioni Publicistiche
Universita di Roma
00158 Rome

Higher Institute of Journalism
State University of Camerino
Via del Bastione
62032 Camerino

Institute for Journalism Studies
Vicolo S. Uffizio 15
90133 Palermo

Scuola de Giornalismo
University of Turin
Via Verdi 8
10124 Turin

Department of Sociology
Universita di Roma "La Sapienza"
Piazzale Aldo Moro 5
00185 Rome

Department of Political Science
Universita di Napoli
Corso Umberto 1
80138 Naples
Department of Journalism
Catholic University of the
  Sacred Heart
Largo Gemell 1
20123 Milan

Netherlands

Instituut voor Preswetenschap
Postbus 9108
Universiteit van Amsterdam
Oude Turfmarkt 151
Amsterdam 1012 CE

Department of Mass Communication
Universiteit van Amsterdam
Oude Hoogstr. 24
1012 CE Amsterdam

Instituut voor Massacommunicatie
Katholieke Universiteit
POB 9102
Comeniuslaan 4
6500 HC Nijmegen

Department of Sociology
State University of Groningen
Grote Markt 23
9418 HR Groningen

Department of Mass Communication
University of Amsterdam
Spui 21
1012 WX Amsterdam

Department of Communication
Tilburg University
Hogeschoolaan 225
POB 90153
5000 LE Tilburg

Department of Communication
University of Utrecht
Heidelberglaan 8
POB 80125
3508 TC Utrecht

Department of Communication
University of Rotterdam
Burgemeester Oudlaan 50
POB 1738
3000 DR Rotterdam

Norway

Norsk Journalisthøgskole
POB 8167 Dep.
0034 Oslo 1

Institute for Journalism
P.O.B. 4084
4601 Kristiansand

NIJ House
Victoria Island
1601 Fredrikstad

Portugal

Faculdade de Letras
Universidade de Lisboa
Lisbon 4

Faculty of Literature
Rua Duques de Braganca 7
Lisbon 2

School of Communication
New University of Lisbon
Praca do Príncipe Real 26
1200 Lisbon

Advanced School of Social
    Communication
Campo dos Mártires da Patria 2
1100 Lisbon

Spain

Facultad de Ciencias de la
    Información
Universidad Autónoma
    de Barcelona
Campus de Bellaterra
08193 Barcelona,

Facultad de Ciencias de
    la Información
Universidad del Pais Vasco
Apartado 644
Bilbao

Center for University Studies
Julian Romea, 23
28003 Madrid

Facultad de Ciencias de
    la Información
Universitas Complutensis
    de Madrid
Ciudad Universitaria
28040 Madrid 3

Radio Television Institute
Dehesa de la Villa
28040 Madrid

Facultad de Ciencias de
    la Información
Universidad de Navara
31080 Pamplona

Sweden

Mass Communication Unit
Department of Political Science
University of Göteborg
402 21 Göteborg

University of Stockholm
Gjorwellsgatan 26
10691 Stockholm

Audience and Programme
    Research Department
Box 5053
10510 Stockholm

NORDICOM-Sweden
Box 5048
University of Göteborg
40221 Göteborg

Department of Information Techniques
University College of Vaxjo
35005 Vaxjo

Department of Sociology
Box 5048
University of Lund
22100 Lund

School of Journalism &
   Mass Communication
University of Göteborg
Vasaparken
41124 Göteborg

Switzerland

Journalism Seminar
University of Zurich
Rämistrasse 71
8006 Zurich

Institut de Journalisme et
   Communication Sociale
Université de Fribourg
1700 Fribourg

Ecole de Journalisme
Université de Neuchâtel
Ave du ler Mars 26
2000 Neuchâtel

Centre Romand de Formation
   des Journalistes
Ave Florimont 1
1006 Lausanne

Medienausbildungzentrum
Villa Krämerstein
St. Niklausen Strasse 59
6047 Kastanienbaum

United Kingdom

Training Department
Reuters News Agency
184 Fleet Street
London EC4 4AJ

The European Institute for the
   Media
University of Manchester
Manchester M13 9PL

International Broadcast Institute
Commonwealth Press Union
Studio House
Tavistock Square
London WCIH 9LG

Graduate Centre for Journalism
City University of London
Northampton Square
London EC1 V 0HB

Centre for Journalism Studies (CJS)
University of Wales
69 Park Place
Cardiff CF1 3AS

BBC Journalist Training
Broadcasting House
London W1A 1AA

The National Film and Television
   School
Station Road
Beaconsfield
Bucks HP9 1 LG

Journalism Department
Napier Polytechnic
Colinton Road
Edinburgh EH 10 5DT

Journalism Department
University of Strathclyde
16 Richmond Street
Glasgow G1 2BP

Journalism Department
Lancashire Polytechnic-Preston
Preston, PR1 2TQ

School of Communication
Polytechnic of Central London
18-22 Riding House Street
London W1P 7PD

Journalism Department
Darlington College of Technology
Cleveland Avenue
Durham DL3 7BB

Journalism Department
Highbury College of Technology
Dover Court Road
Cosham
Portsmouth PO6 2SA

Journalism Department
Harlow College
College Square
The High
Harlow, CM20 1LT

Journalism Department
Stradbroke College
St. Barnabas Centre
Alderson Road
Sheffield 2

School of English Studies,
Journalism and Philosophy
POB 68
University College of Wales-
Cardiff
Cardiff CF1 3XA

EASTERN/CENTRAL EUROPE

Albania

Professional Organization of
    Journalists
Bashkimi i Gazetarve te Shquiperise
Tirana

Czechoslovakia

Faculty of Journalism
Charles University
Smetanovo nabrezi 6
110 01 Prague 1

Department of Journalism
Faculty of Philosophy
Comenius University
Gondova 2
80 601 Bratislava

Hungary

IOJ International Institute for the
    Training of Journalists
Kapy utca 49/B
1025 Budapest

Institute of Mass Communication
Akademia utca 17
1054 Budapest V

Poland

Institute of Journalism
Institute of Arts and Sciences
University of Warsaw
Nowy Swiat 69
00-046 Warszawa 64

Romania

Academia "Stephan Gheorghiu"
B-dul Armata Poporului 1-3
Bucuresti 6

Russia

Journalism Faculty
University of Kiev
Kiev

Faculty of Journalism
University of Leningrad
Leningrad

Faculty of International Journalism
Moscow Institute of International
    Relations
53 Metrostroevskaja st.
Moscow

Faculty of Journalism
Moscow University
Prospect Marxa 20
Moscow K-9

Yugoslavia

Yugoslovenski Institut
   za Novinarstvo
University of Belgrade
Njegoseva 72
POB 541
Belgrade

Fakultet Politickih Nauka (FPN)
Jove Illica 165
11000 Belgrade

**Note: With the changes that
have taken place in Eastern
and Central Europe, this list
may no longer be reliable.**

ASIA/PACIFIC

Afghanistan

Department of Journalism
Faculty of Letters
Kabul University
Kabul

Australia

Australian Film and Television
    School
15 Lyonpark Road
2073 Sydney
NSW

Deakin University
Geelong
Victoria 3217

Training Department
Australian Broadcasting Company
145-153 Elizabeth
2001 Sydney
NSW

Education Department
University of Adelaide
North Terrace
Adelaide

South Australian College of
    Advanced Education
Lorne Avenue
5072 Adelaide
South Australia

Australian Film, Television
    and Radio School
CNR Balaclava Road &
    Epping Highway
North Ryde
2113 Sydney
NSW

Hunter Institute of Higher
    Education
Rankin Drive
Waratah West
2298 New Castle

Journalism Department
South Australian College of
    Advanced Education
5072 Magill
South Australia

Bangladesh

Department of Mass
    Communication and Journalism
University of Dhaka
Ramna
1000 Dhaka

Press Institute of Bangladesh
3 Circuit House Road
Dhaka-2

China

School of Journalism
Department of Languages
Beijing University
Beijing

Institute for Journalistic Research
Academy for Social Sciences
Beijing

School of Journalism
Fudan University
Shanghai

Department of Journalism &
    Communication
Xiamen University
Fujian

Department of Journalism
Wuhan University
Luo Jia Hill
Wuhan

All-China Journalists' Association
50 Xijiaominxiang
Beijing

Department of Journalism
Jinan University
Shipai
Guangzhou

International Journalism Training
    Center
57 Xuenwumen Xidajie
Beijing

Journalism Department
People's University of China
39 Hai Dian Road
Beijing

Fiji

School of Humanities
University of the South Pacific
Suva

Hong Kong

Chinese University of Hong Kong
Shatin, N.T.

India

Department of Journalism
Osmania University
500007 Hyderabad
Andra Pradesh

Department of Jounalism
Saurashtra University
University Campus
360005 Rajkot
Gujarat

Department of Mass
    Communication and Journalism
Karnataka University
Dharavad
580003 Karnataka

Department of Journalism
Marathwada University
Aurangabad
431004 Maharashtra

Department of Journalism and
    Mass Communication
Berhampur University
760007 Berhampur
Ganjam
Orissa

Department of Communication
Punjabi University
147002 Patiala
Punjab

Department of Journalism
University of Kerala
695034 Trivandrum
Kerala

Department of Journalism
Himachal Pradesh University
Summer Hill
171005 Simla

Department of Journalism
University of Poona
Ganeshkhind
411007 Pune
Maharashtra

Department of Communication
Bangalore University
560056 Bangalore
Karnataka State

Department of Journalism
Ranchi University
834008 Ranchi
Bihar

Department of Journalism
University of Punjab
160014 Chandigarh
Union Territory

Department of Journalism
University of Madras
Chepauk
Triplicane Po
600005 Madras
Tamil Nadu

Department of Journalism
University of Calicut
PO Calicut University
673635 Thenhipalam
Kerala

Department of Journalism
University of Mysore
POB 407
570005 Mysore
Karnataka

Film and Television Institute
    of India
Law College Road
Poona 4

All India Radio Staff Training
    Institute
Rosary Lane School
Kingsway Camp
110009 New Delhi

Department of Journalism and
    Mass Communication
Banaras Hindu University
221005 Varanasai

India Institute of Mass
    Communication
D-13, South Extension II
110049 New Delhi

Press Institute of India
Sapru House Annex
Barkhamba Road
110001 New Delhi

Institute of Communication Arts
St. Xavier's College
400001 Bombay

Indonesia

Department of Communication
University of Sumatra
Jl. Universitas 9
Kampus USU
20155 Medan

Department of Communication
University of Hasanuddin
Jl. Mesjid Raya 55
Ujung Pandang

Department of Communication
University of Sebelas Maret
Jl. Ir Sutami 36A
Surakarta

Department of Communication
    Science
University of Airlangga
Jl. Darmawangsa 1
Surabaya

School of Communication
Sekolah Tinggi Ilmu Komunikasi
Semarang

Department of Agricultural
    Communication
Bogor Institute of Agriculture
Jl. Raya Pajajaran
Bogor

School of Journalism
Sekolah Tinggi Ilmu
Kewartawanan
Jakarta

Department of Communication
University of Diponego
Jl. Imam Barjo, Sh. 1-3
POB 270
Semarang

Department of Communication
University of Gadjah Mada
Bulaksumur
55281 Yogyakarta

Faculty of Communication
Jakarta Institute for Social and
    Political Science
Jakarta

Department of Communication
University of Indonesia
POB 295
Jl. Salemba Raya 4
Jakarta

School of Publisistik
Alwashijah University
Berabai
South Kalimantan

Indonesian Institute for
    Press Training
Jalan Abdul Muis 50
Jakarta

Japan

Communication Design Institute
Kyoto Shinyo Kinko Building
Kawaramachi at Oike
Kyoto

Department of Mass
    Communication
Tokai University
1117 Kita kaname Hiratsuka-shi
Kanagawa-Ken

Asian Broadcasting Union
    c/o NHK Broadcasting Centre
Nippon Hoso Kyokai
2-2-1 Jinnan, Shibuya-ku
Tokyo 150

Japan Newspaper Publishers and
    Editors Association (NSK)
2-2-1, Uchisaiwai-cho
Chiyoda-ku
Tokyo 100

School of Journalism
Meiji University
Tokyo

School of Mass Communication
Seijo University
6-1-20 Seijo Setagaya-ku
Tokyo

Faculty of Broadcasting
Konancho Minami Kawachi
Osaka University of Arts
Osaka

Department of Mass
    Communication
Imadegawa Karasumaru
Kamikyoku
Doshisya University
Kyoto

Department of Communication
Faculty of Letters
Sophia University
7 Kioicho Chiyoda-ku
Tokyo
Institute of Communication
    Research
Mita
Keio University
Minato-ku
Tokyo

Department of Journalism
Faculty of Law
Nihon University Tokyo
Tokyo

Malaysia

Communication Program
Universiti Sains Malaysia
Minden
11800 Penang

Organization of Asian News
    Agencies (OANA)
Bangunan Mcoba
Jalan Syed Putra
01002 Kuala Lumpur

National News Agency of
Malaysia (BERNAMA)
50700 Kuala Lumpur

School of Mass Communication
Institut Teknologi Mara
Shah Alam
Selangor Darul Ehsan

Department of Communication
Universiti Kebangsaan Malaysia
43600 Bangi
Selangor

Department of Writing
Universiti Malaya
Lembach Pantai
59100 Kuala Lumpur

Department of Communication
    Development
Universiti Pertanian Malaysia
43400 Serdang
Selangor Darul Ehsan

Mongolia

Department of Journalism
Mongolian State University
Ulan-Bator

Papua New Guinea

School of Journalism
University of Papua New Guinea
UPNG POB 320
Port Moresby

New Zealand

Centre for the Study of
    Educational Communication
    and Media
New Zealand Press Association
Limited (NZPA)
93 Boulcott Street
Wellington

Pakistan

Department of Mass
    Communication
University of Punjab
Quaid-e-Azam Campus
Lahore-20

Press Institute of Pakistan
c/o Pakistan Herald Publications
Haroon House (3F)
Dr Ziauddin Ahmed Rd.
Karachi

Department of Journalism
   & Mass Communication
Gomal University
Dera Ismail Khan

Philippines

Department of English and Mass
   Communication
Angeles City Foundation
   University
Angeles City

Asia Institute of Journalism
Bangkok

Department of Communication
   Arts
Ateneo de Davao University
POB 13
E. Jacinto Street
8000 Davao City

Department of Communication
Ateneo de Manila University
POB 154
Manila

Regional Applied Communication
   Office
Central Luzon State University
Muñoz
Nueva Ecija

Communication Program
College of Arts and Sciences
Centro Escolar University
9 Mendiola St.
San Miguel
Manila

Department of Communication
   Arts
De la Salle University
2401 Taft Ave.
1004 Manila

Mass Communication Department
Divine Word University
   of Tacloban
Veteranos Ave.
Tacloban City
Leyte

Department of Communication
Far Eastern University
POB 609
Manila

School of Development
   Communication
Isabela State University
San Fabian
Echague
1318 Isabela

Department of Development
   Communication
Mariano Marcos State University
Batac
0305 Ilocos Norte

Department of Mass
    Communication
Pamantasan Ng Lungsod Ng
Maynila
Intramuros
Manila

Communication Arts Department
Philippine Women's University
Taft Ave.
1004 Manila

Department of Mass
    Communication
Polytechnic University of the
    Philippines
Anonas St.
Santa Mesa
Manila

School of Communication
Silliman University
6000 Dumaguete City

Department of Mass
    Communication
University of Negros
Occidental-Recoletos
Lizares Ave.
POB 214
6100 Bacolad City

College of Mass Communication
University of the Philippines
Diliman
Quezon City

Department of Development
    Communication
University of the Philippines
Los Baños

Communication Arts Department
Saint Louis University
POB 71
A. Bonifacio St.
2600 Baguio City

DYAR Mass Communication
University of San Jose Recoletos
Crnr. Magallens and P. Lopez
Streets
Cebu City

Journalism Department
University of Santo Tomás
España St.
Manila

Department of Development
    Communication
University of Southern Mindanao
Kabacan
North Cotabato

Communication Department
Xavier University
Misamis Oriental
9000 Cagayan de Oro City
Mindanao

Department of Communication
Ateneo de Cagayan
9000 Cagayan de Oro City
Mindanao

Press Foundation of Asia
P.O.B.1843
1500 Roxas Boulevard
Manila

Singapore

School of Journalism
Times Press Foundation
Times Industrial Building
422 Thomson Road
1129 Singapore

Journalism Course
Department of Government
    and Public Administration
Nanyang University
Upper Jurong Road
22 Singapore

South Korea

Korean Press Institute
Korean Press Center Building,
12th Floor
1-25 Taepyung-Ro
Chung-Ku
Seoul

Sungkok Foundation for
    Journalism
188 Chongjin-dong
Chongro-ku
Seoul, South Korea

Training Department
Seoul Press Foundation
541, Namdaemunno 5-ga
Chung-ug
Seoul, South Korea

Sri Lanka

Department of Mass
    Communication
Faculty of Humanities
University of Sri Lanka
Colombo

Department of Mass
    Communication
Faculty of Humanities
University of Sri Lanka
Vidyalankard Campus
Kelaniya

Worldwide International
Foundation
10 Kinross Avenue
Colombo 4

Thailand

Faculty of Communication Arts
Chulalongkorn University
Phyathai Rd.
10330 Bangkok

Faculty of Journalism and Mass
    Communication
Thammasat University
2 Prachand Rd.
10200 Bangkok

Faculty of Communication Arts
Bangkok University
110/1-4 Prachacheun Rd.
Bangkhen
10210 Bangkok

School of Communication Arts
Sukothai Thammathirat Open
University
9/9 Moo 9
Tambol Bangpood
Pakkred
11120 Nonthaburi

Department of Mass
    Communication
Chiang Mai University
130 Huay Kaew Rd.
Muang District
50002 Chiang Mai

Department of Communication
Kasetsart University
Bangkhen
10900 Bangkok

Department of Communication
Thai Chamber of Commerce
University
126/1 Vipawadee Rangsit Road
Huay Kwang
Phayathai
10400 Bangkok

Division of Communication
Ramkhamhaeng University
Ramkhamhaeng Rd.
Huamark
10240 Bangkok

LATIN AMERICA & THE CARIBBEAN

Argentina

Centro de Estudios de Ciencias
de la Información (CECI)
Libertad 1071
CP Uruguay 680
Buenos Aires

Escuela de Periodismo y
Ciencias de la
Información
Universidad Católica Argentina
Maipú 1369
Rosario. Provincia de Santa Fé

Escuela de Periodismo José M.
Estrada
La Rioja 622
Concordia

Escuela Argentina de
Periodismo
Santa Fé 4320
1425 Buenos Aires

Escuela de Ciencias de la
Información
Universidad Nacional de Río
Cuarto
San Lorenzo 1021
Río Cuarto
Instituto Grafotecnico
Escuela Superior de Periodismo
Moreno 1921
Buenos Aires

Instituto de Periodismo Domingo
F. Sarmiento
Mitre No. 2474
Mar del Plata

Escuela Democratica de
Periodismo
Sarmiento 530
Concordia

School of Journalism and
Communication
John F. Kennedy University
Bartolome Mitre 1411
1087 Buenos Aires

Círculo de la Prensa
Escuela Superior de Periodismo
Instituto de Opinión Pública
Cangallo 2158
Buenos Aires

Departamento de Medios de
Comunicación
Universidad Nacional de Comahue
9 de Octubre 453
Gral. Roca
Provincia de Río Negro

Círculo de la Prensa
Escuela de Periodismo
Rodriguez Peña No. 80
Buenos Aires

Escuela de Comunicación
  Social
Universidad Nacional del
  Rosario
Córdoba 2020
Rosario. Provincia de Santa Fé

Facultad de Ciencias de la
  Educación y de la
  Comunicación Social
Universidad del Salvador
Callao 966
CP 1023
1025 Buenos Aires

Departamento de Ciencias de
  la Comunicación
Facultad de Ciencias Sociales
Universidad Nacional
  de San Juan
Rivadavia 5400
CP 202
San Juan

Instituto de Ciencias de la
  Información
Corrientes 3172
Buenos Aires

Instituto Superior de
  Comunicaciones Sociales
  COSAL (Comunicaciones
  Salesianas)
Don Bosco 400 E
Buenos Aires

Escuela de Ciencias de la
  Información
Universidad Nacional de
  Córdoba
Ciudad Universitaria
5000 Cordoba

Escuela de Periodismo
  "Ovidio Lagos"
Moreno 925
Rosario. Provinicia de Santa Fe

Instituto Católico de Estudios
  Sociales
Junin 3063
CP 34. C. C.
Buenos Aires

Facultad de Ciencias Sociales
Universidad Nacional de
  Lomas de Zamora
Ruta Provincial No. 4.
esq. Juan XXIII
Lomas de Zamora 1832

Escuela Superior De
  Periodismo
Universidad Nacional de la
  Plata
Calle 10 No. 1074
La Plata 1900

Escuela de Periodismo Deportivo
Calle Rodriguez Peña 628
Buenos Aires

Facultad de Ciencias de da
  Información y Opinión
Corrientes 1723
Buenos Aires

Escuela de Periodismo
Instituto de Estudios
  Superiores de Salta
92 Salta
Buenos Aires

Escuela de Ciencias de la
  Comunicación Social
Universidad Nacional
  de Entre Ríos
8 de Junie 600
Concepción del Uraguay
Entre Ríos

Escuela Superior de Periodismo
Belgrano 1041
Mendoza

Bolivia

Departamento de
  Comunicación Social
Universidad Católica Boliviana
Av. 14 de Septiembre 4807
CP 4805
La Paz

Carrera Comunicaciones
Universidad Privada de
  Santa Cruz de la Sierra
España 269
CP 2944
Santa Cruz

Brazil

Curso de Comunicacao Social
  do Ceub
  (Centro de Ensino Unificado
  de Brasilia)
E.U.N. 707/709
Asa Norto. Campus Universitario
70000 D.F.

Departamento de Comunicacao
  Social
Universidad Federal de Minas
  Gerais
Faculdade de Filosofia y
  Ciêncas Humanas
CP 253
3000 M.G. Belo Horizonte

Faculdade de Comunicacao
Universidad Católica
  de Minas Ferais
Av. D. José Gaspar 500
Barrio de Caracao Eucaristico
CP 2685
30000 Belo Horizonte MG.

Curso de Comunicacao
Falculdade Ciêncas y Letras de
  Belo Horizonte
Av. Antonio Carlos 581
30000 Belo Horizonte MG.

Departamento de Comunicacao
Instituto Cultural Newton Paiva
Ferreira
Rua Tarnaios 792
30000 Belo Horizonte MG.

Curso de Comunicacao Social
Universidad Federal
  de Paraná
Instituto de Ciências Humanas
Gal. Carneiro
80000 Curitiba Paraná

Departamento de Comunicacao
  Social
Universidad Federal de Ceará
Faculdade de Ciências Sociales
Rua Romas Aéroly 1505
Aldeota
CP 1257
60000 Fortaleza Ceará

Departamento de Comunicacao
Universidad Federal de Goias
Instituto de Ciências
Humanas y Letras
74000 Goiania GO.

Departamento de Comunicacao
Universidad Federal de Juiz
  de Fora
Faculdade de Doreito
Campos Mortelos
36100 Juis de Fora NG.

Curso de Comunicacao E.
  Journalismo
Universidad Federal de
  Amazonas
Faculdade de Filosofia,
  Ciências e Letras
Rua Monsenhor Coutino
CP 724/734
69000 Manaus AM.

Faculdade de Journalismo
Fundacao José Augusto
Rua Jundfa 641
59000 Natal RGN.

Instituto de Arte e
  Comunicacao Social
Universidad Federal
  Fluminense
Instituto de Arte e
  Comunicacao
Prac del Valonquinho
CP 40
24000 Niteroi
Río de Janeiro

Curso de Comunicacao Social
Universidad Católica de
  Pelotas
Faculdade de Filosofia
Rua Félix da Cunha 412
96100 Pelotas RGS.
Casilla 402

Faculdade de Biblioteconomia
  e Comunicacao
Universidad Federal de RGS
Rua Jacinto Gómez 540
90000 Porto Alegre RGS.

Curso de Comunicacao Social
Universidad Caxias
  de Sul Rua
Francsco Getulio Vargas
CP 1352
95100 Caixas de Sul RGS.

Curso de Comunicacao Social
Universidad Federal de
　Santa María
Centro de Ciêncas Jurídicas
　Económicas y
　Adminstrativas
Rua Floriano Pexoto 1184
97100 Santa María RGS.

Centro Educativos das
　Comunicacaoes Sociales
　do Nordeste (CECOSNE)
Universidad Federal de
　Pernambuco
Rua José Osorio 124
B. Nadalena
50030 Recife, Pernambuco

Derpartamento de
　Comunicacao Social
Universidad Católica de
　Pernambuco
Cenro de Ciêncas Sociales
Rua de Principe
CP 526
50000 Recife, Pernambuco

Escola Superior de Relacoes
　Publicas
Av. Rosa e Silva 891
50000 Recife, Pernambuco

Departamento de Comunicacao
Universidad Federal de Parná
Rua 15 de Nobembro
86100 Londrina-Paraná

Curso de Comunicacao Social
María Liefa de Oliveira
　Candia
Centro de Educacao
Comunicacao e Artes de UCL
Campus Universitario
CP 2111
56100 Londrina Paraná

Escula de Comunicacao
Universidad Federal de
　Río de Janeiro
Av. Pasteur 250. FUNDOS
Río de Janeiro

Departamento de Comunicacao
　Social da PUC/RJ
Pontificia Universidad
　Católica de Río de Janeiro
Rua Marques de Sao Vicante
2000 225 Gánea RS/RG.

Departamento de Comunicacao
　Social
Universidad Estudual de
　Guanabara
Instituto de Psicología e
　Comunicacao
Av. 218 de septembre 111, 2do.
dual
Tijuca ZC11
20000 Río De Janeiro

Faculdade de Comunicacao
　Social
Faculadade Integradas Estacio
Rua de Bispo 83
20000 Río de Janeiro

Faculdade de Comunicacao
e Turismo
Praia de Botafogo 266
20000 Río de Janeiro GB.

Curso de Comunicacao Social
Rua Manoel Vitorino 625
Piendade
30000 Río de Janeiro G.B.

Curso de Journalismo
Faculdade de Filosofía de
Campos
Praca Barao de Rio Branco
CP 15
28100 Campos, Estado de
Río de Janeiro

Departamento de Comunicacao
Universidad Federal de Bahía
Escola de Biblioteconomía e
Comunicacao
Ciudad Universitaria
Vale de Canela
40000 Salvador, Bahía

Escola de Comunicacaoes e
Artes
Universidad de Sao Paulo
Ciudad Universitaria
Butanza Slaes Oliveirra
CP 8191
01000 Sao Paulo

Faculdade de Comunicacao
Fundacao Armando Alvares
Penteado
Rua Alagoas 903
Pacaembú
CP 01242
Sao Paulo

Curso de Relacoes Publicas
Faculdade de Comunicacao
Social
Instituto Educacional
Piracicabano
Rua da Boa Norte 1257
CP 63
13400 Piracicaba, Estado de Sao
Paulo

Faculdade de Comunicacao
Social "Casper Líbero"
Fundacao Casper Líbero
Av. Paulista 900 5te andar
01310 Sao Paulo

Faculdade de Comunicacao
Alcántara Machado
Av. Jabaquara 2180
CP 04046
Sao Paulo 040
Escola Superior de Propaganda
e Marketing
Rua Humaitá 488/489
CP 01321
Sao Paulo

Faculdade de Turismo do
Morumbi
Rua Visconde de Nacar
Sao Paulo

Faculdade Iberoamericana de
   Letras y Ciêncas Humanas
CP 01318
Sao Paulo

Faculdade de Comunicacao
   Social Anhembi
Rua Case de Ator 90
Cepo 04546
Vila Olimpio
01317 Sao Paulo

Curso de Comunicacao
Faculdade de Filosofía
   Ciêncas e Letras
Universidad Católica de
   Campinas
Rua Merecheal Deodoro 1099
13100 Cappinas
Sao Paulo

Faculdade de Comunicacao
   Social
Instituto Metodista de Ensino
   Superior
Rua de Sacremento 2306 B.C.
CP 5.002
09720 San Bernardo de Campo
Sao Paulo

Curso de Relacaoes Publicas
Funducao Morning Basarian
   13200
Itapetininga
Sao Paulo

Federaco das Faculdades Braz
   Cubas
Comunicacao Social
Rua Francisco Franco 133
087 Mogi das Cruzes
Estado de Sao Paulo

Faculadade de Comunicacao
Organizacao Hogiana OMEC
Faculdade de Ciências
   Económicas
Contables Administrativas, R.S.
Jose 141
08700 Hogi das Cruzes
Sao Paulo

Faculdade de Comunicacao de
   Santos
Rua 7 de septembre 34
11100 Santos
Sao Paulo

Federacao de Establecimentos
   de Ensino Superior em
   Novo
Hamburgo Feevale
Escola de Relacoes Públicas
Av. Mauricao Cardese 510
93500-Novo Hamburgo
CP 2121
Rio Grande Do Sul

Departamento de Comunicacao
   e Artes
Fundacao Universidad de
   Maranbao
Instituto de Letras e Artes
Praoa Gonoalvos Días
65000 Sao Luiz
Maranbao

Curso de Comunicacao Social
Escola de Administracao
Publica de Estade de Maranbao
Av. des Franceses
Alemanba
65000 Sao Luiz
Maranbao

Centro de Comunicacao
Universidad de Vale de Rio
    dos Sinos
Praca Tirandentas 35
CP 275
Sao Leopolde R.G.S.

Instituto de Arte de
    Comunicacao
Universidad Católica de
    Petrópolis
CP 944 Petrópolis
25600 Petrópolis
Río de Janeiro

Instituto de Letras de Artes e
    Comunicacao
Universidad Federal do Segipe
Aracalú Segipe
Rua de Campos 177

Chile

Escuela de Peridismo
Universidad Católica de Chile
Facultad de Fiolosofía y
    Ciencias de la Educación
Diagonal Oriente 3300
Santiago
Departamento de Ciencias y
    Tecnicas de la Comunicación
Universidad de Chile
Facultad de Ciencias Sociales
CP 1506
Santiago

Area de Comunicación Visual
Universidad de Chile
Departamento de Diseño
Calle Cochrane 1323
CP 1597
Concepción

Escuela de Periodismo y
    Comunicaciones
Universidad de Concepción
Barros Arana 1769
CP 42-C
Concepción

Escuela de Ciencias de la
    Comunicación Colectiva
Universidad de Chile
    de Valparaiso
Facultad de Ciencias Sociales
Av. Gran Bretania
CP 3740
Valparaiso

Escuela de Comunicación Social
Universidad del Norte
Instituto de Ciencias Sociales
CP 1280
Antofagasta

Colombia

Escuale de Ciencias de la
    Comunicación
Universidad de América
Calle 10 No 644
Bogotá

Facultad de Ciencias de la
    Comunicación Social
Pontificia Universidad
    Javieriana
Carrera 7 No 40-62
Bogotá

Facultad de Ciencias de
    Comunicación Social
Fundación Universidad de
    Bogotá
Jorge Tadeo Lozeno
Calle 23 No. 4-47
CP 34185
Bogotá

Facultad de Comunicación
    Social
Universidad Externado de
    Colombia
Calle 12 No. 1-17 Este
Bogotá

Facultad de Comunicación
    Social
Universidad Pontificia
    Bolivariana
La Playa x Córdoba 1178
CP A.A. 1178
Medellín
Antioquia

Departamento de Ciencias de
    la Comunicación
Universidad de Antioquia
Facultad de Ciencias y
    Humanidades
Ciudad Universitaria
CP 1226
Medellín
Antioquia

Escuela de Ciencias de la
    Comunicaión Social
Universidad Autónoma del
    Caribe
Cra. 46 No 88-26
CP 2754
Barranquilla

Ciencias de la Comunicación
Instituto Superior de Educación
Calle 70 No 11-79
Bogotá

Departamento de Ciencias de
    la Comunicación
División de Humanidades
Universidad del Valle
    Melendez
Facultad de Filosofía y Historia
CP 2188
Cali
Valle

Facultad de Periodismo
Universidad de Sau
  Buenaventura
Cra. 5e. No 9-02
Cali
Valle

Facultad de Comunicación
  Social y Pertiodismo
Universidad de la Sabana
Calle 70 No 11-79
CP 53753
Bogotá

Costa Rica

Central American Autonomous
  University
Av. 11-13, Calle 22 No. 1133
7651-1000 San Jose

Escuela de Periodismo
Facultad de Humanidades
Universidad de Costa Rica
Ciudad Universitaria
San Jose

Escuala de Ciencias de la
  Comunicación Colectiva
Universidad de Costa Rica
Facultad de Ciencias Sociales
Ciudad Universitaria
Rodrigo Facio
San Pedro Montas de Oca

Cuba

Escuela de Periodismo
Universidad de la Habana
Esqu. Av. Universidad
Edificio "Jose Marti"
Vedado Plaza
La Habana 1400

Escuela de Periodismo
Universidad de Oriente
Oriente

Dominican Republic

Departamento de
  Comunicación Social
Facultad de Humanidades
Universitad Autónoma de
  Santo Domingo
Santo Domingo

Instituto Dominicano de
  Periodismo
Condo No 23
Santo Domingo

Centro de Comunicación (CEDIC)
El Conde 203
Edificio Diez apto. 419
CP 2510
Santo Domingo

Ecuador

Escuela de Ciencias de la
    Comunicación
Universidad Central
Ciudad Universitaria
CP 1148
Quito

Escuela de Ciencias de la
    Información
Universidad de Guayaquil
Facultad de Filosofía Letras y
    Ciencias de la Educación
Ciudad Universitaria
CP 471
Guayaquil

Especialización en Ciencias de
    la Información
Universidad de Cuenca
Facultad de Filosofía
Ciudad Universitaria
Av. 12 de Abril
CP 168
Cuenca

El Salvador

Departamento de Periodismo
Universidad Nacional de El
    Salvador
Facultad de Ciencias y
    Humanidades
Ciudad Universitaria
San Salvador

Guatemala

Central American School of
    Journalism
Universidad de San Carlos
Guatemala City

Escuela de Ciencias de la
    Comunicación
Universidad Francisco
    Marroquin
40 Calle "A," 10-01, Zona 8
Guatemala City

Escuela de Ciencias de la
    Comunicación
Universidad de San Carlos
Ciudad Universitaria
Guatemala City

Escuela Centroamericana de
    Periodismo
Universidad Rafael Landivar
Vista Hemmosa 111, Zona 16
Guatemala City

Honduras

Escuela de Peridismo
Universidad Autónoma
    de Honduras
Centro Universitario
    de Estudios Generales
Ciudad Universitaria
Tegucigalpa

Jamaica

Caribbean Institute of Mass
    Communication
University of the West Indies
Mona - Kingston 7

México

Departamento de Ciencias de
    la Comunicación
Universidad Nacional
    Autónoma de México
Facultad de Ciencias Políticas
    y Sociales
Ciudad Universitaria
Villa Obregón
México 20

Escuela de Periodismo
Universidad Femenida
    de México
Escuela de Derecho y Ciencias
    Sociales
Av. Constituyente No 151
México 18

Departamento de
    Comunicación
Universidad Iboamericana
Facultad de Ciencias Sociales
Cerro de las Torres 395
Campestre Churubusco
México 21

Escuela de Comunicación
    Educativa
Instituto Latinoamericano de
    Comunicación Educativa
Auditorio Nacional
Paseo de la Reforma
Luis Vives 200
Col. Polanco
CP 13862
México 18

Departamento de Periodismo
Universidad de las Américas
CP 968
México 1

Escuela de Ciencias de la
    Información Social
Universidad Anahuac
Lomas Anahuac
CP 10-844
México 10

Escuela de Ciencias de la
    Comunicación
Universidad Autónoma de
    Guadalajara
Ciudad Universitaria
CP 1-440
Guadalajara

Escuela de Ciencias y Tecnicas
    de la Comunicación
Instituto des Humanidades
    Pío XII
Av. La Pax 1665
CP 334
Guadalajara

Ciencias de la Comunicación
    Interoccidente
Av. Niños Héroes 1342-8
Guadalajara

Escuela de Ciencias de la
    Información
Universidad de Monterrey
Instituto de Humanidades y
    Ciencias Sociales
Av. Gonzalitos 250, Desp. 124
CP 4442 Suc. H
Monterrey

Facultad de Periodismo
Arista No 633
Esq. Av. Zaragoza
Veracruz

Departamento de Información
Universidad Autónoma de Puebla
Puebla, Pue.

Escuela de Ciencias de la
    Comunicación
Universidad Bajio
Av. Universidad
CP 444
37150 Leon

Escuela de Comunicación y
    Relaciones Públicas
Universidad Latinoamericana
Gabriel Mancera 1402
03100 México

Escuela de Periodismo
Facultad de Filosofía, Letras
    y Periodismo
Universidad de Chihuahua
Chihuahua, Chi.

Nicaragua

Escuela de Periodismo
Arnoldo Quintanilla
Central American University
CP 69
Managua

Facultad de Humanidades
Recinto Universitario
    Rubén Dario
Universidad Nacional
    Autónoma de Nicaragua
CP 665
Managua

Panama

Departamento de Ciencias de
    la Comunicación Social
Universidad Autónoma
Facultad de Filosofía, Letras
    et Educación
CP 3369
Panamá City

Escuela de Periodismo
Universidad Católica
    de Panamá
Panama City

Escuela de Periodismo
Universidad Sta. María
  la Antigua
Av. Ricardo y Alfaro
CP 6-1696
Panamá City 6

Facultad de Comunicación
  Social
Ciudad Universitaria Octavio
  Méndez Pereira
Estafeta Universitaria
Panama City

Paraguay

Departamento de Medios
  Modernos y Comunicación
  Social
Facultad de Filosofia
  y Ciencas Humanas
Universidad Católica
Nuestra Señora de Asunción
CP 1718
Asunción

Sección de Periodismo
Universidad Nacional de
  Asunción
Facultad de Filosofía
Comandante Gamarra y
  Gobernador Irala
Asunción

Peru

Programa Academico de
  Periodismo
Universidad Nacional Mayor
  de San Marcos
Ciudad Universitaria
Av. Venezuela
Lima 1

Programa Academico de
  Periodismo y Comunicación
Universidad San Martín
  de Porras
Santa Cruz 775
Mirablores
Lima

Instituto Superior de
  Periodismo "Jaime
  Bausate y Mesa"
Nicolás Araníbar 661
Santa Beatriz
Lima

Programa de Ciencias de la
  Comunicación
Universidad de Lima
Av. Prolongación Javier
Prado Este
Monterrico
CP 852
Lima

Instituto Superior de
  Periodismo y Relaciones
  Públicas "Carlos Uceda"
San Martín 569
Trujillo

Escuela de Periodismo
Universidad Nacional
   de Trujullo
Facultad de Letras et Educación
Zapita 618
CP 315
Trujillo

Facultad de Ciencias de la
   Comunicación Social
Universidad Católica Santa
   María
CP 1350
Arequipa

Escuela de Periodismo y
   Relaciones Públicas
Universidad Nacional
   San Antonio
Abad del Cuzco
Facultad de Letras y Ciencias
   Humanas
Av. de la Cultura
CP 367
Cuzco

nstituto Superior de
   Periodismo "Jaime Bausate
   y Mesa"
Filial de Huancayo
Callao 179
Huancayo

Programa Academico de la
   Información
Universidad de Piura
CP 353
Piura

Puerto Rico

Programa de Comunicación
Universidad del Sagrado
   Corazón
Calle Rosalez
Cra. San Antonio
Parada 261/2
CP 12383
00920 Santurce

Escuela de Comunicación
   Pública
Universidad de Puerto Rico
Estación de la Universidad
Recinto de Río Piedras
CP 21880
00831 San Juan

Uruguay

Escuela de Periodismo Profesional
Av. 2 de Octubre 2966/1243
Santo Domingo

Venezuela

Escuela de Comunicación
   Social
Universidad Central
Facultad de Humanidades
   y Educación
Ciudad Universitaria
Caracas

Escuela de Comunicación
 Social
Universidad Católica Andrés
 Bello
Facultad de Humanidades
 et Educación
Montalván La Vega
CP 29068
Caracas

Escuela de Comunicación
 Social
Universidad de Zulia
Facultad de Humanidades
 y Educación
Av. Goyica
CP 526
Carrera de Saruna
Maracaibo
Zulia

AFRICA

Benin

Faculté des Sciences de la Santé
Unité Audio Visuelle
POB 188
Cotonou

Burkina Faso

Centre Inter-African D'Etudes en
    Radio Rurale de Ouagadougou
    (CIERRO)
B.P. 385
Ouagadougou

Centre de Formation Professionnelle
    de L'Information
B.P. 7045
Ouagadougou

Burundi

Ecole de Journalisme
B.P. 2393
Bujumbura

Congo

Université Marien Ngouabi
Faculté des Lettres et
    de Sciences Humaines
B.P. 2642
Brazzaville

Département de Journalisme
Ecole Nationale
Brazzaville

Ghana

Ghana Institute of Journalism
POB 667
Accra

Beaconsfield Studios
Ghana Broadcasting Corporation
POB 1633
Accra

Kenya

Centre for African Family Studies
POB 60054
Nairobi

Daystar University College
POB 44400
Nairobi

School of Journalism
University of Nairobi
POB 30917
Nairobi

Broadcast Training Centre
All-African Conference of Churches
POB 14206
Nairobi

AMECEA Communications
POB 21053
Nairobi

Communications Training Centre
Ministry of Information
 and Broadcasting
POB 42422
Nairobi

African Council on Communication
 Education
ACCE
POB 47495
Nairobi

Liberia

University of Liberia
Department of Mass Communication
POB 9020
Monrovia

Mozambique

National School of Journalism
POB 3643
Maputo

Nigeria

Institute of Journalism and
Continuing Education
POB 01120
Enugu
Anambra State

Department of Communication
Calabar Polytechnic
POB 1110
Calabar

Department of Communication
University of Ibadan
Ibadan

Department of Communication
University of Lagos
Lagos

Nigerian Institute of Journalism
 (NIJ)
School of Communications
20 Adeyemo Alakija Street
Lagos

Department of Mass Communication
University of Maiduguri
POB 1069
Maiduguri

Department of Mass Communication
University of Nigeria-Nsukka
Nsukka

Senegal

Pan-African News Agency (PANA)
POB 4056
Dakar

Centre d'Etudes des Sciences et
  Techniques de L'Information
  (CESTI)
University of Dakar
Dakar

Swaziland

University of Swaziland
POB 4
Kwaluseni

Centre for Development
  Communications
POB 750
Mbabane

Tanzania

Tanzania Information Services
POB 9142
Dar-es-Salaam

Lutheran Radio Centre
POB 777
Moshi

Nyegezi Social Training Centre
Journalism Department
POB 307
Mwanza

Tanzania School of Journalism (TSJ)
POB 20131
Lugogo

Togo

Conférences des Eglises de Toute
  L'Afrique(CETA)
B.P. 2268
Lome

Uganda

Uganda School of Journalism
Institute of Public Administration
POB 20131
Lugogo

Zaire

Institut des Sciences et Techniques
  d'Information (ISTI)
Université Nationale du Zaire
B.P. 14998
Kinshasa

Département de Communication
  Sociale
Université Nationale du Zaire
Kinshasa

Studio-Ecole de la Voix du Zaire
B.B. 3164
Kinshasa-Gombe

Zambia

Department of Mass Communication
The University of Zambia
Lusaka

Zimbabwe

Zimbabwe Institute of Mass
    Communication
POB 50516
Causeway
Harare

NORTH AFRICA & MIDDLE EAST

Algeria

Institut National Supérieur de
  Journalisme
Université d'Alger
Alger

Egypt

American University of Cairo
Mass Communication Unit
POB 2511
Sharia Kasr El Ani
Cairo

International Information and
  Communication Consultants
44 Elzahraa St.
Dokki
Cairo

Iran

Institute of Mass Communication
University of Teheran
Teheran

IRAN Communications &
  Development Institute
POB 33183
Tadjrish
Teheran

College of Mass Communication
Ferdowsi Avenue
Teheran

Israel

International Institute for
  Development, Cooperation and
  Labour Studies
16201 7 Nehardea St.
64235 Tel Aviv

Kuwait

Al Qabas Newspaper
Al Qabas Journalism Training
  Center
Al Qabas

Lebanon

Faculty of Information and
  Documentation
Lebanese University
Place du Musée
Beirut

Morocco

Institut Supérieur de Journalisme
Ar-Ribat
Rabat

Sudan

The National Mass Communication
  Training Centre (NMTC)
POB 2894
Khartoum

Department of Journalism &
  Communication
Omburman Islamic University
POB 261
Khartoum

Syria

Institute for Journalism &
  Mass Communication Research
POB 1069
Baghdad Street
Damascus

Radio & TV
Communication Institute
Damascus

Tunisia

Département de Communication
Université de Tunis - Montfleury
7, impasse Mohamed Bachrouch
Tunis

Centre Africain de Perfectionnement
  des Journalistes et des Communicateurs
9, rue Hooker Doolittle
1002 Tunis-Belvedere

Turkey

School of Journalism
  & Broadcasting
University of Ankara
Tandogan
Ankara

School of Journalism & Mass
  Communication
Marmara University
Kayisdagi Caddesi Fikitepe
Kadiköy
Istanbul

School of Journalism
Istanbul University
Beyazil
Istanbul

School of Journalism
Ege University
Bornova
Izmir

Department of Mass
  Communication
Gazi University
Besevler
Ankara

School of Journalism
Anadolu University
Yunus Emre Kampusu
26470 Eskisehir

Yemen [PDR]

State Committee for Information
POB 1409
Tawahi-Aden

Selected Bibliography

Adam, G. Stuart. "The World Next Door: A Commonwealth Perspective." *Gannett Center Journal* 2, no.2 (Spring 1988).

Adams, Paul, and Catherine McKercher. "North America." In *Global Journalism: Survey of International Communication*, 2d ed., edited by John C. Merrill. New York: Longman, 1991.

Adhikarya, Ronny. *Knowledge Transfer and Usage in Communication Studies: The U.S.–ASEAN Case*. Singapore: Asian Mass Communication Research and Information Center, 1983.

Alkali, Mohammad Nur, Jerry Domatob, Yahaya Abubakar and Abubakar Jika, eds. *Mass Communication in Africa: A Book of Readings*. Enugu, Nigeria: Delta Publications, 1988.

Altschull, J. Herbert. *Agents of Power*. New York: Longman, 1984.

Bagdikian, Ben. *The Media Monopoly*. 2d ed. Boston: Beacon Press, 1987.

Barton, Frank. *African Assignment: The Story of IPI's Six-Year Training Program in Tropical Africa*. Zurich: IPI, 1969.

Becker, Lee B., Jeffrey Fruit and Susan Caudill, with Sharon Dunwoody and Leonard Tipton. *The Training and Hiring of Journalists*. Norwood, NJ: Ablex, 1987.

Becker, Lee B. "Enrollments Increase in 1989, but Graduation Rates Drop." *Journalism Educator* 45, no.3 (Autumn 1990): 5.

Bishop, Rober. *Qi Lai! Mobilizing One Billion Chinese: The Chinese Communication System*. Ames: Iowa State University Press, 1989.

Bohère, Georges. *Profession: Journalist*. Geneva: ILO, 1984.

Brod, Donald F. "Classifying the World's Media: The One-Step and Two-Step Approaches." *International Communication Bulletin* 22, nos.3–4 (Fall 1987): 8–11.

Brown, Donald. *International Radio Broadcasting*. New York: Praeger, 1982.

Ceppos, Jerry. "Media Professionals as Teachers." In *Journalism Education: Facing Up to the Challenge of Change*, edited by Robert H. Giles. Washington, DC: American Society of Newspaper Editors Committee on Education for Journalism, 1990.

Chen, Anne Cooper, and Anju Grover Chaudhary. "Asia and the Pacific." In *Global Journalism: A Survey of International Communication*, 2d ed., edited by John C. Merrill. New York: Longman, 1990.

Chimutengwende, Chen C. "The Role of Communications Training and Technology in African Development." In *World Communications: A Handbook*, edited by George Gerbner and Marsha Siefert. New York: Longman, 1984.

Chinese Journalism Handbook. Beijing: People's Daily Publishing House, 1984.

Commission on Freedom of the Press. *A Free and Responsible Press*. Chicago: University of Chicago Press, 1947.

Communications 1990. A report of the Future Committee. Columbia: School of Journalism, University of Missouri-Columbia, 1980.

Cooper, Dennis R. "Basic Training for Third World Journalists." Ph.D. dissertation, University of Tennessee-Knoxville, 1987.

Crook, James A. "Europeans Form Training Association with Help from European Community." *Journalism Educator* 45, no.4 (Winter 1991): 92–96.

Davidson, Terry. "Ed Emery: Teaching Journalism in China." *Community College Journalist* 13, no.4 (Fall 1985): 2–7.

Directory of Communication Training Institutions in Africa. Nairobi: African Council on Communication Education, 1988.

Domatob, Jerry Komia. "Communication Training for Self-Reliance in Black Africa: Challenges and Strategies." *Gazette* 40, no.3 (1987): 167–182.

Eljerary, Abdallah Taher. "The Design of a Mass Media Training Program: The Formulation of a Paradigm for the Developing Nations with Particular Application to the Libyan Example." Ph.D. dissertation, University of Wisconsin-Madison, 1981.

Emery, Edwin, and Joseph McKerns. *AEJMC: 75 Years in the Making*. Journalism Monographs, no. 104. Columbia, SC: AEJMC, 1987.

Emery, Edwin, and Michael Emery. *The Press and America: An Interpretive History of the Mass Media*. 6th ed. Englewood Cliffs, NJ: Prentice-Hall, 1988.

Failing, Lynn. "The Changing Scene in Communication Education." *Media Asia* 13, no.4 (1986): 183–188.

Fischer, Heinz-Dietrich and Otto B. Roegele, eds. *Ausbildung für Kommunikationsberufe in Europa: Praktiken und Perspektiven.* Düsseldorf: Droste Verlag, 1977.

Florangel, Rosario-Braid. "Journalism Education: Responding to New Challenges." *Media Asia* 13, no.4 (1986): 195–199.

Gaunt, Philip. "Developments in Soviet Journalism." *Journalism Quarterly* 64, nos.2–3 (Summer-Autumn 1987): 526–532.

————. *Choosing the News: The Profit Factor in News Selection.* Westport, CT: Greenwood Press, 1990.

————. "Overcoming Obstacles to Regional and International Cooperation for Communication Training." Paper presented to the UNESCO International Meeting of Regional Training Institutes for Communication Development, Paris, June 12–14, 1991.

Government of Canada. *Special Senate Committee on Mass Media* (Davey Commission Report). Ottawa: Queen's Printer, 1970.

————. *Royal Commission on Newspapers* (Kent Commission Report). Hull: Ministry of Supply and Services, 1981.

Hachten, William A. *The World News Prism: Changing Media, Clashing Ideologies,* 2d ed. Ames: Iowa State Press, 1987.

Haquin, Bénédicte. "Les patrons préfèrent embaucher des universitaires." *Le Journaliste* (February-March, 1985): 3.

Head, Sidney W. *World Broadcasting Systems: A Comparative Analysis.* Belmont, CA: Wadsworth, 1985.

Hellack, George. *Newspapers, Radio and Television in the Federal Republic of Germany.* Bonn: Inter Nationes, 1987.

Henningham, J. P. "Comparisons between Australian and U.S. Broadcast Journalists' Professional Values." *Journal of Broadcasting* 28, no.3 (Summer 1984): 331.

Hernett, Isabelle. "Les Ecoles de Communication." *EPP* (June 16, 1986): 60–64.

Hornik, Robert. *Development Communication: Information, Agriculture and Nutrition in the Third World.* White Plains, NY: Longman, 1988.

How Journalists Are Trained. London: National Council for the Training of Journalists, 1989.

Hudec, Vladimir. *Education and Training of Journalists at Higher Educational Establishments in the Czechoslovak Socialist Republic.* Prague: Faculty of Journalism, Charles University, 1984.

Hunter, Frederic N. "Grub Street and Academia: The Relationship between Journalism and Education, 1880–1940." Ph.D. dissertation, City University, London, 1984.

Japanese Press 1952. Tokyo, Nihon Shinbun Kyokai, 1951.

Jimada, Usman. "Nigerian Media Training: An Alternative Model." In *Mass Communication: A Book of Readings,* edited by Mohammad Nur Alkali et al. Enugu, Nigeria: Delta Publications, 1988.

Jingming, Zhang, and Peng Jianan. "Chinese Journalism Education: Slow Progress since 1918." *Journalism Educator* 41, no.4 (Spring 1986): 11–13.

Journalism Career and Scholarship Guide (1991). Princeton, NJ: The Dow Jones Newspaper Fund, Inc., 1990.

Journalistic Training Centers. Prague: International Organization of Journalists, 1986.

Kang, Joon-Mann. "Reporters and Their Professional and Occupational Commitment in a Developing Country." *Gazette* 40, no.1 (1987): 3–20.

Katzen, May. *Mass Communication: Teaching and Studies at Universities*. Paris: UNESCO, 1975.

Keever, Beverly. "Journalism Education Grows by Leaps and Bounds in China." *Journalism Educator* 43, no.1 (Spring 1988): 29–31.

Kirat, Mohamed. "The Algerian News People: A Study of Their Backgrounds, Professional Orientations and Working Conditions." Ph.D. dissertation, Indiana University, 1987.

Koirala, Bharat D. "Mass Communication and Journalism Education in Nepal." In *Communication Education in Asia*, edited by Crispin C. Maslog. The Philippines: Press Foundation of Asia, 1990.

Kopper, Gerd G. "Journalistenrolle und Journalistenausbildung in Japan." In *Ausbildung für Kommunikationsberufe in Europa: Praktiken und Perspektiven*, edited by Heinz-Dietrich Fischer and Otto B. Roegele. Düsseldorf: Droste Verlag, 1977.

Kunczik, Michael. *Concepts of Journalism North and South*. Bonn: Friedrich-Ebert-Stiftung, 1988.

Lent, John A. "Journalism Training in Cuba Emphasizes Politics, Ideology." *Journalism Educator* 39, no.3 (Autumn 1984): 12–15.

Lowenstein, Ralph, and John C. Merrill. *Media, Messages and Men*, 2d ed. New York: Longman, 1979.

Malcolm, Bruce. *To License a Journalist: A Landmark Decision in the Schmidt Case*. New York: Freedom House, 1986.

Martin, L. John. "Africa." In *Global Journalism: Survey of International Communication*, 2d ed., edited by John C. Merrill. New York: Longman, 1991.

Maslog, Crispin C., ed. *Communication Education in Asia*. Manila: Press Foundation of Asia, 1990.

Maslog, Crispin C. "Communication and Journalism Training in India, Indonesia, Malaysia, Nepal, The Philippines and Thailand: An Overview." In *Communication Education in Asia*, edited by Crispin C. Maslog. Manila: Press Foundation of Asia, 1990.

————. "Communication Education and Training in the Philippines." In *Communication Education in Asia*, edited by Crispin C. Maslog. Manila: Press Foundation of Asia, 1990.

McCombs, Maxwell. "Testing the Myths: A Statistical Review 1967–1986." *Gannett Center Journal* 2, no.2 (Spring 1988): 101–108.

McQuail, Denis, and Karen Siune, eds. *New Media Politics: Comparative Perspectives in Western Europe*. Beverly Hills, CA: Sage, 1986.

Merrill, John C. *The Imperative of Freedom*. New York: Hastings House, 1974.

Merrill, John C., ed. *Global Journalism: Survey of International Communication*, 2d ed. White Plains, NY: Longman, 1991.

Mott, Frank Luther. *American Journalism: A History: 1690–1960*, 3d ed. New York: Macmillan, 1982.

Mowlana, Hamid, and Laurie J. Wilson. *Communication Technology and Development*. Reports and Papers on Mass Communication, no. 101. Paris: UNESCO, 1988.

Mujahid, Sharif Al. "Communication Education in Pakistan." Presented at the seminar Communication Education in the Asia-Pacific: Towards 2000, Singapore, January 15, 1990.

Napoli, James J. "In Egypt, Learning U.S. Journalism Can Look Subversive." *Journalism Educator* 41, no.2 (Summer 1986): 31–34.

New Trends in Journalism Education and Practice in Tanzania. Dar-es-Salaam: Ministry of Information, 1980.

Norton, Ray. "J-Education Mexican Style." *Journalism Educator* 27, no.3 (October, 1972): 16–17.

Nordenstreng, Kaarle, ed. *Reports on Journalism Education in Europe*. Tampere: University of Tampere Department of Journalism and Mass Communication, 1990.

Nordenstreng, Kaarle, and Hifzi Topuz, eds. *Journalist: Status, Rights and Responsibilities*. Prague: International Organization of Journalists, 1989.

Ogan, Christine. "Middle East and North Africa." In *Global Journalism: Survey of International Communication*, 2d ed., edited by John C. Merrill. New York: Longman, 1991.

Oreh, Onuma O. "Developmental Journalism and Press Freedom: An African Viewpoint." *Gazette* 24, no.1 (1978): 36–40.

Paraschos, Manny. "Europe." In *Global Journalism: Survey of International Communication*, 2d ed., edited by John C. Merrill. New York: Longman, 1991.

Picard, Robert G. *The Press and the Decline of Democracy*. Westport, CT: Greenwood Press, 1985.

Pisarek, Walery. "Central and East European Countries: Overview." In *Reports on Journalism Education in Europe*, edited by Kaarle Nordenstreng. Tampere: University of Tampere Department of Journalism and Mass Communication, 1990.

Pool, Ithiel de Sola. *Technologies of Freedom*. Cambridge, MA: Belknap Press/Harvard University Press, 1983.

Rajan, R. V. "A Paper on India." Presented at the seminar Communication Education in the Asia-Pacific: Towards 2000, Singapore, January 15, 1990.

Ramanathan, Sankaran, and Katherine T. Frith. "Mass Comm Young and Grow-
  ing in Malaysia." *Journalism Educator* 42, no.4 (Winter 1988): 10–12.
Ramsey, Doug. "Educating Professional Journalists: Their Wants and Needs."
  Newspaper Research Journal 11, no.4 (Fall 1990): 72–79.
Raudsepp, Enn. "Reinventing Journalism Education." *Canadian Journal of
  Communication* 14, no.2 (May 1989): 1–14.
Rogers, Everett. *Communication and Development: Critical Perspectives*. Bev-
  erly Hills, CA: Sage, 1976.
Rugh, William. *The Arab Press*. Syracuse, NY: Syracuse University Press,
  1979.
Ruotólo, A. Carlos. "Professional Orientation among Journalists in Three Latin
  American Countries." *Gazette* 40, no.2 (1987): 131–142.
Sala-Balust, Ramon. "Journalists' Training: A FIEJ Survey." *FIEJ Bulletin* 144
  (September 1985): 9–12.
Salayakanond, Wirasak. "Mass Communiction and Journalism Education in
  Thailand." In *Communication Education in Asia*, edited by Crispin C.
  Maslog. Manila: Press Foundation of Asia, 1990.
Sandford, John. *The Mass Media of the German-speaking Countries*. London:
  Oswald Wolff, 1976.
Sarkar, Chancal. "Mass Communication and Journalism Education in India." In
  Communication Education in Asia, edited by Crispin C. Maslog. Ma-
  nila: Press Foundation of Asia, 1990.
Savary, Jean. "Les écoles de journalisme: permis de conduire ou leçon de
  conduite?" *Presse-Actualité* (June-July 1985): 19.
Scheibel, Robert. "Five Dimensions Explain Differences in British-American
  Journalism Education." *Community College Journalist* 15, no.4 (Fall
  1988): 10–11.
Schillinger, Elizabeth. "Journalism at Moscow State: The Impact of Glasnost."
  Journalism Educator 43, no.2 (Summer 1988): 52–56.
Siebert, Frederick, Theodore Peterson and Wilbur Schramm. *Four Theories of
  the Press*. Urbana: University of Illinois Press, 1956.
Sparks, Colin, and Slavko Splichal. "Journalistic Education and Professional
  Socialization." *Gazette* 43 (1989): 31–52.
Stephenson, Hugh, and Pierre Mory, *Journalism Training in Europe*. Brussels:
  Commission of the European Communities, 1990.
Stevenson, Robert L. *Communication, Development and the Third World*. White
  Plains, NY: Longman, 1988.
Story of the Press Institute of India. New Delhi: Press Institute of India, 1988.
Suparto, Ina Mariana. "Mass Communication and Journalism Education in
  Indonesia." In *Communication Education in Asia*, edited by Crispin C.
  Maslog. Manila: Press Foundation of Asia, 1990.
Taylor, Larry. "Journalism Education at the Times of India." *Community Col-
  lege Journalist* 15, no.2 (Spring 1987): 3.
Thornburg, Ron. "The Liberal Arts and Sciences." In *Journalism Education:
  Facing Up to the Challenge of Change*, edited by Robert H. Giles.

Washington, DC: American Society of Newspaper Editors Committee on Education for Journalism, 1990.

Tulloch, John. "The United Kingdom." In *Reports on Journalism Education in Europe*, edited by Kaarle Nordenstreng. Tampere: University of Tampere Department of Journalism and Mass Communication, 1990.

Tunstall, Jeremy. *Journalists at Work*. London: Constable, 1971.

UNESCO. *Education for Journalism*. Reports and Papers on Mass Communication, no. 8. Paris: UNESCO, 1954.

_____ . *The Training of Journalists: A World-wide Study on the Training of Personnel for the Mass Media*. Paris: UNESCO, 1958.

_____ . *Professional Training for Mass Communication*. Reports and Papers on Mass Communication, no. 45. Paris: UNESCO, 1965.

_____ . *Training for Mass Communication*. Reports and Papers on Mass Communication, no. 73. Paris: UNESCO, 1975.

_____ . *Communication in Africa*. Paris: UNESCO, 1977.

_____ . *Perspectives for Regional and International Cooperation*. Conference Document CII-91/CONF CC-609. Paris: UNESCO, April 30, 1991.

Urdininea, José Baldivia, Mario Planet, Javier Solís and Tomás Guerra Rivas. *La Formación des los Periodistas en América Latina: México, Chile, Costa Rica*. Mexico City: Editorial Nueva Imagen, S.A., 1981.

Voyenne, Bernard. *Les Journalistes Français: D'où viennent-ils? Qui sont-ils? Que font-ils?* Paris: Les Editions CFPJ, 1985.

Warren, John, and Adchara Khotanan. "Communication Education at Thai Universities." *Journalism Educator* 45, no.4 (Winter 1991): 28–33.

Weaver, David H., and G. Cleveland Wilhoit. "A Profile of JMC Educators: Traits, Attitudes and Values." *Journalism Educator* 43, no.2 (Summer 1988): 15–41.

_____ . *The American Journalist: A Portrait of U.S. News People and Their Work*, 2d ed. Bloomington: Indiana University Press, 1991.

Weerackody, Irvin. "The Sri Lanka Situation." Presented at the seminar Communication Education in the Asia-Pacific: Towards 2000, Singapore, January 15, 1990.

Williams, Raymond. *Communications*, 3d ed. Harmondsworth, Middlesex, U.K.: Penguin Books, 1976.

Woolford, Don. "Third World Journalism Training." *Australian Journalism Review* 6, no.1 (January 1984): 63–67.

Index

About the Author

PHILIP GAUNT is Director of Research at the Elliott School of Communication, Wichita State University. He is the author of *Choosing the News* (Greenwood, 1990) as well as numerous articles in *Journalism Quarterly, Media Culture and Society* and other scholarly publications.